Resilience of Democracy

Illiberalism and authoritarianism have become major threats to democracy across the world. In response to this development, research on the causes and processes of democratic declines has blossomed. Much less scholarly attention has been devoted to the issue of democratic resilience. Why are some democracies more resilient than others to the current trend of autocratization? What role do institutions, actors and structural factors play in this regard? What options do democratic actors have to address illiberal and authoritarian challenges? This book addresses all these questions.

The present introduction sets the stage by developing a new concept of democratic resilience as the ability of a democratic system, its institutions, political actors, and citizens to prevent or react to external and internal challenges, stresses, and assaults. The book posits three potential reactions of democratic regimes: to withstand without changes, to adapt through internal changes, and to recover without losing the democratic character of its regime and its constitutive core institutions, organizations, and processes. The more democracies are resilient on all four levels of the political system (political community, institutions, actors, citizens) the less vulnerable they turn out to be in the present and future.

This edited volume will be of great value to students, academics, and researchers interested in politics, political regimes and theories, democracy and democratization, autocracy and autocratization, polarization, social democracy, and comparative government. The chapters in this book were originally published as a special issue of *Democratization*.

Anna Lührmann has been Associate Professor of Political Science at the University of Gothenburg, Sweden, and since 2021 serves as a Member of the German Bundestag and Minister of State at the Federal Foreign Office.

Wolfgang Merkel is Professor Emeritus at Humboldt University, Berlin, Germany, and Director Emeritus at WZB Berlin Social Science Center. He serves as Senior Scholar at the Democracy Institute at Central University in Budapest. His research focuses on Transformation of political regimes, (defective) democracy and democratization, political parties, and social democracy in power. He co-edited *The Oxford Handbook of Political, Social, and Economic Transformation* (OUP 2019).

Resilience of Democracy
Responses to Illiberal and Authoritarian Challenges

Edited by
Anna Lührmann and Wolfgang Merkel

LONDON AND NEW YORK

First published 2023
by Routledge
4 Park Square, Milton Park, Abingdon, Oxon OX14 4RN

and by Routledge
605 Third Avenue, New York, NY 10158

Routledge is an imprint of the Taylor & Francis Group, an informa business

Introduction, Chapters 2–6 © 2023 Taylor & Francis
Chapter 1 © 2021 Vanessa A. Boese, Amanda B. Edgell, Sebastian Hellmeier, Seraphine F. Maerz and Staffan I. Lindberg. Originally published as Open Access.
Chapter 7 © 2021 Anna Lührmann. Originally published as Open Access.

With the exception of Chapters 1 and 7, no part of this book may be reprinted or reproduced or utilised in any form or by any electronic, mechanical, or other means, now known or hereafter invented, including photocopying and recording, or in any information storage or retrieval system, without permission in writing from the publishers. For details on the rights for Chapters 1 and 7, please see the chapters' Open Access footnotes.

Trademark notice: Product or corporate names may be trademarks or registered trademarks, and are used only for identification and explanation without intent to infringe.

British Library Cataloguing in Publication Data
A catalogue record for this book is available from the British Library

ISBN13: 978-1-032-42615-0 (hbk)
ISBN13: 978-1-032-42616-7 (pbk)
ISBN13: 978-1-003-36350-7 (ebk)

DOI: 10.4324/9781003363507

Typeset in Minion Pro
by Newgen Publishing UK

Publisher's Note
The publisher accepts responsibility for any inconsistencies that may have arisen during the conversion of this book from journal articles to book chapters, namely the inclusion of journal terminology.

Disclaimer
Every effort has been made to contact copyright holders for their permission to reprint material in this book. The publishers would be grateful to hear from any copyright holder who is not here acknowledged and will undertake to rectify any errors or omissions in future editions of this book.

Contents

Citation Information	vii
Notes on Contributors	ix

Introduction—Resilience of democracies: responses to illiberal and
authoritarian challenges   1
Wolfgang Merkel and Anna Lührmann

1   How democracies prevail: democratic resilience as a two-stage process   17
*Vanessa A. Boese, Amanda B. Edgell, Sebastian Hellmeier, Seraphine F.
Maerz and Staffan I. Lindberg*

2   What halts democratic erosion? The changing role of accountability   40
Melis G. Laebens and Anna Lührmann

3   Pernicious polarization, autocratization and opposition strategies   61
Murat Somer, Jennifer L. McCoy and Russell E. Luke

4   Negative partisanship towards the populist radical right and democratic
resilience in Western Europe   81
Carlos Meléndez and Cristóbal Rovira Kaltwasser

5   The supply and demand model of civic education: evidence from a field
experiment in the Democratic Republic of Congo   102
Steven E. Finkel and Junghyun Lim

6   Democratic Horizons: what value change reveals about the
future of democracy   124
Christian Welzel

7   Disrupting the autocratization sequence: towards democratic resilience   149
    Anna Lührmann

    Index   172

Citation Information

The chapters in this book were originally published in the journal *Democratization*, volume 28, issue 5 (2021). When citing this material, please use the original page numbering for each article, as follows:

Introduction

Resilience of democracies: responses to illiberal and authoritarian challenges
Wolfgang Merkel and Anna Lührmann
Democratization, volume 28, issue 5 (2021), pp. 869–884

Chapter 1

How democracies prevail: democratic resilience as a two-stage process
Vanessa A. Boese, Amanda B. Edgell, Sebastian Hellmeier, Seraphine F. Maerz and Staffan I. Lindberg
Democratization, volume 28, issue 5 (2021), pp. 885–907

Chapter 2

What halts democratic erosion? The changing role of accountability
Melis G. Laebens and Anna Lührmann
Democratization, volume 28, issue 5 (2021), pp. 908–928

Chapter 3

Pernicious polarization, autocratization and opposition strategies
Murat Somer, Jennifer L. McCoy and Russell E. Luke
Democratization, volume 28, issue 5 (2021), pp. 929–948

Chapter 4

Negative partisanship towards the populist radical right and democratic resilience in Western Europe
Carlos Meléndez and Cristóbal Rovira Kaltwasser
Democratization, volume 28, issue 5 (2021), pp. 949–969

Chapter 5

The supply and demand model of civic education: evidence from a field experiment in the Democratic Republic of Congo
Steven E. Finkel and Junghyun Lim
Democratization, volume 28, issue 5 (2021), pp. 970–991

Chapter 6

Democratic Horizons: what value change reveals about the future of democracy
Christian Welzel
Democratization, volume 28, issue 5 (2021), pp. 992–1016

Chapter 7

Disrupting the autocratization sequence: towards democratic resilience
Anna Lührmann
Democratization, volume 28, issue 5 (2021), pp. 1017–1039

For any permission-related enquiries please visit:
www.tandfonline.com/page/help/permissions

Notes on Contributors

Vanessa A. Boese is Assistant Professor at the Department of Political Science, University of Gothenburg, Sweden. Her research covers how to (not) measure democracy in quantitative studies, macro-economic models of trade, development, democracy, and peace, as well as panel data methods.

Amanda B. Edgell is Assistant Professor of Political Science at the University of Alabama, USA, and Research Associate at the Varieties of Democracy (V-Dem) Institute, Sweden. Her research on electoral institutions, authoritarianism, and foreign aid has appeared in the *European Journal of Political Research*, *Democratization*, and the *African Studies Review*.

Steven E. Finkel is the Daniel Wallace Professor of Political Science at the University of Pittsburgh. His areas of expertise include comparative political behavior, public opinion, democratization, and quantitative methods. He is the author of *Causal Analysis* with Panel Data (1995) as well as numerous articles on political participation, voting behavior, and civic education in new and established democracies.

Sebastian Hellmeier is Postdoc at the WZB Berlin Social Science Center, Germany. His work on mass mobilization and authoritarian regimes has been published in *Comparative Political Studies*, *Political Communication*, and the *European Journal of International Relations*.

Cristóbal Rovira Kaltwasser is Professor of Political Science at Universidad Diego Portales in Santiago de Chile and Associate Researcher at the Centre for Social Conflict and Cohesion Studies (COES). His main area of research is comparative politics, and he has a special interest in the ambivalent relationship between populism and democracy.

Melis G. Laebens is Postdoctoral Prize Research Fellow in Politics and International Relations at the Nuffield College, University of Oxford, UK. Her work has focused on contemporary democratic backsliding and incumbent takeovers as well as on party politics and partisanship with a focus on Turkey, Ecuador, and Poland.

Junghyun Lim is PhD candidate at the Department of Political Science, University of Pittsburgh, USA. Her research focuses on globalization politics, international migration, and democratic backsliding. Her research has appeared in *Electoral Studies*.

Staffan I. Lindberg is Professor of Political Science and Director of the V-Dem Institute at the University of Gothenburg, Sweden; founding Principal Investigator of Varieties of Democracy (V-Dem); Wallenberg Academy Fellow; author of *Democracy and Elections in Africa* as well as over fifty articles on issues such as democracy, elections and democratization, accountability, clientelism, sequence analysis methods, women's representation, and voting behavior, and extensive experience as consultant and advisor to international organizations.

Anna Lührmann has been Associate Professor of Political Science at the University of Gothenburg, Sweden, and since 2021 serves as a Member of the German Bundestag and Minister of State at the Federal Foreign Office.

Russell E. Luke is PhD Candidate at the Department of Political Science, Georgia State University, USA. His current research projects develop the spatial model of politics, analyze the impact of voter ID laws on communities of color, and examine the political determinates of COVID-19 behaviors.

Seraphine F. Maerz is Research Fellow at the Institute of Political Science, Goethe University Frankfurt, Germany. Her research on authoritarian survival strategies and public communication in autocracies and democracies has been published among others in *Government and Opposition*, *Quality and Quantity*, *Political Research Exchange*, and the *Journal of Political Ideologies*.

Jennifer L. McCoy is Political Science Professor at Georgia State University and non-resident scholar at the Carnegie Endowment for International Peace. A specialist on democratization and polarization, mediation and conflict prevention, election processes and election observation, and Latin American politics, Dr. McCoy has authored or edited six books and dozens of articles. Her latest volume is *Polarizing Polities: A Global Threat to Democracy*, co-edited with Murat Somer (2019).

Carlos Meléndez is Post-Doctoral Researcher at the Centre for Social Conflict and Cohesion Studies (COES) and Associate Researcher at Instituto de Investigación en Ciencias Sociales – Universidad Diego Portales in Santiago de Chile. His research work is focused on political linkages in systems with low institutionalization, with special emphasis on the Andean Region and Central America.

Wolfgang Merkel is Professor Emeritus at Humboldt University, Berlin, Germany, and Director Emeritus at WZB Berlin Social Science Center. He serves as Senior Scholar at the Democracy Institute at Central University in Budapest. His research focuses on Transformation of political regimes, (defective) democracy and democratization, political parties, and social democracy in power. Among his latest books he co-edited: *The Oxford Handbook of Political, Social, and Economic Transformation* (2019).

Murat Somer is Professor of Political Science and International Relations at Koç University, Istanbul, Turkey, and an expert on polarization and de-polarization, religious and secular politics, ethnic conflicts, autocratization, and democratization.

Christian Welzel, member of the German Academy of Sciences (Leopoldina), is the Political Culture Research Professor at Leuphana University in Lueneburg, Germany, and Program Director at the National Research University – Higher School of Economics in Moscow, Russia. His research focuses on human empowerment, emancipative values, cultural change, and democratization. His most recent book includes *Democratization* (with Christian Haerpfer, Ronald Inglehart and Patrick Bernhagen, 2019).

INTRODUCTION

Resilience of democracies: responses to illiberal and authoritarian challenges

Wolfgang Merkel and Anna Lührmann ⓘ

ABSTRACT
Illiberalism and authoritarianism have become major threats to democracy across the world. In response to this development, research on the causes and processes of democratic declines has blossomed. Much less scholarly attention has been devoted to the issue of democratic resilience. Why are some democracies more resilient than others to the current trend of autocratization? What role do institutions, actors and structural factors play in this regard? What options do democratic actors have to address illiberal and authoritarian challenges? This Special Issue addresses these questions. The present introduction sets the stage by developing a new concept of democratic resilience as the ability of a democratic system, its institutions, political actors, and citizens to prevent or react to external and internal challenges, stresses, and assaults. We sketch three potential reactions of democratic regimes: to withstand without changes, to adapt through internal changes, and to recover without losing the democratic character of its regime and its constitutive core institutions, organizations, and processes. The more democracies are resilient on all four levels of the political system (political community, institutions, actors, citizens) the less vulnerable they turn out to be in the present and future.

Introduction

Illiberalism and authoritarianism have become major threats to democracy across the world. In the wake of this global development, the literature on the challenges, erosion, decline, and crisis of democracy has greatly proliferated.[1] These contributions differ in their analyses of the causes and consequences, but they make one common observation: the main contemporary challenge to democracy is its gradual demise after illiberal or authoritarian-leaning political leaders come to power in elections and aggrandize their prerogatives at the cost of parliaments and independent judiciaries.[2] We denote here "authoritarian" actors as being those that are openly in opposition to the democratic regime. Their intention is to transform democracy into some sort of autocracy. In established democracies, illiberal or "semi-loyal"[3] actors who are not fully committed to the norms and institutions within democracies that constrain the executive and enforce civil liberties and the rule of law within democracy are more common.[4] Though they might not attack the electoral regime as such, they often try to dismantle the liberal dimensions of the democratic regime.[5] Often they do not follow a strategic masterplan, but the sum of their decisions and their style of governance leads to defective democracies, that is, those with increasingly illiberal characteristics.[6] However, if the illiberal virus persists long enough, it transforms the liberal dimension, polarizes the political space, and may affect the institutional core of democracies as well. This results in a further step from a liberal democratic towards an autocratic regime.

In fact, opinion surveys and polls suggest that citizens' trust in core democratic institutions such as parliaments and governments has declined in many western societies.[7] Fewer citizens in established democracies trust those institutions they can vote for (parties, parliaments, governments) than those institutions that they cannot vote for, such as the military, judiciary, bureaucracy.[8] This might indicate citizens' preferences towards technocratic governance, rapid top-down decisions and expertise and a shift away from pluralistic competition and parliamentary deliberation. Further, the COVID-19 pandemic has fostered a technocratic turn when most of the executives in democracies used executive decrees and emergency rules.[9] Yet, we wholeheartedly agree with Adam Przeworski that "one should not draw inferences about the survival of democracy from answers to survey questions".[10] In Western Europe for instance, there is a peculiar tension between the worrying survey results on trust in majoritarian institutions and the actual robustness and resilience of democracies, which continue to be strong, and unambiguously democratic political parties still win elections with wide margins.[11] One reason for this might be that support for democratic norms and values is still at high levels but trust in specific democratic institutions such as political parties and parliament is declining or simply very low.

Conceptualizing democratic resilience

We define democracies as political regimes that were established in free and fair multiparty elections taking place in a context where freedom of speech, association, and universal suffrage were guaranteed.[12] However, *liberal* democracies need more: their survival and quality depend also on institutionalized checks and balances that check the power of those who govern.[13] The well constitutionalized horizontal accountability of such democracies is particularly relevant in times when the challenges and assaults on democracy are coming from within, often from democratically elected executives, presidents and prime ministers alike.[14]

Autocratization denotes a relevant decline of democratic regime attributes that may – but do not have to – result in democratic breakdown.[15] Though "autocratization" describes political regime developments on a continuum from democracy to autocracy, it can start from and stop at any point on the regime continuum. In their comprehensive conceptualization of autocratization, Maerz et al. included two different starting zones on the regime continuum. They use the term "democratic regression" for autocratization that occurs within the limits of democracy; and call it "autocratic regression" when some remaining democratic traits decline within the demarcation lines of autocratic regimes and move closer to the autocratic end of the regime continuum.[16] If such processes start and end in democracies with lower democratic quality, they are often termed "democratic erosion".[17] If they are less liberal, individual and minority rights are restricted, and checks and balances do not work satisfactorily anymore, those regimes can be called "electoral" or "defective democracies".[18] If democratic erosion does not come to a halt on the slippery slope of de-democratization, "democratic breakdown" could be the consequence.[19]

Autocratization is not a historically new phenomenon – there have been prior waves of autocratization in the twentieth century.[20] The current "third wave of autocratization" started – slowly but surely – more than a quarter of a century ago.[21] As historical and contemporary cases of autocratization demonstrate, autocratization can be stopped in each phase and point in time. Nevertheless, the more advanced it has become before it is stopped, the more difficult it will be to return to the democratic status quo ante. The sooner it can be stopped, the more likely democratic continuity will be.

Little scholarly attention has been devoted to the issue of democratic resilience in the current period of democratic uncertainty, but the issue will be a decisive one for the quality of democracy and its capacity to survive, both in the present and in the future. While one finds abundant literature on "erosion", "decline", "de-democratization", "de-consolidation" of democracy and the like, it is hard to find studies that analyse the resilience of democracy since 2010. An early exception is a 1999 *Democratization* special issue edited by Burnell and Calvert.[22] Further, Costa Pinto and Teixeira argue that most aspects of democracy in Portugal have stayed resilient after the 2008 financial crisis.[23] Cornell, Møller and Skaaning analysed sources of democratic resilience in Northwest Europe during the 1920s–1930s.[24] Additional case studies of good democratic performers such as the Nordic countries, Switzerland, Costa Rica or Canada are largely missing. The dominant inquiry has always been about democratic decline and its causes. In a recent issue of *Democratization,* mainly on regression of democracy, the contributions of Larry Diamond and Ding and Slater[25] hint at some point to the "resilience" of democracy but without spelling the notion out conceptually.

The few extant explicit treatments of democratic resilience in political science tend to define democratic resilience as commitment to democratic norms and values. For instance, Burnell and Calvert view democratic resilience as an "attachment to democratic ideals (…), in spite of hostility from the officially prescribed values and norms and apparent indifference from many elements in society".[26] In a book on Japan's foreign policy, Teo defines democratic resilience as: "Japanese people's regard for the constitution and democracy".[27] In a broader perspective, Guasti conceptualizes democratic resilience as "the ability of the institutional guardrails and civil society to withstand the attempts of technocratic populists to erode accountability".[28]

In a physical sense, resilience means "the capability of a strained body to recover its size and shape after deformation caused especially by compressive stress [; and] an ability to recover from or adjust easily to misfortune or change".[29] There is no consensus across the sciences on what resilience means. In psychology, resilience means "the process of adapting well in the face of adversity, trauma, tragedy, threats or significant sources of stress".[30] In engineering and architecture, resilience is defined by the "the ability of a building, facility, or community to both prevent damage and to recover from damage".[31] The closeness of that technical understanding to organization theory, where resilience is defined as the ability of a system "to withstand changes in its environment and still function",[32] is not surprising; in urban planning, resilience means the "ability (...) to maintain or rapidly return to desired functions in the face of a disturbance, to adapt to change, and to quickly transform systems that limit current or future adaptive capacity".[33] Taking these insights from across the sciences and transferring them to the context of political regimes, one can define democratic resilience as follows: *Democratic resilience is the ability of a political regime to prevent or react to challenges without losing its democratic character.*

Nevertheless, definitions are still a long way from being analytical concepts or usable "focused theory frames"[34] that allow us to reduce the complex real world of existing phenomena, order them into types or classes, and to formulate assumptions about the causal powers the core dimensions have when they interact with the outside world.[35] From a functionalist point of view,[36] one can distinguish three possible reactions of political regimes to internal and external challenges[37]:

(1) The first stresses the ability to withstand without (major) changes.
(2) The second emphasizes the ability to adapt through internal changes.
(3) The third adds the ability to recover after initial damage and disorder.

These three "abilities" of resilience are neither *all* required by a democracy in order to be resilient nor are they mutually exclusive; rather they can coexist in various constellations. But they are useful as the "functionalist" building blocks for constructing a "usable" concept of democratic resilience.

However, the functionalist perspective, i.e. the ability to withstand, adapt, or recover, is only one constitutive element of democratic resilience – but not a sufficient one. It has to be complemented by two additional constitutive dimensions, namely structural and actor-centred perspectives.[38] First, we need to scrutinize those rules and institutions which are relevant for the survival and democratic quality of the regime, in particular the institutional relationships between the legislature, the executive, and the judiciary. Here we do not have to "re-invent the wheel". The debate on the "perils and virtues" of presidential and parliamentary regimes by Juan Linz and its critics[39] is a useful foundation on which to build.

Second, below those macro-institutions, we should scrutinize the level of the most relevant political actors, namely political parties: Do democratic, semi-democratic or undemocratic parties structure political competition? The more semi- or undemocratic parties impact race and relevant policies, the higher is the centrifugal dynamic of the party system[40] and the lower is democratic resilience; the more democratic parties and actors dominate the competitive dynamic of the party system, the more resilient is democracy.

Below the level of constitutional powers and political parties there is a third level, namely civic culture and civil society. Citizens' attitudes and behaviours are also relevant for democratic resilience. The more widespread and anchored democratic values and attitudes are in a society and the more vital and active civil society is, the more immune is democracy to external shocks and external challenges. In the famous chapter on "mores" in his "Democracy in America", Tocqueville argued that "mores", seen as the internalization of democratic norms into the collective consciousness of a society, may serve as a bulwark against non-democratic tendencies.[41] As Maletz points out "[t]hese mores, if adapted to new conditions, may help to support effective democratic practice".[42] The deeper democratic principles are rooted in the traditions and mores of a society, the better they translate into open, participatory and effective institutions. The more stable the consensus among elites to play by the basic democratic rules of the political game and the fairer the policy output and outcomes of political decisions are perceived to be by the citizens, the more resilient a democratic regime will be. If such a consensus has waned as in the United States during the Trump era; all depends on whether the institutions are strong enough to absorb the undemocratic behaviour of powerful political actors.

The fourth and most fundamental level concerns the political community of citizens.[43] The more cohesive, the less unequal, conflictual and polarized the political community is, the easier it will be for political elites to accept compromises and play by the constitutional rules of democracy. Polarization increases and cleavages deepen the more citizens' common sense of belong evaporates and political communities are jeopardized. To modify Barrington Moores famous saying: no political community, no democracy.

If we take into account the different structures and actors and their relative ability to withstand, adapt to, and recover from challenges and turbulences, we may understand the internal dynamic within a democratic regime better. As an example: if the particular inability and unwillingness of a government to play by the rules can be countered by a strong parliament or an independent and "resilient" judiciary, the executive's attempt to aggrandize its power might be stopped and neutralized right in an initial phase. If the parliament is controlled by the government and does not oppose "executive aggrandizement"[44] beyond the constitutional constraints, and the judiciary is packed by government partisans, the virus of autocratization might spread fast through politics and society and erode democratic resilience on several or all four levels. Boese et al.[45] distinguish in their contribution to this special issue between *onset resilience* and *breakdown resilience*. *Onset resilience* means that democratic regimes resist episodes of autocratization right from the beginning. *Breakdown resilience* describes the potential of a democracy already on the slippery slope of autocratization to resist regime breakdown. The authors call this a "two stage concept of democratic resilience". Their empirical studies show that legislative constraints in particular prevent the executive from engaging in undemocratic aggrandizement, whereas it is the autonomous power of the judiciary t strengthens the resilience against breakdown considerably.

The two-stage concept of democratic resilience can be insightfully applied in large n-analyses. The four-level approach above is particularly applicable to case studies and small n-comparisons where the interactions on each and between the four levels can be observed. The two-stage concept reveals correlation patterns between the particular democratic resilience of specific forms of accountability in specific stages of regime development. The "four-level approach" (see previous section: constitutional powers, political parties, civil society, political community) can trace the virus of autocratization through the different levels of the democratic regimes, can identify the most vulnerable or resilient parts of it, and can discover its main drivers and opponents among the political actors. It is the sum of interdependencies between actors (elites and masses, democrats and antidemocrats) and the functioning of institutions that determine the overall resilience of a democracy. Moreover, it allows us to recognize who the challengers to democracy are and the strong sources of democratic resilience. Both seem to us to be essential for pro-democratic interventions in turbulent times. The concept of resilience understood as a "focused theory frame"[46] amplified by functions, structures and actors can now fully be defined as follows.

A structural-functionalist concept of resilience

Democratic resilience is the ability of a democratic system, its institutions, political actors, and citizens to prevent or react to external and internal challenges, stresses, and assaults through one or more of the three potential reactions: to withstand without changes, to adapt through internal changes, and to recover without losing the democratic character of its regime and its constitutive core institutions, organizations, and processes. The more resilient democracies are on all four levels of the political system (political community, institutions, actors, citizens) the less vulnerable they turn out to be in the present and future.

From an aggregated statistics point of view (e.g. the V-Dem data set), one can argue that democracies are resilient if they manage to preserve the same or a similar level of democratic quality overall and in each of their core dimensions when faced with severe challenges. The same level of quality, however, does not necessarily mean the same processes, institutions, and actors.[47] On the contrary, we can assume that most democracies have to transform and adapt their traditional processes and strategies to changed and changing environments in order to fulfil their democratic functions designed by their respective constitutions.[48] We emphasize that practices, procedures, and even institutions have to adapt to keep the democratic quality of the political regime as a whole. The same does not apply to democratic principles such as individual liberty, popular sovereignty, equal political rights, and constitutional checks and balances as such. Institutions, procedures, and actors may change, but the core principles of democracy have to remain the same. Otherwise, democracy moves down the slippery slope of autocratization.

Moreover, political regimes should not simply adapt to external changes; they should also preventively shape their external environment in order to safeguard the invariant core of democratic principles and thus minimize present and future challenges. A democracy's economic, social, and politico-institutional preventive capacity is causal to its overall resilience. It is not only about institutions and actors but also about the regime's policy performance, which either strengthens or weakens the legitimacy of a (democratic) regime. Knowing that, the erosion of democracy can be seen as the mirror image of consolidating resilience. Several contributions to the special issue (e.g. Boese et al. and Welzel) confirm different versions of modernization theory from Lipset through Przeworski to Inglehart, Norris, and Welzel – that the level of socio-economic development in a democracy – directly or through its mobilization of cognitive resources – can serve as a bulwark for *onset resilience* and economic growth against the danger of regime breakdown.

Erosion is not inevitable

The erosion of democracy can be prevented or stopped by democratic resilience, which in turn can be constructed and strengthened through intelligent democratic reforms. There are multiple entry points to intervene and strengthen single elements and thereby the whole of the democracy. To explore those entry points, develop intervention strategies, and to evaluate their resilience effects on working democracies is a major new research field for countering the present challenges most democracies are facing.

In previous sections, we sketched the general elements of the concept of democratic resilience. We ought to clarify what the central internal factors and external preconditions of democratic resilience are, though the contributions in this special issue discuss in more detail how specific structures, processes, actors, policies and (un)democratic outcomes of the democratic system as a whole interact in specific circumstances at a certain point in time. A recent example, which is affecting all democracies, is the COVID-19 pandemic. Some governments have used the pandemic as an excuse to disproportionally limit democratic rights and freedoms in violation of international standards for emergency responses. Such "pandemic backsliding" has mainly affected countries with an already weak democratic systems such as El Salvador and Sri Lanka.[49] Many democratic governments have reacted to the pandemic by accelerating their processes of authoritative decision-making and diminishing the parliament's involvement in order to fight the pandemic effectively as it has been the case in well-established democracies such as France, Germany, and Austria. Those measures were based on scientific advice from virologists, epidemiologists and public health experts. They were guided by the moral goal of saving human lives in most countries. The goal is understandable, but the concrete measures have temporarily limited individual rights and marginalized parliamentary legislation and control. Thus, even in well-established democracies emergency policies cause some democratic limitations, at least temporarily. First, they accelerate the already latent power shift from the legislature to the executive. Parliaments, the institutional core of representative democracies, were often degraded to ex post rubber stamping institutions after the decision was already made by the executive. It was the hour of the executive, where medical safety trumped political liberties.[50] Second, to contain the spread of the virus, democratically elected governments applied emergency powers and legislation, which temporarily limited basic human rights in particular the freedom of movement and the free exercise of profession.[51] Third, such emergency measures were typically accepted by parts of the parliamentary opposition in 2020. Fourth, the majority of the people (the represented) accepted the emergency policies albeit with shrinking margins as the crisis went on in 2021.

The political response to the pandemic shows how institutions, actors, procedures, and the public is interdependently connected to each other. Moreover, it provides an inside view on how the democratic quality of governance may decrease in deep crises with majoritarian consent – even in well-established democracies. That certainly does not mean that we can identify a script for "how democracies die",[52] since well-established democracies do have sufficient resilience even in times of emergency politics. Immediately after the pandemic, the time for "resilient recovery" has to come. But it may also be too optimistic to assume that all democracies simply turn the switch back to the status quo before the crisis at the end of 2019. It remains to be seen how fast political actors (especially in the executive), institutions, and the people can "forget" those emergency practices and recover, turning back towards the high standards of working liberal democracies.

On the one hand, there remains the danger of a "*ratchet effect*" of measures and policies implemented by governments during COVID-19, meaning that they be hard to undo after the pandemic abates. Even though some measures to surveil citizens appear to be legitimately needed to protect the public from COVID-19 today, they are prone to misuse by authorities in the future.[53] On the other hand, the standards for democratically acceptable and legitimate practices of governance during man-made disasters might shift permanently. What is legitimate during the Corona crisis may also seem justifiable during other deep crises, such as global warming. The damage to democracy may then be minimized as acceptable collateral damage of governance in a permanent state of crisis.

On the way back to working democracies in "normal" times the third dimension of resilience, namely "recovery" will be called upon.

The contributions to this special issue

The contributions to the special issue address the themes of democratic erosion and democratic resilience from various perspectives. Vanessa A. Boese and her co-authors investigate the resilience of democracy since 1900. They define democratic resilience in a minimalist way as the ability to prevent substantial regression in the quality of democratic institutions and practices. They differentiate between "*onset resilience*" and "*breakdown resilience*" and position it in a "two-stage concept of democratic resilience". The two-stage concept allows for interesting new insights into the specific impact of resilience at different stages of regime transformation. Over the period of almost 120 years, onset resilience, i.e. the ability of a democracy to withstand significant erosion, turned out to be rather high. Nevertheless, the worrisome finding is that democratic resilience weakened after 1989 when new democracies emerged from the collapsed Soviet Union. Compared to *onset resilience,* the second stage, i.e. *breakdown resilience*, proved to be much weaker since 1900. The authors test the impact of the classical determinants of regime development such as economic factors, neighbourhood effects, and previous democratic experience, thereby confirming many of the findings of the previous consolidation literature.[54] But the very new finding is that a strong legislature is important for safeguarding democracy and providing *onset resilience*, where the judicial control works as "democracy's last line of defence" against breakdown,[55] fighting against autocratizers in the executive. It is interesting to note that this runs to some extent counter to what we know about the *onset resilience* of a democracy during the COVID-19 crisis when it was above all the judiciary that controlled the executive much more effectively than the parliament, which accepted many of the emergency decisions of the government. This happened in Germany alone more than 150 times during the first year of the pandemic.

Melis G. Laebens and Anna Lührmann take up the question of what can stop democratic erosion and relate it to different spheres of accountability conceived as the institutional core of democratic resilience. Building on earlier works, their analysis distinguishes between three types of accountability: vertical, diagonal, and horizontal. All three types can impact a democracy's fate on their own, but they are more powerful the more they act jointly and simultaneously. As the two authors argue, incumbents are afraid to be voted out of power. That fear sometimes constrains their autocratic ambitions of governments. Protest, unrest, or an organized "monitory civil society"[56] may also prevent or stop the autocratic ambitions of the incumbents. They make clandestine autocratization apparent to a wider public. Independent media play an important role; that is why the first actions of autocratizers are often directed against non-governmental organizations and the media. The judiciary can stop repressive policies against the independence of the media and punish autocratizers for corruption. A strong parliamentary opposition challenges the power aggrandizement of the executive and makes it apparent to the citizens. Based on a comparison of three dissimilar cases and constructed analytic narratives of severe episodes of democratic erosion Laebens and Lührmann's analysis suggest that accountability mechanism may prevent the breakdown of democracy if institutional constraints work together with civil society. They constitute an effective bulwark against democratic breakdown particularly if contextual factors change in disfavour of the incumbent – for example due to economic crisis and corruption scandals.

Murat Somer, Jennifer McCoy and Russell Luke focus on one of the major shortfalls of contemporaneous democracies: polarization, or more precisely "pernicious polarization". Accepting that some polarization inextricably exists and may even be necessary in pluralist democracies and unequal capitalist societies, the three authors claim that democratic polarization transforms into toxic or pernicious polarization when the political interplay between opponents transforms into a political war between "Us and Them" and political opponents become enemies. That is what Carl Schmitt conceived as the essence of "the political". Almost one century later, at the beginning of the 2020s, Somer, McCoy and Luke claim that polarization – especially severe *levels* of sustained polarization rather than temporary surges in the *rate* of polarization – mostly fosters trends towards the decline of liberal democracy and benefits the radical actors in politics and society. However, the three authors go beyond the empirical confirmation of that trend and ask which strategies in the conflict between incumbents and opposition lead to polarization or can trigger the opposite, namely depolarization. They identify an "endogenous explanation of polarization" and strategic ways to escape the pernicious dynamic of increasing polarization. Agency matters, according to the authors. Democratic resilience depends considerably on what kind of polarizing or de-polarizing strategies political oppositions employ against the incumbent autocratizers, and how. Depolarizing strategies might avoid the "pitfalls of pernicious polarization-cum-autocratization".[57] More importantly, it matters whether actors employ generative, rather than preservative, strategies, shifting the axis of politics to new issues and cleavages that weaken the basis of polarizing politics. Thus, regenerative strategies of "active-depolarizing" and "transformative-repolarizing" strategies are most promising "to improve a country's resilience to autocratizing pressures".[58] Hence, the authors go beyond the level of pure (analytical) description and dare to move into the sphere of prescription providing analysts and political elites with a set of strategies and tools to use against pernicious polarization. Similar to Boese et al. and Laebens and Lührmann, Somer, McCoy and Luke consider those tools and strategies to be determined by time and timing. Tools and strategies have to be contextualized to the phase of democratic erosion. If, for example, the erosion of democracy has progressed and the checks and balances of parliament and the courts do not have the de facto constitutional power or perceived legitimacy to prevent the illegal aggrandizement of power by the executive, then the combination of oppositional mobilization and protest in the streets (or at the workplace) with concerted opposition during electoral campaigns may stop even seemingly unassailable incumbents from further autocratization.

But who are the most pernicious actors driving polarization in Europe, the US, India, Turkey, and parts of Latin America? Populism, mostly right-wing populism, represents powerfully the Zeitgeist of polarization and propagates politics as a political zero-sum game between *Friends and Foes* or *Them and Us*. Carlos Meléndez and

Cristóbal Rovira Kaltwasser analyse the emergence and the potential limits of the new radical populist key players in gaining majoritarian support from the voters. In order to balance the autocratizing power of the populist radical right (PRR) against the resilience of democracy, the authors follow a rather new approach in party research. They do not focus primarily on the voters and sympathizers of the PRR (positive partisanship), but on those citizens who wholeheartedly reject them, called negative partisanship. Negative partisanship implies a deeply anchored antipathy and rejection of the populist radical right. It is combined with the conviction of individual voters that they cannot imagine ever voting for any party of the PRR. To investigate those forms of partisanship, the two authors have chosen the empirical sample of 10 Western European countries. Their findings show that on average around 10% of citizens in those Western European democracies have a clear positive partisanship in relation to the PRR, in part due to its illiberal leanings and in part due to its open authoritarian values and attitudes. But what is the ceiling of electoral support for the PRR? Can those parties extend their electoral influence significantly? Rovira Kaltwasser and Meléndez are sceptical. They hint at approximately 50% of voters with a marked negative partisanship in relation to the PRR. Moreover, that negative partisanship is accompanied by a positive identification with liberal democracy and the defense of immigration, European integration, and minority rights. At least for the moment, these empirical facts call for a less ubiquitous alarmist attitude to the challenge of the PRR to democracy in the public discourse in Western Europe.[59] They maintain that activating and mobilizing negative partisanship towards the PRR is an important remedy to limit the electoral growth of this party family. Another idea for an institutional remedy for stabilizing or even lowering the ceiling for the PRR could be compulsory voting. It would not only diminish the relative percentage of the PRR vote since the radical right mobilizes their voters much more efficiently than centre parties, but also counter the undemocratic underrepresentation of the lower classes.

After analysing the erosion and resilience of democracy on the macro-level of institutions and the meso-level of political actors, the micro-level of individual behaviour and democratic learning is still missing. Steven Finkel and Junghyun Lim are filling this gap. Their research question goes to a core desideratum of sustainable resilience when they ask: "Can democratic orientations and political participation in fragile democracies be fostered through civic education?" If this were the case, then we would have found one major piece of the puzzle of self-reproducing democratic resilience. The authors report that early work ascribed the generally positive effects to civic education, whereas more recent work has become increasingly sceptical. They set up an experiment in the Democratic Republic of Congo to try to get insight into the question in a field experiment. The results to some extent reproduce the assumptions and findings of the older and more recent research. On the one hand, the experiment shows a negative effect of civic education on support for decentralization and individuals' satisfaction with democracy. On the other hand, the participants in the experiment displayed positive democratic effects in the form of non-electoral participation and "democratic orientations such as knowledge, efficacy, and political tolerance". In times where we observe "pernicious polarization" in many democracies (cf. Somer, McCoy and Luke in this issue), an increase in political tolerance appears to be key to democratic resilience. Accordingly, Finkel and Lim conclude that "civic education programs continue to have the potential to deepen democratic engagement and values, even in fragile or backsliding democratic settings" (Finkel and Lim in this issue). This is a hopeful message for democracies in challenging times: civic education may enhance democratic resilience even under unlikely circumstances.

Cristian Welzel is also optimistic with regard to the future of democracy in his contribution. His research is firmly rooted in modernization theory ranging from Seymour Martin Lipset to Ronald Inglehart and Pippa Norris. But Welzel gives his approach his own special twist. It is not simply economic development, but more specifically the steady increase of "emancipative values" which speaks for the resilience of a democracy, at least in the long run. Against the *Zeitgeist* of current research on democratic backsliding, he criticizes much of the "democracy-in-crisis-literature" as being negligent about the cultural foundations of autocracy versus democracy. He argues that the country's membership in higher and lower emancipative "culture zones" explains about 70% of the global variation in autocracy versus democracy. And he affirms that this variation remained highly stable over time. According to Welzel, democratic backsliding is overwhelmingly limited to countries with low levels of emancipative values. The author emphasizes that the prospects for democracy depend on the further development of emancipative values among the citizens of a country. At least in the long run, there are good reasons to be optimistic. Nevertheless, the author concedes that there can be democratic backsliding in the short run. But seen from the perspective of the ascendant emancipative development as a generational profile, Welzel argues that the current episode of democratic erosion will stand out "as a temporary downward cycle (rather) than a lasting downward trajectory" (Welzel in this issue).

Not all authors in this issue would subscribe to this strong optimism. They have based their analyses not on long-term cultural perspectives, but on rather short-term observations with a strong leaning towards neo-institutionalist approaches. They emphasize political actors and actions. The contributors see the challenges of democratic erosion and take them seriously, but they do not join the chorus intoning the inevitable crisis in democracy almost everywhere. On the contrary, almost all of the contributions diagnose erosions, but they also see and propose ways out of democracy's malaise. The message is that political agency matters. At least in the more developed democracies, most of the institutions and political agents are more prone to democracy than to autocracy. There is a spirit of reasonable, well-grounded, but cautious optimism that connects the contributions of this special issue. The more we know about democratic resilience, the more we can advise politics how to strengthen it.

Notes

1. See for example, Merkel and Kneip, "Introduction", "Conclusion"; Lührmann and Lindberg, "A Third Wave of Autocratization is Here"; Diamond, *Ill Winds*; Mounck, *The People vs Democracy*; Urbinati, *Democracy Difigured*, Svolik, "Polarization versus Democracy"; Keane, *The New Despotisms*; Maerz et al. "State of the World 2020"; Diamond, "Democratic Regression in Comparative Perspective".
2. E.g. Bermeo, "Reflections"; Norris and Inglehart, *Cultural Backlash*; Levitsky and Ziblatt, *How Democracies Die.*
3. Linz, *The Breakdown.*
4. Lührmann and Hellmeier, "Populismus, Nationalismus und Illiberalisums".
5. See for example Merkel and Kneip, "Democracy and Crisis"; Mounk, *The People vs Democracy*; Lührmann and Lindberg, "A Third Wave".
6. Merkel, "Embedded and Defective Democracies"; Levitsky and Ziblatt, *How Democracies Die.*

7. Based on Eurobarometer data, Merkel and Krause show an average decline in trust in governments and parliaments in Europe between 1994 and 2013. Petraca, Sanhueza and Weßels point out that while trust decreased somewhat at the end of the 2000s, there is no "common" pattern of decline in Europe in trust in parliaments and parties until 2018 using the Eurobarometer and GovElec data; see Merkel and Krause, "Krise der Demokratie?" 59. Petrarca, Sanhueza and Weßels, "Support for Insider," 8.
8. For Europe see Merkel and Krause, "Krise der Demokratie?" 59; for other OECD countries see: Schäfer and Zürn, "Demokratische Regression," 105.
9. Merkel, "Who Governs in Deep Crisis?"
10. Przeworski, *Crisis of Democracy*, 102.
11. Merkel and Kneip, "Democracy and Crisis"; Maerz, et al., "State of the World"; Morlino et al., "What Is the Impact of the Economic Crisis on Democracy?" 618.
12. See Dahl, "A Preface to Democratic Theory"; Dahl, "Polyarchy"; Lührmann et al., "Regimes of the World".
13. See for example O'Donnell, "Horizontal Accountability in New Democracies"; Merkel, "Embedded and Defective Democracies".
14. See for example Levitsky and Ziblatt 2018; Keane, "The New Despotisms".
15. Lührmann and Lindberg, "A Third Wave"; Maerz et al., "Understanding Regime Transformation".
16. Maerz et al., "Understanding Regime Transformation", 7.
17. See Laebens and Lührmann, "Halting Erosion".
18. Merkel, "Embedded and Defective Democracies".
19. Such a process from a liberal democracy to a closed autocracy can occur in a rather short period of time is historically shown in the last years of the Weimar Republic by the erosion (1929–1932) and breakdown (1933) of (liberal) democracy, followed by the closing of its autocratic regime in 1934. Classical on democratic breakdown is Linz, *Breakdown*.
20. Huntington, *The Third Wave*, 17.
21. Lührmann and Lindberg, "A Third Wave".
22. Burnell and Calvert, "The Resilience of Democracy."
23. Costa Pinto and Teixeira, "Portugal Before and After".
24. Cornell, Møller, and Skaaning, *Democratic Stability in an Age of Crisis*.
25. Diamond, "Democratic Regression"; Dinng and Slater, "Democratic Decoupling".
26. Burnell and Calvert, "The Resilience of Democracy," 4.
27. Teo, *Japan's Arduous Rejuvenation*, 23.
28. Guasti, "Populism in Power and Democracy," 476.
29. https://www.merriam-webster.com/dictionary/resilience.
30. American Psychological Association, *The Road to Resilience*, 1.
31. American Institute of Architects, *Architectural Graphic Standards*, 72.
32. McCarthy et al, "Adaptive Organizational Resilience," 33.
33. Meerow et al., "Defining Urban Resilience," 39.
34. Rueschemeyer, *Usable Theory*, 29.
35. Goertz, *Social Science Concept*, 28.
36. Easton, *System Analysis*.
37. On the distinction between exogenous and endogenous threats to regime stability see also Gerschewski, "Explanations of Institutional Change". Many contemporary challenges to regime stability come from actors, which are within the regime itself (e.g. elected executives undermining media freedom).
38. Scharpf, *Games Real Actors Play*.
39. Linz, "Perils"; Linz, "Virtues"; Linz and Stepan, "Problems"; Przeworski et al., "Democratic Development"; Nohlen, "El Contexto"; Cheibub et al., "Beyond presidentialism".
40. Sartori, *Parties and Party Systems*.
41. Tocqueville, Amerika, 183.
42. Maletz, "Tocqueville on Mores and the Preservation of Republics," 1.
43. Easton, "A Systems Analysis".
44. Bermeo, "Democratic Backsliding," 6.
45. Boese et al., "How Democracies Prevail".
46. Rueschemeyer, *Usable Theory*, 28.

RESILIENCE OF DEMOCRACY   13

47. This is due to democracy being multi-dimensional. A given level of democracy can reflect a wide variety of configurations of institutions, actors etc. See Boese et al., "Visualizing Authority Patterns".
48. See: Lührmann, "Conclusion," in this issue.
49. Kolvani et al. "Pandemic Backsliding".
50. Merkel, "Who Governs in Deep Crisis".
51. The time we are writing this is the end of March 2021. In most democracies, some sort of emergency measures still remain in place.
52. Levitsky and Ziblatt, *How Democracies Die*.
53. Smith and Cheeseman, "Authoritarians are Exploiting the Corona Virus".
54. See for example Linz and Stepan, *Problems of Democratic Transition and Consolidation*; Merkel, "Consolidation"; Morlino, *Democracy between Consolidation and Crisis*; Morlino; "Democratic Consolidation".
55. See Boese et al., in this issue.
56. Keane, "Monitory Democracy?" 212.
57. Somer, McCoy and Luke in this issue.
58. Ibid.
59. There are hints that the assault of right and left-wing populism on liberal democracy is more frequent and successful in presidential systems in North and Latin America.

Acknowledgements

This issue builds on the discussions at the Berlin Democracy Conference in November 2019, which was a collaboration between the Varieties of Democracy Institute (V-Dem), the Berlin Social Science Center (WZB) and the Open Society Foundations (OSF). We would like to express our gratitude to everyone involved in these debates; in particular to Palina Kolvani and Kilian Lüders for their skillful research assistance. We are grateful for helpful comments to earlier versions of this article from the authors of this issue and editors of Democratization.

Disclosure statement

No potential conflict of interest was reported by the author(s).

Funding

The Berlin Democracy Conference has been funded by the Open Society Initiative for Europe (OSIFE, Grant OR2018-45627). Anna Lührmann's work on the special issue has been supported by the Vetenskapsrådet [grant number 2018-01614].

ORCID

Anna Lührmann   http://orcid.org/0000-0003-4258-1088

Bibliography

American Psychological Association. *The Road to Resilience*. Washington, DC: American Psychological Association, 2014.

American Institute of Architects. *Architectural Graphic Standards*. 12th ed. New York: John Wiley & Sons, 2016.

Bermeo, Nancy. "Reflections: Can American Democracy Still be Saved?" *The ANNALS of the American Academy of Political and Social Science* 681, no. 1 (2019): 228–234. doi:10.1177%2F0002716218818083.

Boese, Vanessa, Scott Gates, Carl-Hendrik Knutsen, Harvard Nygård, and Harvard Strand. "Visualizing Authority Patterns over Space and Time." V-Dem Working Paper 96 (2020).

Boese, Vanessa A., Amanda B. Edgell, Sebastian Hellmeier, Seraphine F. Maerz, and Staffan I. Lindberg. "How Democracies Prevail: Democratic Resilience as a Two-Stage Process." *Democratization* 5 (2021). doi:10.1080/13510347.2021.1891413.

Burnell, Peter, and Peter Calvert. "The Resilience of Democracy: An Introduction." *Democratization* 6, no. 1 (1999): 1–32. doi:10.1080/13510349908403594.

Cheibub, José Antonio, Zachary Elkins, and Tom Ginsburg. "Beyond Presidentialism and Parliamentarism." *British Journal of Political Science* 44, no. 3 (2014): 515–544. doi:10.1017/S000712341300032X.

Cornell, Agnes, Jørgen Møller, and Svend-Erik Skaaning. *Democratic Stability in an Age of Crisis: Reassessing the Interwar Period*. Oxford: Oxford University Press, 2020.

Costa Pinto, António, and Conceição Pequito Teixeira. "Portugal Before and After the 'Great Recession': A Resilient Democracy?" In *Political Institutions and Democracy in Portugal: Assessing the Impact of the Eurocrisis*, edited by António Costa Pinto, and Conceição Pequito Teixeira, 1–12. Cham: Springer International Publishing, 2019.

Dahl, Robert A. *A Preface to Democratic Theory*. Chicago: The University of Chicago Press, 1956.

Dahl, Robert A. *Polyarchy: Participation and Opposition*. Connecticut: Yale UP, 1971.

Diamond, Larry. *Ill Winds: Saving Democracy from Russian Rage, Chinese Ambition, and American Complacency*. New York: Penguin, 2019.

Diamond, Larry. "Democratic Regression in Comparative Perspective: Scope, Methods, and Causes." *Democratization* 28, no. 1 (2021): 22–42.

Easton, David. *A System Analysis of Political Life*. New York: John Wiley and Sons, Inc, 1965.

Finkel, Steven E., and Junghyun Lim. "The Supply and Demand Model of Civic Education: Evidence from a Field Experiment in the Democratic Republic of Congo." *Democratization* 5 (2020). doi:10.1080/13510347.2020.1843156.

Gerschewski, Johannes. "Explanations of Institutional Change: Reflecting on a Missing Diagonal." *American Political Science Review* 115 (2021): 218–233. doi:10.1017/S0003055420000751

Goertz, Gary. *Social Science Concepts*. Princeton: PUC, 2006.

Guasti, Petra. "Populism in Power and Democracy: Democratic Decay and Resilience in the Czech Republic." *Politics and Governance* 8, no. 4S3 (2020): 473–484. doi:10.17645/pag.v8i4.3420.

Huntington, Samuel P. *The Third Wave. Democratization in the Late Twentieth Century*. Oklahoma: Oklahoma University Press, 1991.

Jones, Clive. "Israel's Democracy at Fifty: From Resilience to Residue?" *Democratization* 6, no. 1 (1999): 155–178. doi:10.1080/13510349908403601.

Keane, John. "Monitory Democracy?" In *The Future of Representative Democracy*, edited by Sonia Alonso, John Keane, and Wolfgang Merkel, 212–235. Cambridge: Cambridge UP, 2011. doi:10.1017/CBO9780511770883.010

Keane, John. *The New Despotisms*. Cambridge: Harvard UP, 2020.

Kelsen, Hans. *Allgemeine Staatslehre*. Tübingen: Mohr Siebeck, 1925.

Krause, Werner, and Wolfgang Merkel. "Crisis of Democracy? Views of Experts and Citizens." In *Democracy and Crisis. Challenges in Turbulent Times*, edited by Wolfgang Merkel and Sascha Kneip, 31–47. Cham: Springer, 2018.

Laebens, Melisa, and Anna Lührmann. "What Halts Democratic Erosion? The Changing Role of Accountability." *Democratization* 5 (2021). doi:10.1080/13510347.2021.1897109.

Levitsky, Steve, and Daniel Ziblatt. *How Democracies Die*. New York: Penguin, 2018.

Linz, Juan, and Alfred Stepan. *Problems of Democratic Transition and Consolidation: Southern Europe, South America and Post-Communist Europe*. Baltimore: JHU-Press, 1996.

Linz, Juan. "The Perils of Presidentialism." *Journal of Democracy* 1, no. 1 (1990): 51–69. . muse.j-hu.edu/article/225694.

Linz, Juan. *The Breakdown of Democratic Regimes: Crisis, Breakdown & Reequilibration.* Baltimore: Johns Hopkins University Press, 1978.

Kolvani, Palina, Martin Lundstedt, Seraphine F. Maerz, Anna Lührmann, Jean Lachapelle, Sandra Grahn, and Amanda B. Edgell. "Pandemic Backsliding: Democracy and Disinformation Seven Months into the Covid-19 Pandemic." V-Dem Policy Brief 25 (2020). https://www.v-dem.net/en/publications/briefing-papers/.

Lührmann, Anna, Marcus Tannenberg, und Staffan I. Lindberg. 2018. "Regimes of the World (RoW): Opening New Avenues for the Comparative Study of Political Regimes." *Politics and Governance* 6 (1): 1–18.

Lührmann, Anna, und Staffan I. Lindberg. 2019. "A Third Wave of Autocratization is Here: What is New about It?" *Democratization* 26 (7): 1095-1113.

Maerz, Seraphine F., Amanda Edgell, Matthew C. Wilson, Sebastian Hellmeier, and Staffan I. Lindberg. "A Framework for Understanding Regime Transformation: Introducing the ERT Dataset." V-Dem Working Paper 113 (2021). doi:10.2139/ssrn.3781485

Maletz, Donald J. ": Tocqueville on Mores and the Preservation of Republics." *American Journal of Political Science* 49, no. 1 (2005): 1–15.

McCarthy, Ian P, Mark Collard, and Michael Johnson. "Adaptive Organizational Resilience: An Evolutionary Perspective." *Current Opinion in Environmental Sustainability* 28 (2017): 33–40. doi:10.1016/j.cosust.2017.07.005.

McCoy, Jennifer, and Murat Somer. "Toward a Theory of Pernicious Polarization and How It Harms Democracies: Comparative Evidence and Possible Remedies." *The Annals of the American Academy of Political and Social Science* 681, no. 1 (2019): 234–271.

McCoy, Jennifer, and Murat Somer, eds. "Special Issue on Polarized Polities: A Global Threat to Democracy." *Annals of the American Academy of Political and Social Science* 681, no. 1 (2019): 8–271.

Meerow, Sara, Joshua P. Newell, and Melissa Stults. "Defining Urban Resilience: A Review." *Landscape and Urban Planning* 147 (2016): 38–49.

Meléndez, Carlos, and Cristóbal Rovira Kaltwasser. "Negative Partisanship Towards the Populist Radical Right and Democratic Resilience in Western Europe." *Democratization* 5 (2021). doi:10.1080/13510347.2021.1883002.

Merkel, Wolfgang. "The Consolidation of Post-Autocratic Democracies: A Multi-Level Model." *Democratization* 5, no. 3 (1998): 33–67. doi:10.1080/13510349808403572.

Merkel, Wolfgang. "Embedded and Defective Democracies." *Democratization* 11, no. 5 (2004): 33–58. doi:10.1080/13510340412331304598.

Merkel, Wolfgang. "Who Governs in Deep Crises? The Case of Germany." *Democratic Theory* 7, no. 2 (2020): 1–11. doi:10.3167/dt.2020.070202.

Merkel, Wolfgang and Kneip, Sascha, eds. *Democracy and Crisis. Challenges in Turbulent Times.* Cham: Springer, 2018.

Merkel, Wolfgang, and Werner Krause. "Krise der Demokratie? Ansichten von Experten und Bürgern." In *Demokratie und Krise. Zum schwierigen Verhältnis von Theorie und Empirie*, edited by Wolfgang Merkel, 45–65. Wiesbaden: Springer VS, 2015.

Mitra, Subrata Kumar, and Mike Enskat. "Parties and the People: India's Changing Party System and the Resilience of Democracy." *Democratization* 6, no. 1 (1999): 123–154. doi:10.1080/13510349908403600.

Morlino, Leonardo. *Democracy Between Consolidation and Crisis.* Oxford: OUP, 1998.

Morlino, Leonardo. "Democratic Consolidation." In *The Handbook of Political, Social, and Economic Transformation*, edited by Wolfgang Merkel, Raj Kollmorgen, and Han-Jürgen Wagener, 459–464. Oxford: OUP, 2019.

Morlino, Leonardo, Mario Quaranta, Marianne Kneuer, Brigitte Geissel, and Hans-Joachim Lauth. "What is the Impact of the Economic Crisis on Democracy? Evidence from Europe." *IPSR* 37, no. 5 (2016): 618–633. doi:10.1177%2F0192512116639747

Nohlen, Dieter. *El Contexto Hace la Diferencia: Reformas Institucionales y el Enfoque Histórico-empírico.* México: Universidad Nacional Autónoma de México, Instituto de Investigaciones Jurídicas: Tribunal Electoral del Poder Judicial de la Federación, 2003.

Norris, Pippa, and Ronald Inglehart. *Cultural Backlash: Trump, Brexit, and Authoritarian Populism.* Cambridge: Cambridge UP, 2019.

O'Donnell, Guillermo. "Horizontal Accountability in New Democracies." *Journal of Democracy* 9, no. 3 (1998): 112–126. doi:10.1353/jod.1998.0051.

O'Donnell, Guillermo, Philippe C. Schmitter, and Lawrence Whitehead. *Transitions from Authoritarian Rule. Tentative Conclusions about Uncertain Democracies.* Baltimore: JHU-Press, 1986.

Petrarca, Constanza Sanhueza, Heiko Giebler, and Bernhard Weßels. "Support for Insider Parties: The Role of Political Trust in a Longitudinal-Comparative Perspective." *Party Politics* (2020). doi:10.1177/1354068820976920

Przeworski, Adam. *Crises of Democracy.* Cambridge: CUP, 2019.

Przeworski, Adam, Michael E. Alvarez, José Antonio Cheibub, and Fernando Limongi. *Democracy and Development. Political Institutions and Well-Being in the World, 1950–1990.* Cambridge: Cambridge UP, 2000.

Rueschemeyer, Dietrich. *Usable Theory: Analytical Tools for Social and Political Research.* Princeton: PUC, 2009.

Sartori, Giovanni. *Parties and Party Systems: A Framework for Analysis.* Cambridge: CUP, 1976.

Schäfer, Armin, and Michael Zürn. *Die Demokratische Regression.* Frankfurt: Suhrkamp, 2021.

Scharpf, Fritz W. *Games Real Actors Play.* New York: Routledge, 1997.

Schmitt, Carl. *The Concept of the Political, 1932.* Chicago: The University of Chicago Press, 1996.

Schmotz, Alexander. "Hybrid Regimes." In *Handbook of Political, Social, and Economic Transformation*, edited by Wolfgang Merkel, Raj Kollmorgen, and Hans-Jürgen Wagener, 521–525. Oxford: OUP, 2019.

Somer, Murat, Jennifer McCoy and Russell Evan Luke IV. "Pernicious Polarization, Autocratization and Opposition Strategies." *Democratization* 5 (2021). doi:10.1080/13510347.2020.1865316.

Smith, Jeffrey, and Nic Cheeseman. "Authoritarians Are Exploiting the Coronavirus. Democracies Must Not Follow Suit." *Foreign Policy*, April 28, 2020. https://foreignpolicy.com/2020/04/28/authoritarians-exploiting-coronavirus-undermine-civil-liberties-democracies/.

Svolik, Milan. "Polarization versus Democracy." *Journal of Democracy* 30, no. 3 (2019): 20–32. doi:10.1353/jod.2019.0039.

Teo, Victor. *Japan's Arduous Rejuvenation as a Global Power: Democratic Resilience and the US-China Challenge.* Singapore: Springer Nature, 2019.

Tocqueville, Alexis de. *Über die Demokratie in America* [Democracy in America], 1835. Stuttgart: Reclam, 1985.

Urbinati, Nadia. *Democracy Disfigured: Opinion, Truth, and the People.* Cambridge: Harvard UP, 2014.

Welzel, Christian. "Democratic Horizons: What Value Change Reveals about the Future of Democracy." *Democratization* 5 (2021). doi:10.1080/13510347.2021.1883001.

OPEN ACCESS

How democracies prevail: democratic resilience as a two-stage process

Vanessa A. Boese ⑩, Amanda B. Edgell ⑩, Sebastian Hellmeier ⑩, Seraphine F. Maerz ⑩ and Staffan I. Lindberg ⑩

ABSTRACT
This article introduces a novel conceptualization of democratic resilience - a two-stage process where democracies avoid democratic declines altogether or avert democratic breakdown given that such autocratization is ongoing. Drawing on the Episodes of Regime Transformation (ERT) dataset, we find that democracies have had a high level of resilience to onset of autocratization since 1900. Nevertheless, democratic resilience has become substantially weaker since the end of the Cold War. Fifty-nine episodes of sustained and substantial declines in democratic practices have occurred since 1993, leading to the unprecedented breakdown of 36 democratic regimes. Ominously, we find that once autocratization begins, only one in five democracies manage to avert breakdown. We also analyse which factors are associated with each stage of democratic resilience. The results suggest that democracies are more resilient when strong judicial constraints on the executive are present and democratic institutions were strong in the past. Conversely and adding nuance to the literature, economic development is only associated with resilience to onset of autocratization, not to resilience against breakdown once autocratization has begun.

Introduction

Democracy is under threat globally. Over 20% of countries in the world[1] and one-third of the global population are now experiencing substantial and sustained declines in democracy amounting to a "third wave" of autocratization.[2] Since 1992, 36 democratic regimes have broken down. What distinguishes democracies that prevail against a global wave of autocratization from those that do not?

ⓑ Supplemental data for this article can be accessed at https://doi.org/10.1080/13510347.2021.1891413.

This is an Open Access article distributed under the terms of the Creative Commons Attribution License (http://creativecommons.org/licenses/by/4.0/), which permits unrestricted use, distribution, and reproduction in any medium, provided the original work is properly cited.

Understanding "democratic resilience" – the ability to prevent substantial regression in the quality of democratic institutions and practices – is now more important than ever.[3] Yet, the term presently lacks a clear specification in the literature, making it prone to becoming yet another buzzword in democracy promotion. We offer a new conceptualization of democratic resilience with two stages that are distinct. In the first stage – *onset resilience* – some democracies are resilient by preventing autocratization altogether, meaning they have not experienced substantial or sustained declines in democratic qualities (such as Switzerland and Canada). If onset resilience fails, democracies experience an episode of autocratization. A democracy may then exhibit *breakdown resilience* by avoiding democratic breakdown in the second stage (such as South Korea from 2008–2016, and Benin from 2007–2012).

This two-stage concept of democratic resilience is pragmatic and empirically observable, allowing us to assess which democracies withstand the forces of autocratization (that is, have high onset resilience – at least thus far) and which have breakdown resilience once autocratization has begun.

We make use of the new Episodes of Regime Transformation (ERT) dataset[4] that identifies episodes of substantial and sustained changes in levels of democracy for most political units from 1900 to 2019 drawing on the V-Dem electoral democracy index (EDI).[5] This episodes approach enables us to empirically observe the two-stage process of democratic resilience that provides a better concept-measurement validity compared to data on annual changes in levels or discrete regime types.[6]

We then provide a comprehensive overview of global trends in both stages of democratic resilience since 1900. This descriptive analysis offers several new insights. First, it shows that onset resilience is very high among democracies. There have been only 96 episodes of autocratization in 64 democratic countries from 1900 to 2019. Second, however, we find that democracies are increasingly susceptible to onset of autocratization and the period since the end of the Cold War is the worst on record. Third, once a democracy enters an autocratization episode, the fatality rate is distressingly high: since 1900 a mere 19 episodes (23%) managed to avert breakdown at the end of the episode. Fourth, the two-stage approach to democratic resilience demonstrates an important methodological insight: what is typically treated as a quandary of measurement (levels vs. discrete changes) is actually the equifinality of democratic survival.

Finally, we provide a novel set of analyses by modelling how economic and political factors identified as determinants of autocratization in the literature are related to each stage of the democratic resilience process. Judicial constraints on the executive and a country's past experience with democracy (democratic stock) are positively associated with onset and breakdown resilience. Thus, our results support views that see the judiciary as the last bulwark against autocracy. Contrarily, economic development is only associated with resilience to onset of autocratization, not to resilience against breakdown once autocratization has begun. Higher levels of democracy in neighbouring countries, by contrast, are positively related to resilience against breakdown but not to onset resilience. The main takeaway from these empirical correlations is that different factors seem to matter for onset and breakdown resilience, respectively. By adopting an episode approach rather than measuring regime transitions as events, we can distinguish between these factors.

Conceptualizing democratic resilience

In general, we define democratic resilience as the persistence of democratic institutions and practices. Empirically, resilience is measured as the continuation of democracy, without substantial or sustained declines in its quality, that is, the avoidance of autocratization.[7] We speak of *episodes* of autocratization to capture periods with a definitive start and end date during which substantial and sustained declines in democratic qualities take place.[8] Such declines may result in democratic breakdown, or the regime could avert breakdown by reversing the trend and sustain minimal levels of democracy necessary to be considered democratic.

For this reason, we conceptualize democratic resilience as a two-stage process (see Figure 1). In the first stage, democracies exhibit resilience by maintaining or improving their level of democracy. Put differently, first-stage resilient democracies avoid the onset of autocratization. For this reason, we refer to the first stage as *onset resilience*. In the second stage, democracies that are experiencing autocratization can demonstrate resilience by averting democratic breakdown. This second stage of democratic resilience thus involves avoiding a regime change. We refer to this second stage as *breakdown resilience*. Because a democracy can only exhibit breakdown resilience if it has failed to demonstrate onset resilience, these two stages of resilience may have different drivers. What happens after a democratic breakdown, lies outside the scope of this study.

Importantly, we can only observe whether a democracy has exhibited onset or breakdown resilience *until now*. We may also not yet know if a democracy currently undergoing autocratization will exhibit resilience breakdown because the episode is still ongoing (as is the case for the 12 "censored" episodes in our sample). In either case, this does not necessarily mean that the regime itself will be onset or breakdown resilient in the future.[9] In other words, our approach avoids making assumptions about resilience at the regime level.

This departs from earlier literature on democratic consolidation, that sought to label democratic regimes as "consolidated" based on predictions about their propensity to survive.[10] A democracy is typically considered consolidated if it is unlikely to revert to authoritarianism in the future.[11] Thus, democratic consolidation remains an inherently fuzzy term that relies on causal inferences about democratic stability or survival

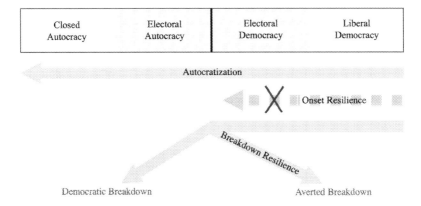

Figure 1. Conceptualization of onset and breakdown resilience.

drawn from observations about the regime duration and its correlates.[12] Yet, this ignores the fact that all "consolidated democracies" somehow managed to survive from year-to-year before they became consolidated, and that "unconsolidated democracies" often survive for several years (or decades) before ultimately breaking down.[13] This is why it is preferable to use "resilience" based on empirics rather than the future-orientated and therefore largely unobservable concept of "consolidation".[14] We thus provide an important corrective to previous research on democratic consolidation.[15]

If anything, recent failures of onset resilience in cases like the United States, India, and Brazil, as well as failures of breakdown resilience in Hungary and Venezuela, highlight the dangers of forecasting regimes as "consolidated" based on their past. Whether regimes that have previously shown breakdown resilience are more likely to exhibit onset or breakdown resilience in the future is an empirical question yet to be explored. Elsewhere in this special issue, Laebens and Lührmann[16] provide a detailed qualitative analysis of such breakdown-resilient democracies where autocratization stopped short of a regime transition.

Consider, for example, the case of Mali (Figure 2). Despite Mali's rapid democratization from 1991–1993, early observers warned that it could yield yet another failed democratic experiment.[17] Prior to 1992, the country was persistently authoritarian, having endured spells of military and one-party rule since independence in 1960. Scepticism about Mali's democratic resilience initially appeared warranted. Widespread irregularities and opposition boycotts marred the 1997 parliamentary elections, forcing the Constitutional Court to invalidate the poll and order a re-run. Against all odds, however, Mali exhibited breakdown resilience and further democratized throughout the mid-1990s and early 2000s. By 2012, it appeared poised for a third peaceful transition of power through multiparty presidential elections. While on the outside Mali had become "one of Africa's model democracies",[18] on the inside, its

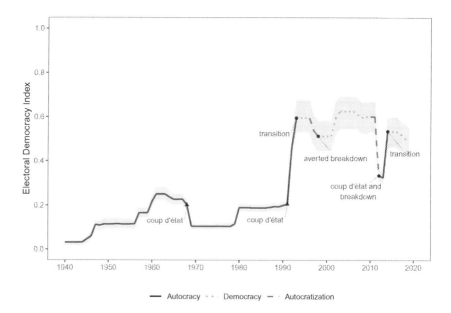

Figure 2. Electoral democracy, coups, and regime transitions in Mali, 1940–2019.

democratic resilience was only as hollow as its institutions. Systemic corruption, strong presidentialism, and weak political parties combined produced rising popular discontent. Meanwhile, the regime's undermining of decentralization spurred a resurgent rebellion in the North. These factors eventually culminated in military coup d'état in March 2012 and a complete failure of democratic resilience.

The fate of Mail's third republic serves as a cautionary tale for those studying democratic resilience or consolidation. In 1997–1998, we see effective breakdown resilience in the face of a political crisis, despite a long history of authoritarian rule. By contrast, after twenty years of democratic elections, the complete failure of democratic resilience (at both stages) in 2012 caught many observers by surprise because they had been fooled by the "consolidation mirage".[19]

Our conceptualization of democratic resilience also resolves a long-standing discussion in the literature about the relative value of continuous versus categorical regime typologies. We recognize the merits of both approaches, viewing regime characteristics along a continuum from democracy to autocracy (liberal to closed), while also acknowledging the empirical clustering of regimes along this continuum as distinct subtypes. At the most general level, we consider the divide between democracy and autocracy to be a meaningful distinction.

Previous insights on democratic resilience tend to measure regime transitions as events, with survival or durability as the absence of a breakdown in a given year.[20] This approach overlooks the important conceptual distinction between the avoidance of autocratization altogether and the ability to avert breakdown once autocratization has begun. A rich comparative literature suggests that democratic breakdowns are the culmination of processes of regime transformation producing substantial declines in democracy that often unfold over an extended period,[21] and do not always culminate in complete democratic breakdown.[22] Focusing on democratic breakdowns "blind [s] us to potentially important and theoretically revealing cases".[23] From a methodological perspective, this also leads to questions about selection bias, especially if factors influencing the experience of autocratization are correlated with the outcome. The other standard quantitative approach is to measure resilience as unchanged year-to-year scores on an index in time-series cross-sectional designs.[24] Yet, this approach makes it impossible to distinguish democratic decline from breakdown. As such, existing theories about democratic resilience remain incomplete until we simultaneously account for its two stages: onset and breakdown resilience.

Operationalizing democratic resilience

We make use of the new Episodes of Regime Transformation (ERT) dataset where episodes of autocratization are measured as periods of substantial and sustained declines on the V-Dem electoral democracy index (EDI), which is based on Dahl's conceptualization of polyarchy.[25] It provides identification of the onset and end dates as well as the outcome of autocratization in democracies (that is, whether democratic breakdown occurred or was averted). The ERT considers substantial and sustained declines (that is, autocratization episode onset) to begin with an annual EDI drop of at least 0.01, followed by an overall decline of at least 0.10 throughout the episode. Autocratization is considered ongoing so long as (I) annual EDI declines continue for at least one out of every five consecutive years, (II) the EDI does not increase by 0.03 or greater in a given year, and (III) the EDI does not gradually increase by 0.10 over a five-year period. The end date of all episodes is the year the case experienced an annual decline of at least 0.01 after episode onset and prior to experiencing one of these three conditions for termination. Breakdown occurs if a country (a) becomes a closed autocracy as defined by the Regimes of the World classification (b) becomes an electoral autocracy for at least one election, or (c) becomes an electoral autocracy for at least five years. Ongoing episodes are censored.[26]

For our purposes here, *onset resilience* is indicated by the absence of an autocratization episode within a given democratic country-year. *Breakdown resilience* is indicated by the absence of a democratic breakdown within an ongoing episode of autocratization. Thus, the ERT allows us to attain a high degree of concept-measure validity when compared to discrete regime type datasets or annual changes on interval democracy measures.

Democratic resilience over space and time

This section offers a panoramic overview of global trends in democratic resilience from 1900 to 2019. We report on three main findings: First, democracies have been highly resilient to onset of autocratization, but second, this resilience is now substantially weaker in the period after the Cold War. Third, fatality rates are very high once autocratization has started; only slightly more than one in five (23%) regressing democracies avert breakdown. The increasing number of democracies undergoing autocratization, including major G20-countries such as Brazil, India, Indonesia, and the United States, could therefore signal the global democratic tide is turning.

In Table 1, we report statistics for onset resilience before (1900–1992) and after (1993–2019) the end of the Cold War. We chose these two periods because (a) they reflect changing international norms about liberal democracy and (b) they roughly correspond to the period before and during the present wave of autocratization identified by Lührmann and Lindberg.[27]

Table 1 demonstrates first that democracies exhibit high onset resilience, avoiding autocratization more than 98% of the time. Out of 4,374 democratic country-years at risk of autocratization (that is, not currently experiencing an episode), 4,278 did not experience episode onset. Put differently, there are only 96 episodes of autocratization affecting 516 democratic country-years in 64 countries from 1900 to 2019.

Second, onset resilience among democracies has deteriorated since the end of the Cold War. From 1900–1992 and 1993–2019, we see fairly similar numbers of democratic country-years at risk of autocratization onset. In the former, democracies showed onset resilience about 98% of the time, as compared to a slight decrease to 97% in the post-Cold War period. However, these numbers obscure a key finding when looking at data from the episode level. We find that 59 (61%) of the autocratization episodes began between 1993 and 2019. This amounts to about 2.27 new

Table 1. Onset resilience.

Period	Lack of onset resilience (episodes)		Onset resilience (country-years)		
	N onset	% onset	N risk*	N resilient	% resilient
1900–1992	37	39%	2 186	2 149	98%
1993–2019	59	61%	2 188	2 129	97%
Total	96	100%	4 374	4 278	98%

* Risk set includes democratic country-years not in an ongoing episode.

autocratization episodes in democracies per year since 1993, as compared to just 0.4 per year in the preceding period. Apart from cases in the 1930s, the failure of onset resilience is overwhelmingly a post-Cold War phenomenon, lending support to arguments that despite (or perhaps because of) a global democratic "zeitgeist",[28] democratic resilience is on the decline.

The decline in onset resilience appears to be irrespective of geopolitical region. Figure 3 plots the number of democratic countries exhibiting onset resilience in a given year (thin, blue lines) against the total number of democracies in that region (thick, orange lines) from 1900 to 2019. The gap between these two lines corresponds to the number of democracies in the region that lacks onset resilience. For most of the regions, we observe the post-Cold War decrease in onset resilience, particularly since the late 1990s. In Eastern Europe and Central Asia (EECA), this is most pronounced, with just 56% of democracies in the region exhibiting onset resilience at its low point in 2007. While onset resilience in EECA has since increased to 76% in 2019, this might be tied to fewer democracies in the region due to breakdowns in Hungary, Serbia, and Ukraine. Asia and the Pacific (AP) and sub-Saharan Africa (SSA) also show faltering onset resilience since the late 1990s. Meanwhile autocratization in Israel and Turkey threaten democratic resilience in the Middle East and North Africa (MENA), where levels of democracy already tend to be quite low. By contrast, for Western countries, where democracy is arguably the oldest and most prevalent, onset resilience remains fairly robust, aside from the United States which began autocratizing in 2016.

Third and finally, breakdown resilience is very low. As shown in Table 2, among the 84 episodes that had ended by December 2019 – 12 of the 96 are ongoing with unknown outcome – only 19 (23%) exhibited breakdown resilience. In short, once democracies begin autocratizing, their fatality rate is very high. Here we find similar levels of breakdown resilience in the post-1993 period as in the 1900–1992 period (23% and 22%, respectively), but the unknown fates of twelve censored episodes may alter this

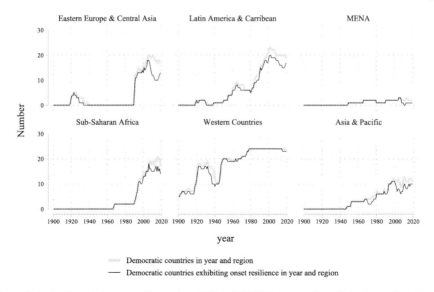

Figure 3. Regional trends in onset resilience from 1900 to 2019. Thick, orange lines depict the total number of democratic countries in each region by year, while the thin, blue lines indicate the number of onset-resilient democratic countries (that is, those not experiencing autocratization in that year).

Table 2. Breakdown resilience.

	Episodes				Episode-country-year		
Period	Completed episodes	Averted breakdown N	%	Mean duration (years)	Total years	Resilient N	%
1900–1992	37	8	22%	4.92	153	124	81%
1993–2019	47	11	23%	4.60	298	262	88%
total	84	19	23%	4.74	451	386	100%

Completed episodes and mean duration columns exclude 12 censored episodes ongoing in 2019 for which the outcome is unknown. Mean duration is calculated for all episode years occurring in democracies. For episodes that encounter a breakdown and subsequent autocratic regression, non-democratic years after the breakdown are excluded.

finding in the future. So far however, two-thirds of the episodes in which breakdown resilience failed, occurred in the period after 1992.[29]

Figures 4 and 5 provide additional detail on the trajectories of democracies undergoing autocratization, divided into those that did and did not exhibit breakdown-resilience, respectively.[30] A similar plot for censored episodes where the outcome is not known, including present periods for Brazil and the United States, is found in the Appendix (Section B, Figure 7). The clustering of observations in these figures further illustrates the high prevalence of autocratization in post-Cold War period, regardless of outcome. These plots also reveal wide variation in the quality of democracy at the onset of autocratization, in the extent of democratic decline, and the duration of the episode. This demonstrates that taking democratic survival, breakdown, or annual changes at a given point in time would obscure this variation and potentially vital information on patterns that could help us better understand democratic resilience.

When taken together, these findings provide us with the grim observation that democracies have become less resilient in the post-Cold War period. More democracies

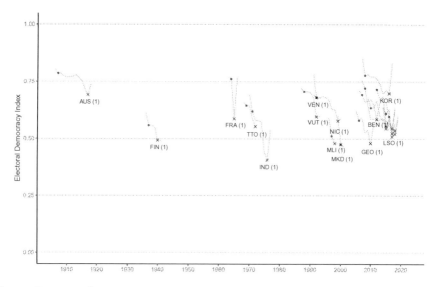

Figure 4. Trajectories of autocratization episodes in democracies that exhibit breakdown resilience throughout the episode, that is, that ended without democratic breakdown. Black dots mark the start year of an episode and the crosses mark the end year. Plots include the pre- and post-episode year. Number of episodes by country in brackets.

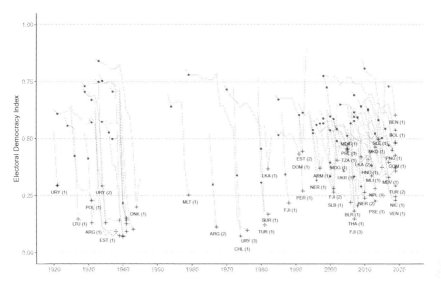

Figure 5. Trajectories of autocratization episodes in democracies that ended with democratic breakdown. Black dots mark the start year of an episode and the crosses mark the end year. Plots include the pre- and post-episode year. Number of episode by country in brackets.

are experiencing autocratization episodes, and they continue to exhibit a low resilience to breakdown once autocratization has begun. Accordingly, the post-Cold War period has seen the breakdown of an unprecedented 36 democratic regimes. As a result, over 700 million people have lost access to democratic institutions and freedoms.

But what distinguishes the correlates of onset and breakdown resilience, respectively? While we cannot pursue a full-scale explanatory analysis here, in the next section we explore several main factors suggested by the literature.

Existing insights into determinants of democratic resilience

The literature on democratic breakdown and survival informs much of what we know about resilience. Scholars in this field typically test for the effects of factors on the probability of democratic survival or breakdown as events,[31] or incrementally using annual changes in levels of democracy.[32] We suggest a different approach and combine an onset model as well as a selection model following our conceptualization described above, and focus on four of the main factors identified in these two literatures: institutional constraints on the executive, economic factors, neighbouring regimes, and previous democratic experience. We draw on extensive theories in the literature which provide some causal basis to the regressions reported below. In places, we may adopt the causal language which is standard practice in reporting regression models. Nevertheless, acknowledging the limits our analysis due to observational data and statistical techniques, we do not make any firm causal claims here.

Constraints on the executive

A prominent body of work concerns the "perils of presidentialism".[33] According to Linz, separate legislative and executive elections create a dual legitimacy and individual mandate of the executive that predisposes political actors to view presidential systems as a zero-sum game. This discourages coalitions while concentrating substantial powers in one individual.[34] In effect, presidential systems are more prone to political polarization, deadlock, personalization of politics, and exclusion of losers compared to parliamentary democracies, thus furthering military coups and other types of breakdown.[35]

Noting that the United States is the only long-lasting presidential democracy,[36] several large-N studies find a negative relationship between presidentialism and rates of democratic survival.[37] Case evidence suggests that executives in presidential democracies are likely to "rule at the edge of the constitution" because the legislature has limited removal powers.[38]

Recent trends suggest that attacks on democracy are often driven by a concentration of power in the executive, even in parliamentary democracies. This calls for revisiting Linz's focus on the effects of weak constraints on the executive as the chief mechanism linking presidentialism to democratic instability. The extent to which the executive is constrained *de facto* varies considerably, and executive aggrandizement affects both presidential and parliamentary systems.[39] In effect, the phenomenon of "presidential hegemony" poses a potential risk to democratic resilience across systems.[40]

The Linz thesis is yet to be tested using granular data on the specific causal mechanism of weak constraints on the executive. Our expectation is that stronger constraints on the executive by the legislature and the judiciary are positively associated with both a lower likelihood of autocratization episodes in democracies (onset resilience) and greater resilience to democratic breakdown once such an episode has begun.

Economic factors

Since Lipset's seminal work on the societal effects of economic development, questions about the links between economics and democratic stability have preoccupied the discipline.[41] Lipset's original focus is actually on democratic resilience when arguing that "the more the well-to-do a nation, the greater the chances that it will *sustain* democracy" (emphasis added).[42] Some tests of Lipset's theory such as by Przeworski and Limongi suggest that democracies become resilient to breakdown once they are above a certain threshold level of income.[43] Several studies find that positive economic growth predicts democratic survival,[44] but this may be good for the stability of any regime, including autocracies[45] because a better quality of life makes people more likely to support the status quo over those seeking to undo the existing order.

Indicators of economic development are now standard practice in models estimating democratization, democratic breakdown, and democratic survival.[46] In line with the bulk of previous studies, we expect that higher levels of economic development will make democracies more resilient to experiencing an autocratization episode (onset). We remain agnostic about the association between development and breakdown resilience.

Neighbourhood effects

Several studies provide evidence of diffusion effects across countries. This is often described as a "pull towards the regional mean" – or a tendency for countries "left behind" to eventually adapt to regional norms about institutional configurations for autocratic as well as democratic regimes by way of diffusion, emulation, spill-over, or demonstration effects.[47] In light of the gradual nature of autocratization during the third wave, we expect at most small neighbourhood effects on the probability of experiencing an episode. Once a democracy opts into an episode of autocratization, however, we hypothesize a greater breakdown resilience because dismantling of democracy in stage two should be more difficult for aspiring autocrats in more democratic regions.

Previous democratic experience

Previous experience under democracy may reinforce democratic resilience through the "construction of solid links between the democratic institutions and society".[48] Some scholars suggest that the institutionalization of party systems and judicial institutions[49] helps to handle "problems of monitoring and social coordination that complicate democratic compromise".[50] Others claim that election cycles have a self-reinforcing, self-improving quality, altering the incentives to accept the rules of the game.[51] Indeed, everyday experiences living under democracy seem to promote democratic attitudes within society, making successful challenges to democracy less likely.[52] We expect that previous experience with democracy will be associated with a higher onset resilience, as well as with greater resilience to breakdown in stage two.

Modelling correlates of the two stages of democratic resilience

To estimate onset resilience, we use a standard onset model (probit model with Firth's method of bias reduction)[53] in which resilient democratic country-years (that is, those not experiencing the beginning of an autocratization episode) are treated as ones. The onset of an episode as given by the ERT is coded as zero and democratic country-years in ongoing episodes are excluded.[54] To estimate breakdown resilience in stage two, we use a standard bivariate probit model with non-random sample selection.[55] The first "selection" stage estimates the probability that a given democratic country-year falls within an autocratization episode, that is, it lacks onset resilience, using the sample of democratic country-years in the ERT dataset (estimation sample: 3,864 observations). The second "outcome" stage includes the subsample of country years that are not onset resilient (352 observations in the estimation sample) and estimates the probability of breakdown resilience, thus accounting for selection bias estimated in the first stage. The outcome variable is coded as one for each episode-year in which democratic breakdown does *not* occur and zero for breakdown years.

We focus on factors from the literature discussed above. To capture the key mechanism in the "perils of presidentialism", we include two *de facto* measures of executive constraints provided by the V-Dem dataset: the judicial constraints on the executive index and the legislative constraints on the executive index.[56] The former measures judicial independence and whether the executive respects court rulings and the constitution. The latter indicates the degree to which the legislature and government agencies exercise oversight of the executive.[57] Second, we include measures of inflation-adjusted GDP per capita and economic growth from the Maddison project[58] to capture the level of economic development and economic performance, respectively. Third, to address spatial clustering of regimes and potential neighbourhood effects found in the literature, we include the average scores of V-Dem's EDI for all other countries in the region using the tenfold geo-political classification scheme in V-Dem.[59] Fourth, to capture past democratic experience, we draw on a recently developed measure of democratic stock.[60] Finally, we add a nonlinear time trend to control for unobserved factors that changed over time.

In addition, we include a series of other well-known correlates of democratic resilience. Because military coups are one of the main threats to democracy,[61] we use information on the occurrence of one or more military coups in a country (binary indicator) by combining information from two coup datasets.[62] We include population size from the Maddison project[63] as it might affect a polity's susceptibility to conflict and autocratization. We also count the cumulative number of previous episodes of autocratization in democracies. A large number of previous episodes should be indicative of a general vulnerability to autocratization. To account for global trends, we add the percentage of countries with ongoing democratization and autocratization episodes for each year. We include region dummies to control for unobserved time-invariant factors. Finally, a linear time trend accounts for global trends in autocratization and decade dummies account for global shocks such as the two World Wars simultaneously affecting a large number of countries. Due to missing economic and population data, we exclude 14 episodes in the ERT from our analysis.[64] We provide summary statistics for all variables in the different samples used in the analysis in Table 8, 9 and 10 in Section E of the Appendix. To reduce concerns of simultaneity bias, that could arise if aspiring autocrats dismantle institutional checks and balances, we lag all variables (except for coups) by one year.

Results

The main results are summarized in Table 3. Model 1 identifies factors associated with higher levels of onset resilience. In line with scholarly work on the importance of judges and courts for democracy, we find that stronger judicial constraints on the executive are significantly associated with greater democratic resilience to experiencing autocratization. We do not observe a similar relationship for legislative constraints. In line with the literature, we find that economic development and a greater democratic stock are also associated with significantly higher onset resilience. Furthermore, Model 1 shows that coups, previous episodes of autocratization, and a larger population may significantly decrease the likelihood of onset resilience. The significant coefficient for the share of democratizing countries suggests that global trends in democratization has a positive association with onset resilience in individual countries.

Model 2 contains the results from the two-stage Heckman model that we use to assess factors associated with breakdown resilience. The model takes into account that only countries that were not onset resilient can display breakdown resilience. As required by the model assumptions, we include some predictors for "selection into" autocratization in the first model stage but not in the second stage. We argue that the number of previous autocratization episodes and a greater number of concurrent episodes of regime transformations (democratization and autocratization) in other democracies should be expected to influence whether a democracy is more likely to lose onset resilience but that they should be substantively unrelated to the outcome once an episode is ongoing. We also control for the duration of the episode in the second stage, by including the number of years since episode onset and its square term, as shorter or longer episodes may be more prone to breakdown.[65]

Table 3. Main results: correlates of onset and breakdown resilience.

	Model 1	Model 2	
	Onset resilience	[I]	Breakdown resilience
Judicial constraints on executive	1.52**	−2.51***	1.89**
	(0.54)	(0.75)	(0.70)
Legislative constraints on executive	0.08	−1.43***	−0.05
	(0.38)	(0.51)	(0.48)
GDP per capita (log)	0.33†	−0.95***	0.05
	(0.20)	(0.23)	(0.32)
GDP growth (5-year avg.)	0.00	−0.04*	0.02
	(0.01)	(0.02)	(0.02)
Regional democracy levels	−0.02	−0.16	4.77†
	(0.87)	(1.33)	(2.45)
Democratic stock	5.45***	1.76†	3.33**
	(1.04)	(0.99)	(1.20)
Coup	−1.48***	1.54***	−2.47***
	(0.27)	(0.31)	(0.52)
Population (log)	−0.05	0.03	0.10
	(0.06)	(0.08)	(0.10)
Previous autocratization episode	−1.23***	1.30***	
	(0.14)	(0.16)	
Autocratizing countries (%, global)	0.02	−0.01	
	(0.01)	(0.02)	
Democratizing countries (%, global)	0.02*	−0.04***	
	(0.01)	(0.01)	
Episode duration			−0.20***
			(0.06)
Episode duration^2			0.01*
			(0.00)
Intercept	−4.54**	10.04***	−4.08
	(1.72)	(1.78)	(3.90)
P	−		0.03
Region dummies	yes		yes
Nonlinear time trend	yes		yes
AIC	522.04		1526.38
BIC	679.05		1805.63
Log Likelihood	−236.02		−719.19
Total obs.	3,946		4,216
Censored obs.	−		3,864
Obs. in outcome stage	−		352

Note: Probit model with Firth's bias reduction (Model 1) and Heckman-style selection model (Model 2). Dependent variable in selection equation [I]: ongoing autocratization in a democracy. Dependent variable in outcome equation: breakdown resilience in current episode-year. Standard errors clustered at the country-level. Time since last autocratization episode (t, t^2, t^3) omitted from Table. Significance levels ***$p < 0.001$, **$p < 0.01$, *$p < 0.05$, †$p < 0.1$.

The right column of Model 2 shows the results for breakdown resilience in the second stage. Similar to the onset model, judicial constraints on the executive are associated with significant increases in the likelihood of resilience to breakdown. However, legislative constraints are not significant at conventional thresholds ($p>0.10$). This finding supports recent work claiming that judicial institutions can act as the "last bulwark" against democratic breakdown[66], while the legislature can do little to stop autocratization once it has started.

The results for economic factors are less clear across the two stages of autocratization. Economic development is significantly associated with onset resilience but not with breakdown resilience. These results could suggest that long-term economic development could make people less inclined to support actors inclined to derail democracy but once autocratization has started, economic factors are less relevant.

Higher levels of democratic stock are significantly associated with increases in resilience to both onset and breakdown. More democratic neighbours are significantly related to higher resilience against breakdown. These results illustrate that factors the literature suggest as causally related to survival and breakdown may have

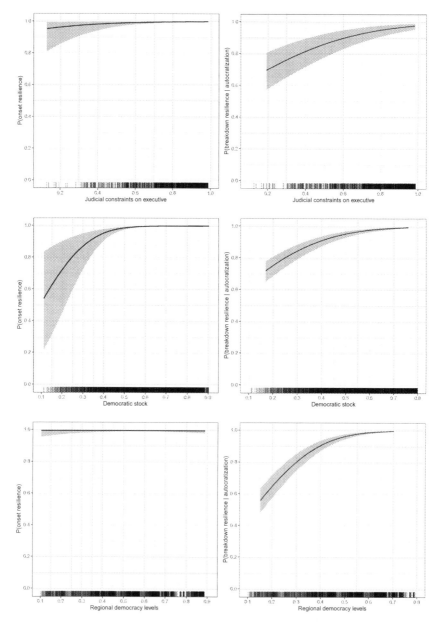

Figure 6. Predicted probabilities of onset resilience (left panel) and breakdown resilience (right panel) over the range of selected explanatory variables. Estimates and 95% confidence intervals are based on simulations from the model parameters.

varying relationships to the two stages of resilience. Although we cannot compare both models directly, they suggest that a different set of explanatory factors for each stage of resilience is needed to understand variation in levels of democratic resilience.

To illustrate the results more substantively, we simulate predicted probabilities for both stages of resilience based on our model estimates and plot them over the range of the key independent variables in Figure 6. The plots on the left show how the probability of onset resilience varies with judicial constraints on the executive, democratic stock, and regional levels of democracy. Country-years where the de facto constraints on the executive are greater have a higher likelihood of onset resilience. However, the differences are relatively small. Onset resilience is high even at moderate levels of judicial constraints.

The relationship between democratic stock and onset resilience is more pronounced. Democracies with a short history of democracy like Tunisia (0.38 in 2019) or Nepal (0.39 in 2019) face a considerable risk of experiencing autocratization whereas countries with longstanding democratic institutions are highly resilient. Given the rarity of autocratization onset and democratic breakdown, these differences are quite substantial. For regional levels of democracy, the plots show little differences in onset resilience. A comparison of the plots on the left and right underlines the importance of separating onset- and breakdown resilience. In the second stage, judicial constraints are clearly related to a higher likelihood of breakdown resilience. The predicted probability of resilience against breakdown is much lower for countries with low-to-medium levels of judicial constraints. While the effect of democratic stock is comparable to the onset stage, regional levels of democracies only make a difference for breakdown resilience. Thus, different factors matter for the different stages of democratic resilience.

A series of robustness tests give substantially unchanged results (see Appendix, section E Robustness Checks for details). For instance, we run different model specifications, decompose the legislative and judicial constraints indices and apply different thresholds for the starting and end dates of autocratization episodes. A more general challenge is the small number of episodes and the rarity of autocratization onset and democratic breakdown. Thus, including a large number of explanatory variables can be problematic, as can the exclusion or inclusion of influential episode cases. However, our main findings are robust to different modelling choices and operationalization of autocratization episodes. Across models, judicial constraints and democratic stock are significantly associated with both types of resilience. The results for economic factors are not consistent across stages; economic development matters only for onset resilience. Regional levels of democracy appear to be relevant only when autocratization is already ongoing. Coups are associated with lower levels of resilience in both stages.

Conclusions

Existing quantitative studies of democratic resilience typically operationalize democratic breakdown as events. This disregards conceptual and empirical differences between those democracies that never experience autocratization and those that – having begun autocratizing – somehow manage to avert breakdown. This article conceptualizes and analyses democratic resilience as a two-stage process – either by avoiding the onset of autocratization altogether or, once it has started by avoiding a full breakdown.

With this novel conceptualization and using the ERT dataset, this article offers a first panoramic overview of global trends in democratic resilience from 1900 to 2019. We show that overall, resilience to the onset of autocratization among democracies is high. There have been only 96 cases of episodes of autocratization in 70 democratic countries over the 120 years of available data. Democracies are resilient over 90% of the time.

Second, we also demonstrate that democratic resilience to onset has gone down markedly, and autocratization in democracies is overwhelmingly a post-Cold War phenomenon. Of all the episodes, 59 (61%) began after 1992.

Third, we show that once democracies "select in" to autocratization, breakdown resilience is weaker. The global fatality rate is 77% – only 19 of the 84 completed episodes managed to change the course and avert breakdown. Thus far, the third wave of autocratization has led to the breakdown of 36 democratic regimes, with only eleven cases showing resilience to breakdown. In sum, during the present period democracies are less resilient to onset than before, while the fatality rate remains very high once a democracy experiences autocratization.

In the second part of the article, we examine how some of the prime suspects or covariates from the literatures on democratic survival/breakdown relate to a two-stage understanding of democratic resilience. Modelling both onset and breakdown resilience, we analyse the correlates of resilience. We find corroboration for claims that view the judiciary as the "last bulwark" against democratic breakdown. Judicial constraints are positively and significantly associated with resilience to the onset of autocratization and to democratic breakdown once autocratization has begun. As also discussed elsewhere in this special issue, judicial institutions seem to play an important role as democracy's last line of defence against aspiring dictators. Our results also point to the importance of a country's past experience with democracy, which is consistently associated with higher levels of resilience in both stages.

In a contribution to the literature on the role of economic development for endurance of democracy, we can also nuance the picture. We find that higher level of economic development is associated with a greater onset resilience but has zero influence on avoiding breakdown once an episode has begun. This is an important corrective to what we know from the previous literature that did not distinguish between the two forms of resilience. For breakdown resilience, what seems to matter more is having democratic neighbours and longer previous democratic experiences. This means that our existing theories remain incomplete until we account for the two-stage nature of democratic resilience.

This study further underscores the need for more nuanced research on the role of factors – endogenous or exogenous[67] – in different stages of democratic resilience. For practitioners in democracy promotion and pro-democracy activists, the spectre of autocratization requires different responses depending on whether the process has already begun. Only then can democracies prevail.

Notes

1. We use "countries" for ease while acknowledging V-Dem's data include semi-autonomous units and colonies in the dataset.
2. Maerz et al., "State of the world 2019"; Lührmann and Lindberg, "A Third Wave of Autocratization."

3. This builds on concepts of democratic durability and resilience as defined by Burnell and Calvert, "The Resilience of Democracy."
4. Edgell et al., "Episodes of Regime Transformation." The attached ERT Codebook provides more information on content and scope of the ERT dataset.
5. Coppedge et al., "V-Dem Dataset V10."
6. Svolik, "Authoritarian Reversals"; Bernhard, Nordstrom, and Reenock, "Economic Performance"; Alemán and Yang, "A Duration Analysis."
7. In many cases, this means democratic stability, but it also includes regimes undergoing democratic deepening, or reforms to institutions and practices resulting in even higher levels of democracy.
8. Edgell et al., "Episodes of Regime Transformation"; Lührmann and Lindberg, "A Third Wave of Autocratization"; Wilson et al., "Successful and Failed Episodes."
9. More technically democratic resilience (r) is divided into *onset resilience* (r^1) and *breakdown resilience* (r^2). In a given year (i), a democracy (j) is either onset resilient $(r^1_{i,j} = 1)$ or experiences autocratization $(r^1_{i,j}=0)$. We observe whether a democracy has exhibited onset resilience *until now* $(\min[r^1_{1,j} \ldots r^1_{k,j}] = 1)$. Likewise, in a given year, democracies experiencing autocratization are either breakdown resilient $(r^2_{i,j}=1)$ or experience a transition to autocracy $(r^2_{i,j}=0)$. We know the outcome of the *episode* of autocratization for 84 episodes in our sample in terms of breakdown resilience (i.e. $r^2_{i,e}=1$) or not (i.e. they resulted in breakdown, $r^2_{i,e} = 0$).
10. The literature on democratic consolidation discusses various dimensions of consolidation, e.g. behavioural aspects (Foa and Mounck, "The Danger of Deconsolidation" or Chull Shin, "Democratic Deconsolidation in East Asia") or institutional factors (Merkel, "Embedded and Defective Democracies"). For a discussion of the issues of consolidation as a future-orientated concept, see Schedler, "What Is Democratic Consolidation?", 91, or Schedler, "Measuring Democratic Consolidation."
11. Houle, "Inequality and Democracy"; Svolik, "Authoritarian Reversals"; Svolik, "Which Democracies Will Last?".
12. Schedler, "What Is Democratic Consolidation?", 91, or Schedler, "Measuring Democratic Consolidation".
13. Svolik, "Authoritarian Reversals" for a related discussion.
14. For further criticism on the concept consolidation see O'Donnell, "Illusions About Consolidation" and Svolik, "Authoritarian Reversals."
15. Svolik, "Authoritarian Reversals"; Gasiorowski and Power, "The Structural Determinants".
16. Laebens and Lührmann, "What Stops Erosion?".
17. Vengroff, "Governance and the Transition to Democracy."
18. Wing, "Mali: Politics of Crisis."
19. Greene, "Coups and the Consolidation Mirage."
20. Alemán and Yang, "A Duration Analysis"; Bernhard, Nordstrom, and Reenock, "Economic Performance"; Gasiorowski, "Economic Crisis"; Gates et al., "Institutional Inconsistency."
21. See Cassani and Tomini, "Reversing Regimes and Concepts", 18. Levitsky and Ziblatt, "How Democracies Die."
22. See Przeworski, *Crises of Democracy* for a discussion of two cases of averted democratic breakdown: France during the 1950s and 1960s and the US under Nixon.
23. Ziblatt, "How Did Europe Democratize?" 326.
24. E.g. Teorell, *Determinants of Democratization*.
25. Dahl, *Polyarchy*; Teorell, Lindberg and Skaaning, "Measuring Polyarchy."
26. Edgell et al., "Episodes of Regime Transformation". For more technical details on the ERT, see the attached ERT codebook. The authors of the ERT provide an R-package that replicates all episodes based on the most recent V-Dem dataset. The package allows for further robustness tests and has flexible parameter settings to redefine the episode data: Maerz et al., "ERT – an R package."
27. Lührmann and Lindberg, "A Third Wave of Autocratization".
28. Linz and Stepan, *Problems of Democratic Transition*.
29. Section C of the Appendix lists all episodes by outcome.
30. The supplemental material includes additional interactive plots that allows the reader to take a closer look at individual country trajectories.

31. E.g. Svolik, "Authoritarian Reversals"; Hollyer, Rosendorff, and Vreeland, "Transparency, Protest"; Bernhard, Nordstrom, and Reenock, "Economic Performance".
32. E.g. Ginsburg and Huq, *How to Save*; Erdmann, "Transition from Democracy"; Mechkova, Lührmann, and Lindberg, "How Much Democratic Backsliding?"
33. Linz, "The Perils of Presidentialism."
34. Ibid; Linz, *The Breakdown of Democratic Regimes*; Linz and Valenzuela, *The Failure of Presidential Democracy*.
35. Kaufman and Haggard, "Democratic Decline."
36. E.g. Cheibub, *Presidentialism, Parliamentarism, and Democracy*."
37. Mainwaring, "Presidentialism, Multipartism, and Democracy"; Bernhard, Nordstrom, and Reenock, "Economic performance"; Riggs, "Presidentialism versus Parliamentarism"; Svolik, "Which Democracies Will Last?".
38. Stepan and Skach, "Constitutional Frameworks". However, several critiques contend that the relationship is spurious, e.g. Cheibub, *Presidentialism, Parliamentarism, and Democracy*; Hiroi and Omori, "Perils of Parliamentarism?"
39. Bermeo, "On Democratic Backsliding."
40. Pérez-Liñán, Schmidt, and Vairo, "Presidential Hegemony."
41. Lipset, *Some Social Requisites*.
42. Ibid., 75.
43. Przeworski and Limongi, "Modernization: Theories and Facts"; also see Boix and Stokes, "Endogenous Democratization"; Burkhart and Lewis-Beck, "Comparative Democracy"; Epstein et al., "Democratic Transitions"; Przeworski et al., *Democracy and Development*; Teorell, *Determinants of Democratization*.
44. Gasiorowski, "Economic Crisis"; Gates et al., "Institutional Inconsistency"; Morlino and Quaranta, "What Is the Impact."
45. Alemán and Yang, "A Duration Analysis"; Feng, "Democracy, Political Stability and Economic Growth"; Gates et al., "Institutional Inconsistency"; Svolik, "Authoritarian Reversals."
46. Morlino and Quaranta, "What Is the Impact"; Olson, "Dictatorship, Democracy, and Development"; Teorell, *Determinants of Democratization*.
47. E.g. Bader, Grävingholt, and Kästner, "Would Autocracies Promote Autocracy?"; Brinks and Coppedge, "Diffusion Is No Illusion"; Gates et al., "Institutional Inconsistency"; Gleditsch, *All International Politics Is Local*; Gleditsch and Ward, "Diffusion"; Houle and Kayser, "The Two-step Model"; Risse and Babayan, "Democracy Promotion"; Tansey, Koehler, and Schmotz, "Ties to the Rest."
48. Tomini and Wagemann, "Varieties of Contemporary Democratic Breakdown and Regression", 690.
49. Pérez-Liñán and Mainwaring, "Regime Legacies."
50. Reenock, Staton, and Radean, "Legal Institutions and Democratic Survival," 491.
51. Lindberg, *Democracy and Elections in Africa*, 144.
52. Grosfeld and Zhuravskaya, "Cultural vs. Economic Legacies"; Guiso, Sapienza, and Zingales, "Long-term Persistence"; Persson and Tabellini, "Democratic Capital"; Putnam, *Making Democracy Work*.
53. Kosmidis and Firth, "Jeffreys-prior penalty"; McGrath, "Estimating Onsets."
54. Due to listwise deletion, we end up with 82 onset cases in our estimation sample.
55. Heckman, "Sample Selection Bias"; Marra and Radice, "GJRM."
56. Linz, "The Perils of Presidentialism."
57. While both indices are part of the Liberal Component Index, there is no overlap with the EDI that is used to determine the start and end of autocratization episodes. For the full list of all variables included in the two indices, see Coppedge et al., "V-Dem Codebook v10", 357.
58. Bold et al., "Maddison Style Estimates". We use a five-year moving average of GDP growth to make sure our results are not driven by short-term fluctuations. We also use linear interpolation to replace missing values in the data.
59. Brinks and Coppedge, "Diffusion Is No Illusion."
60. Edgell et al., "Democratic Legacies."
61. Marinov and Goemans, "Coups and Democracy."
62. Powell and Thyne, "Global Instances"; Przeworski et al., Political Institutions and Political Events.

63. Bold et al., "Maddison Style Estimates."
64. A full list can be found in Table 7 in Section A of the Appendix.
65. The second stage is similar to a regular duration model, which is why we add a variable for the duration of the ongoing episode as well as its squared term.
66. Staton et al., *Can Courts be Bulwarks?*
67. For a conceptual differentiation between endogenous and exogenous factors see Gerschewski, "Erosion or Decay?"

Acknowledgements

We thank Anna Lührmann, Wolfgang Merkel, two anonymous reviewers and seminar participants at the V-Dem Research Seminar at the University of Gothenburg for excellent comments and suggestions. We are also grateful to Natalia Natsika for skillful research assistance.

All co-authors contributed equally to the design of the study, the conceptual innovation, as well as writing – including original draft preparation, review, and editing. Boese took responsibility as the lead author; Boese and Edgell led the theory development; Edgell and Maerz led the data curation; Hellmeier led the data analysis and visualizations. All co-authors provided extensive input on each aspect during the process.

Disclosure statement

No potential conflict of interest was reported by the author(s).

Funding

We recognize support by the Swedish Research Council, Grant 2018-01614, PI: Anna Lührmann; by Knut and Alice Wallenberg Foundation to Wallenberg Academy Fellow Staffan I. Lindberg, Grant 2018.0144; by European Research Council, Grant 724191, PI: Staffan I. Lindberg; as well as by internal grants from the Vice- Chancellor's office, the Dean of the College of Social Sciences, and the Department of Political Science at University of Gothenburg. The computations of expert data were enabled by the Swedish National Infrastructure for Computing (SNIC) at National Supercomputer Centre, Linköping University, partially funded by the Swedish Research Council through grant agreement no. 2019/3-516.

ORCID

Vanessa A. Boese (iD) http://orcid.org/0000-0002-1680-0745
Amanda B. Edgell (iD) http://orcid.org/0000-0002-3029-691X
Sebastian Hellmeier (iD) http://orcid.org/0000-0002-9423-7150
Seraphine F. Maerz (iD) http://orcid.org/0000-0002-7173-9617
Staffan I. Lindberg (iD) http://orcid.org/0000-0003-0386-7390

Bibliography

Alemán, José, and David D. Yang. "A Duration Analysis of Democratic Transitions and Authoritarian Backslides." *Comparative Political Studies* 44, no. 9 (2011): 1123–1151.

Bader, Julia, Jörn Grävingholt, and Antje Kästner. "Would Autocracies Promote Autocracy? A Political Economy Perspective on Regime-Type Export in Regional Neighbourhoods." *Contemporary Politics* 16, no. 1 (2010): 81–100.

Bermeo, Nancy. "On Democratic Backsliding." *Journal of Democracy* 27, no. 1 (2016): 5–19.

Bermeo, Nancy. *Ordinary People in Extraordinary Times: The Citizenry and the Breakdown of Democracy.* New Jersey: Princeton University Press, 2003.

Bernhard, Michael, Timothy Nordstrom, and Christopher Reenock. "Economic Performance, Institutional Intermediation, and Democratic Survival." *Journal of Politics* 63, no. 3 (2001): 775–803.

Boix, Carles, and Susan C. Stokes. "Endogenous Democratization." *World Politics* 55, no. 4 (2003): 517–549.

Bold, Jutta, and Jan Luiten van Zanden. "Maddison Style Estimates of the Evolution of the World Economy. A New 2020 Update." *Maddison Project Working Paper* 15 (2020): 1–43.

Brinks, Daniel, and Michael Coppedge. "Diffusion Is No Illusion: Neighbor Emulation in the Third Wave of Democracy." *Comparative Political Studies* 39, no. 4 (2006): 463–489.

Burkhart, Ross E., and Michael S. Lewis-Beck. "Comparative Democracy: The Economic Development Thesis." *American Political Science Review* 88, no. 4 (1994): 903–910.

Burnell, Peter, and Peter Calvert. "The Resilience of Democracy: An Introduction." *Democratization* 6, no. 1 (1999): 1–32.

Cassani, Andrea, and Luca Tomini. "Reversing Regimes and Concepts: From Democratization to Autocratization." *European Political Science* 19 (2020): 272–287.

Cheibub, José Antonio. *Presidentialism, Parliamentarism, and Democracy.* New York: Cambridge University Press, 2007.

Chull Shin, Doh. "Democratic Deconsolidation in East Asia: Exploring System Realignments in Japan, Korea, and Taiwan." *Democratization* 28, no. 1 (2021): 142–160. doi:10.1080/13510347.2020. 1826438.

Coppedge, Michael. "Eroding Regimes: What, Where, and When?" *V-Dem Working Paper Series* 57 (2017): 1–405.

Coppedge, Michael, John Gerring, Carl Henrik Knutsen, Staffan I. Lindberg, Jan Teorell, David Altman, Michael Bernhard, et al. "V-Dem Codebook v10." *Varieties of Democracy (V-Dem) Project* (2020).

Dahl, Robert A. *Polyarchy: Participation and Opposition.* New Haven: Yale University Press, 1971.

Edgell, Amanda B., Seraphine F. Maerz, Laura Maxwell, Richard Morgan, Juraj Medzihorsky, Matthew C. Wilson, Vanessa Boese, Sebastian Hellmeier, Jean Lachapelle, Patrik Lindenfors,

Anna Lührmann, and Staffan I. Lindberg. (2020). Episodes of Regime Transformation Dataset (v2.2) Codebook.

Edgell, Amanda B., Matthew C. Wilson, Vanessa A. Boese, and Sandra Grahn. "Democratic Legacies: Using Democratic Stock to Assess Norms, Growth, and Regime Trajectories." *V-Dem Users Working Paper Series* 100, (2020): 1–38.

Epstein, David L, Robert Bates, Jack Goldstone, Ida Kristensen, and Sharyn O'Halloran. "Democratic Transitions." *American Journal of Political Science* 50, no. 3 (2006): 551–569.

Erdmann, Gero. "Transition from Democracy. Loss of Quality, Hybridisation and Breakdown of Democracy." *Comparative Governance and Politics* 1 (2011): 21–58.

Feng, Yi. "Democracy, Political Stability and Economic Growth." *British Journal of Political Science* 27, no. 3 (1997): 391–418.

Foa, Roberto Stefan, and Yascha Mounk. "The Danger of Deconsolidation: The Democratic Disconnect." *Journal of Democracy* 27, no. 3 (2016): 5–17.

Gasiorowski, Mark J. "Economic Crisis and Political Regime Change: An Event History Analysis." *American Political Science Review* 89, no. 4 (1995): 882–897.

Gasiorowski, Mark J., and Timothy J. Power. "The Structural Determinants of Democratic Consolidation: Evidence from the Third World." *Comparative Political Studies* 31, no. 6 (1998): 740–771.

Gates, Scott, Håvard Hegre, Mark P. Jones, and Håvard Strand. "Institutional Inconsistency and Political Instability: Polity Duration, 1800–2000." *American Journal of Political Science* 50, no. 4 (2006): 893–908.

Gerschewski, Johannes. "Erosion or Decay? Conceptualizing Causes and Mechanisms of Democratic Regression." *Democratization* 28, no. 1 (2021): 43–62. doi:10.1080/13510347.2020.1826935

Ginsburg, Tom, and Aziz Z. Huq. *How to Save a Constitutional Democracy.* Chicago: University of Chicago Press, 2018.

Gleditsch, Kristian Skrede. *All International Politics Is Local: The Diffusion of Conflict, Integration, and Democratization.* Ann Arbor: University of Michigan Press, 2009.

Gleditsch, Kristian Skrede, and Michael D. Ward. "Diffusion and the International Context of Democratization." *International Organization* 60, no. 4 (2006): 911–933.

Greene, Samuel R. "Coups and the Consolidation Mirage: Lessons for Stability in New Democracies." *Democratization* 27, no. 7 (2020): 1280–1300.

Grosfeld, Irena, and Ekaterina Zhuravskaya. "Cultural vs. Economic Legacies of Empires: Evidence from the Partition of Poland." *Journal of Comparative Economics* 43, no. 1 (2015): 55–75.

Guiso, Luigi, Paola Sapienza, and Luigi Zingales. "Long-term Persistence." *Journal of the European Economic Association* 14, no. 6 (2016): 1401–1436.

Heckman, James J. "Sample Selection Bias as Specification Error." *Econometrica* 47, no. 1 (1979): 153–161.

Hiroi, Taeko, and Sawa Omori. "Perils of Parliamentarism? Political Systems and the Stability of Democracy Revisited." *Democratization* 16, no. 3 (2009): 485–507.

Hollyer, James R., Peter B. Rosendorff, and James R. Vreeland. "Transparency, Protest and Democratic Stability." *British Journal of Political Science* 49, no. 4 (2019): 1251–1277.

Houle, Christian. "Inequality and Democracy: Why Inequality Harms Consolidation but Does not Affect Democratization." *World Politics* 61 (2009): 589.

Houle, Christian, and Mark A. Kayser. "The Two-Step Model of Clustered Democratization." *Journal of Conflict Resolution* 63, no. 10 (2019): 2421–2437.

Huntington, Samuel P. "Democracy's Third Wave." *Journal of Democracy* 2, no. 2 (1991): 12–34.

Kasuya, Yuko, and Kota Mori. "Better Regime Cutoffs for Continuous Democracy Measures." *V-Dem Users Working Paper Series* 25 (2019): 1–31.

Kaufman, Robert R., and Stephan Haggard. "Democratic Decline in the United States: What Can We Learn from Middle-Income Backsliding?" *Perspectives on Politics* 17, no. 2 (2019): 417–432.

Kosmidis, Ioannis, and David Firth. "Jeffreys-prior Penalty, Finiteness and Shrinkage in Binomial-Response Generalized Linear Models." *Biometrika* 108, no. 1 (2021): 71–82. https://doi.org/10.1093/biomet/asaa052.

Laebens, Melis, and Anna Lührmann. "What Stops Democratic Erosion? The Role of Institutions of Accountability." Paper prepared for the Berlin Democracy Conference, Berlin, November 11–12, 2019.

Levitsky, Steven, and Daniel Ziblatt. How Democracies Die. New York: Broadway Books, 2018.

Lindberg, Staffan I. *Democracy and Elections in Africa*. Baltimore, MD: Johns Hopkins University Press, 2006.

Linz, Juan J. *The Breakdown of Democratic Regimes*. Maryland: Johns Hopkins University Press, 1978.

Linz, Juan J. "The Perils OfPresidentialism." *Journal of Democracy* 1, no. 1 (1990): 51–69.

Linz, Juan J., and Arturo Valenzuela. *The Failure of Presidential Democracy. Vol. 1*. Baltimore, MD: Johns Hopkins University Press, 1994.

Lipset, Seymour Martin. "Some Social Requisites of Democracy: Economic Development and Political Legitimacy." *American Political Science Review* 53, no. 1 (1959): 69–105.

Lührmann, Anna, and Staffan I. Lindberg. "A Third Wave of Autocratization Is Here: What Is New About It?" *Democratization* 26, no. 7 (2019): 1095–1113.

Lührmann, Anna, Marcus Tannenberg, and Staffan I. Lindberg. "Regimes of the World (RoW): Opening New Avenues for the Comparative Study of Political Regimes." *Politics & Governance* 6, no. 1 (2018): 60–77.

Maerz, Seraphine F., Amanda B. Edgell, Joshua Krusell, Laura Maxwell, and Sebastian Hellmeier. (2020). ERT – an R package to load, explore and work with the Episodes of Regime Transformation dataset. Available at: https://github.com/vdeminstitute/ERT.

Maerz, Seraphine F., Anna Lührmann, Sebastian Hellmeier, Sandra Grahn, and Staffan I. Lindberg. "State of the World 2019: Autocratization Surges - Resistance Grows." *Democratization* 27, no. 6 (2020): 909–927.

Mainwaring, Scott. "Presidentialism, Multipartism, and Democracy: The Difficult Combination." *Comparative Political Studies* 26, no. 2 (1993): 198–228.

Marinov, Nikolay, and Hein Goemans. "Coups and Democracy." *British Journal of Political Science* 44, no. 4 (2014): 799–825.

Marra, Giampiero, and Rosalba Radice. "GJRM: Generalised Joint Regression Modelling. R Package Version 0.2-2 (2020). https://CRAN.R-project.org/package=GJRM.

McGrath, Liam F. "Estimating Onsets of Binary Events in Panel Data." *Political Analysis* 23, no. 4 (2015): 534–549.

Mechkova, Valeriya, Anna Lührmann, and Staffan I. Lindberg. "How Much Democratic Backsliding?" *Journal of Democracy* 28, no. 4 (2017): 162–169.

Merkel, Wolfgang. "Embedded and Defective Democracies." *Democratization* 11, no. 5 (2004): 33–58.

Morlino, Leonardo, and Mario Quaranta. "What Is the Impact of the Economic Crisis on Democracy? Evidence from Europe." *International Political Science Review* 37, no. 5 (2016): 618–633.

O'Donnell, Guillermo A. "Illusions About Consolidation." *Journal of Democracy* 7, no. 2 (1996): 34–51.

Olson, Mancur. "Dictatorship, Democracy, and Development." *American Political Science Review* 87, no. 3 (1993): 567–576.

Pemstein, Daniel, Kyle L. Marquardt, Eitan Tzelgov, Yi-ting Wang, Juraj Medzihorsky, Joshua Krusell, Farhad Miri, and Johannes von Römer. "The V-Dem Measurement Model: Latent Variable Analysis for Cross-National and Cross-Temporal Expert-Coded Data." *V-Dem Working Paper Series* 21 (2019). 4th edition.

Pérez-Liñán, Aníbal, and Scott Mainwaring. "Regime Legacies and Levels of Democracy: Evidence from Latin America." *Comparative Politics* 45, no. 4 (2013): 379–397.

Pérez-Liñán, Aníbal, Nicolás Schmidt, and Daniela Vairo. "Presidential Hegemony and Demo- Cratic Backsliding in Latin America, 1925–2016." *Democratization* 26, no. 4 (2019): 606–625.

Persson, Torsten, and Guido Tabellini. "Democratic Capital: The Nexus of Political and Economic Change." *American Economic Journal: Macroeconomics* 1, no. 2 (2009): 88–126.

Powell, Jonathan M., and Clayton L. Thyne. "Global Instances of Coups from 1950 to 2010: A New Dataset." *Journal of Peace Research* 48, no. 2 (2011): 249–259.

Przeworski, Adam. *Crises of Democracy*. New York: Cambridge University Press, 2019.

Przeworski, Adam, R. Michael Alvarez, Michael E. Alvarez, Jose Antonio Cheibub, and Fernando Limongi. *Democracy and Development: Political Institutions and Well-Being in the World, 1950–1990. Vol. 3*. New York: Cambridge University Press, 2000.

Przeworski, Adam, and Fernando Limongi. "Modernization: Theories and Facts." *World Politics* 49, no. 2 (1997): 155–183.

Przeworski, Adam, Lindsay S. Newman, S. K. Park, Didac Queralt, Gonzalo Rivero, and Kong Joo Shin. "Political Institutions and Political Events (PIPE) Data Set." *Department of Politics, New York University, New York* (2013).

Putnam, Robert. *Making Democracy Work: Civic Traditions in Modern Italy. 1–280.* Princeton: Princeton University Press, 1993.

Reenock, Christopher, Jeffrey K. Staton, and Marius Radean. "Legal Institutions and Democratic Survival." *The Journal of Politics* 75, no. 2 (2013): 491–505.

Riggs, Fred W. "Presidentialism Versus Parliamentarism: Implications for Representativeness and Legitimacy." *International Political Science Review* 18, no. 3 (1997): 253–278.

Risse, Thomas, and Nelli Babayan. "Democracy Promotion and the Challenges of Illiberal Regional Powers: Introduction to the Special Issue." *Democratization* 22, no. 3 (2015): 381–399.

Schedler, Andreas. "Measuring Democratic Consolidation." *Studies in Comparative International Development* 36, no. 1 (2001): 66–92.

Schedler, Andreas. "What Is Democratic Consolidation?" Journal of Democracy 9, no .2 (1998): 91–107.

Staton, Jeffrey, Christopher Reenock, and Jordan Holsinger. *Can Courts be Bulwarks of Democracy? Judges and the Politics of Prudence.* Cambridge: Cambridge University Press, Forthcoming.

Stepan, Alfred, and Cindy Skach. "Constitutional Frameworks and Democratic Consolidation: Parliamentarianism Versus Presidentialism." *World Politics* 46, no. 1 (1993): 1–22.

Svolik, Milan. "Authoritarian Reversals and Democratic Consolidation." *American Political Science Review* 102, no. 2 (2008): 153–168.

Svolik, Milan. "Which Democracies Will Last? Coups, Incumbent Takeovers, and the Dynamic of Democratic Consolidation." *British Journal of Political Science* 45, no. 4 (2015): 715–738.

Tansey, Oisín, Kevin Koehler, and Alexander Schmotz. "Ties to the Rest: Autocratic Linkages and Regime Survival." *Comparative Political Studies* 50, no. 9 (2017): 1221–1254.

Teorell, Jan. *Determinants of Democratization: Explaining Regime Change in the World, 1972– 2006.* New York: Cambridge University Press, 2010.

Teorell, Jan, Michael Coppedge, Staffan I. Lindberg, and Svend-Erik Skaaning. "Measuring Polyarchy Across the Globe, 1900–2017." *Studies in Comparative International Development* 54, no. 1 (2019): 71–95.

Tomini, Luca, and Claudius Wagemann. "Varieties of Contemporary Democratic Breakdown and Regression: A Comparative Analysis." *European Journal of Political Research* 57, no. 3 (2018): 687–716.

Vengroff, Richard. "Governance and the Transition to Democracy: Political Parties and the Party System in Mali." *Journal of Modern African Studies* 31, no. 4 (1993): 541–562.

Wilson, Matthew C., Richard Morgan, Juraj Medzihorsky, Laura Maxwell, Seraphine F. Maerz, Anna Lührmann, Patrik Lindenfors, Amanda B. Edgell, Vanessa Boese, and Staffan I. Lindberg. "Successful and Failed Episodes of Democratization: Conceptualization, Identification, and Description." *V-Dem Working Paper Series* 97 (2020): 1–47.

Wing, Susanna D. "Mali: Politics of Crisis." *African Affairs 112* 448 (2013): 476–485.

Ziblatt, Daniel. "How Did Europe Democratize?" *World Politics* 58, no. 2 (2006): 311–338.

What halts democratic erosion? The changing role of accountability

Melis G. Laebens [ID] and Anna Lührmann [ID]

ABSTRACT
Worldwide, democratic erosion is on the rise, with incumbents slowly undermining the pillars of democratic competition such as political freedoms, clean elections, and a free press. While such gradual erosion frequently culminates in democratic breakdown, this is not always the case. How can accountability mechanisms contribute to halting democratic erosion before breakdown, even if they could not prevent the onset of erosion? To study this question, we use the V-Dem Electoral Democracy Index to systematically identify three recent cases – Benin (2007–2012), Ecuador (2008–2010), and South Korea (2008–2016) – where substantial democratic erosion happened but democracy did not break down. Studying these cases in depth we find that accountability mechanism – parliamentary and judicial oversight (horizontal accountability), pressures from civil society and the media (diagonal accountability), or electoral competition between parties and within parties (vertical accountability) – played a part in halting democratic erosion in all of them. They effectively halted erosion when institutional constraints – such as presidential term limits or judicial independence – and contextual factors – in particular economic downturns and public outrage about corruption scandals – worked together to create simultaneous pressures on the incumbents from civil society and from vertical or horizontal accountability actors.

Introduction

Worldwide, democracy is in a new recession. Unlike in past periods of global democratic reversal, democracies today are tending to not break down abruptly. Rather, they are being gradually eroded as incumbents slowly undermine the pillars of democratic competition, such as political freedoms, civil society, a free press, and the rule of law.[1] While gradual change is pernicious because it can be hard to detect and react to for voters, parties and the media, a slow process of democratic erosion also provides opportunities for resistance.

Mechanisms of accountability can play a prominent role in defending democratic institutions against governments' attempts to undermine them. Accountability

---

[B] Supplemental data for this article can be accessed https://doi.org/10.1080/13510347.2021.1897109.

constrains the use of political power.[2] Vertical accountability – elections and political parties – can help remove from office incumbents who abuse their powers. Horizontal accountability enables other state actors to oversee, sanction, and coordinate against the executive. Actors enforcing diagonal accountability – the media and civil society – may mobilize against autocratizing incumbents and provide information to other political agents.

How do these different mechanisms of accountability contribute to halting democratic erosion, even when they were not able to prevent its onset? In this article, we address this question by shedding light on three relevant cases where substantial democratic erosion occurred but was halted before breakdown. Democratic erosion is a process during which incumbents who accessed power in democratic elections gradually but substantially undermine democratic institutions.[3] We systematically identify three cases of substantial democratic erosion that was stopped before democratic breakdown using the concept of "autocratization episodes"[4] – periods of democratic decline – and data from the Varieties of Democracy Institute.[5] We limit our study to the post-Cold War era because democratic erosion has been a prevalent form of democratic reversal only in this more recent period.

Studying three cases that experienced democratic erosion but have evaded breakdown – Benin (2007–2012), Ecuador (2008–2010), and South Korea (2008–2016) – we find support for the idea that mechanisms of accountability have helped to halt democratic erosion and we develop hypotheses about why accountability mechanisms were effective in halting erosion, even though they could not prevent its onset. We suggest that in the cases we analysed, erosion was halted thanks to a combination of diagonal accountability pressures with either vertical or horizontal accountability. In other words, democratic erosion could be halted when civil society successfully mobilized to oppose the incumbent's behaviour, *and* elites coordinated to sanction the incumbent through the judiciary and the legislature, or at the ballot box. The moment in which accountability pressures were successful in sanctioning the incumbent depended on the pre-existing strength of democratic institutions, as well. In South Korea, with its "high-quality" democracy and relatively strong democratic institutions, accountability mechanisms were triggered soon after the incumbent abused her powers.[6] In Benin and Ecuador, however, accountability mechanisms were only able to work once the incumbent was politically weakened by contextual factors such as the end of the incumbent's constitutional term, economic downturn, or corruption scandals. We hypothesize that in these "low-quality" democracies, changing circumstances gave accountability actors greater leverage to sanction the incumbent.

Focusing only on cases without democratic breakdown allows us to study the accountability mechanisms in detail, but we cannot draw cross-case causal inference about what stabilized these democracies after periods of erosion. We do not aim to provide this kind of causal explanation. Rather, our goal is to build theory by isolating the mechanisms by which aggrandizement and abuse of power by incumbents was contained in our specific cases and thus to generate insights about accountability as a possible source of democratic resilience in countries that are experiencing democratic erosion.

The article proceeds as follows. We first define the problem of democratic erosion. Following that, we review the literature and develop theoretical expectations concerning what might halt democratic erosion. Then we discuss methods for identifying three relevant cases of halted erosion and analyse them. Finally, we summarize our findings

The problem of democratic erosion

A slow but sustained decline in levels of freedom and democracy worldwide is driving widespread concern.[7] Democratic reversal in today's world – where international norms favour democratic multiparty elections – is often gradual and results from piecemeal state actions that erode the freedom and fairness of the democratic electoral process and its supporting institutions.[8]

The threat to democracy has typically taken the form of a gradual concentration of power in the hands of the executive branch, and especially its leader, at the expense of other branches of government and of citizens' rights. Bermeo calls this phenomenon "executive aggrandizement", emphasizing that as the incumbent leader gradually expands his or her powers in this way, he or she also weakens the ability of the opposition to compete in elections, gradually making these less free and less fair.[9] This process sometimes also involves the "strategic manipulation" of elections, for example by excluding opposition candidates from the ballot, manipulating electoral rolls or election rules, and using government resources for electoral campaigns.

We focus on these kinds of processes which, following Lührmann and Lindberg, we call democratic erosion.[10] Building on their definition, we consider there to be democratic erosion when a democratically elected incumbent substantially undermines democratic institutions (that is, causes autocratization) by expanding or abusing their powers, but does not suspend or abolish them altogether. We consider democratic institutions to have been *substantially undermined* – or autocratization to have taken place – when there is a substantive decline in the extent to which the regime fulfils the criteria for polyarchy proposed by Dahl – free, fair and consequential elections, access to independent information, respect for individual freedoms of expression and association and for the right to compete in elections, and universal suffrage.[11] If these institutions are eroded to such an extent that the country becomes classified as an (electoral) autocracy, we consider key democratic institutions suspended or abolished.[12] Democratic erosion is a subtype of autocratization processes. It starts in democracies and ends without causing a democratic breakdown and is driven primarily by the democratically elected incumbent's self-serving actions. Excluding from our study autocratization processes that happen primarily for other reasons – such as abuses by the judiciary or the legislature, civil unrest, or international interventions – allows us to generate more precise theoretical insights.

Table 1. Concepts of democratic decline.

	Starts in	Driver
Democratic Erosion (also used in Lührmann/Lindberg 2019)	Democracies	(Elected) incumbents
Executive aggrandizement (Bermeo 2016)	Democracies	(Elected) incumbents
Democratic Backsliding (Bermeo 2016)	Democracies	State-led
Autocratization (Lührmann/Lindberg 2019)	Any regime type	Open
Autocratization (Cassani/Tomini 2020)	Any regime type	Open
Democratic Backsliding (Waldner/Lust 2018)	Any regime type	Open

Table 1 situates democratic erosion with respect to concepts used in some influential works in the literature. Democratic erosion starts in democracies and is driven mainly by the incumbent, who was elected democratically. This concept is similar to Bermeo's notion of executive aggrandizement.[13] Bermeo also uses the broader term democratic backsliding to denote all processes of democratic decline occurring in democracies. Other concepts, such as autocratization[14] and democratic backsliding as defined by Lust and Waldner,[15] are broader and capture any form of decline in the democratic qualities of regimes. In all concepts discussed here, democratic breakdown may be included but does not have to be.

How do democracies survive erosion?

Lührmann and Lindberg have pointed out that the majority of substantial processes of democratic erosion culminate in democratic breakdown.[16] However, given the gradual nature of today's democratic declines, processes of erosion can sometimes be halted, and democratic breakdown can be averted. How did some democracies manage to halt this process of gradual regime change? Given the existence of many cases of ongoing democratic erosion in our contemporary world, even among those democracies that were considered firmly established, there is both scholarly and practical value in understanding how some democracies have survived a period of erosion.

Our research question is related to a broader question that has incited rich scholarly discussion: What makes democracies resilient? Much of the research on this issue has focused on the role of structural factors, particularly income,[17] but also the structure of the economy[18] and ethnic, religious or political "subcultures" among the country's population.[19] Another branch of scholarship has explored the importance of institutional design for overcoming the challenges that democracies face. Parliamentary versus presidential forms of government, majoritarian versus consociational institutions, unitary versus decentralized or federal administrative structures and the features of party systems have been studied with respect to their contributions to democratic stability and consolidation.[20]

We propose a different approach to studying democratic resilience, one that focuses on the mechanisms that stabilize democracy in the face of gradual attacks by incumbent leaders on democratic institutions. Thus, instead of analysing the effects of particular institutional or structural configurations on the survival of democracy, we study how democratic regimes survived erosion brought about by incumbents abusing and expanding their powers. In so doing, our approach is similar to that used by Linz in his classical analysis of democratic breakdown.[21] While Linz analysed regime crises to describe the anatomy of democratic breakdown, we analyse a particular kind of political crisis to shed light on how democratic regimes could avoid being dismantled by incumbents, even when they have caused considerable damage to democratic institutions.

To generate insights into how democratic erosion can be halted, we turn to the incumbent's political environment and the probability that the incumbent's behaviour will be sanctioned. While incumbents' normative preferences might be relevant for explaining why democracies are eroded, they can rarely account for how democratic erosion is halted in the absence of a leadership change, as preferences should be generally stable across time. The probability that the incumbent is sanctioned, however, changes over time. Dahl argued that ruling elites allow democratization if the costs of toleration are lower than the costs of suppressing the demand for democracy.[22] Extending this axiom to the context of democratic erosion implies that ruling elites in a democracy weigh the cost of the status quo against the cost of engaging in democratic erosion. The cost of the status quo is quite high for incumbents, since – as Przeworski famously stated "democracy is a system in which parties lose elections".[23] At the same time, the potential costs of engaging in democratic erosion may also be high for incumbents in democracies. They may not only lose elections but also face impeachment, prosecution, jail, exile, and even threats to their lives as a result of their actions.

Erosion may be costly for incumbents because democratic institutions disperse power, make its exercise more transparent, and create a framework where those in power can be peacefully replaced. We use Lührmann et al.'s framework of political accountability to discuss these constraining forces. Following the general practice in the literature, they distinguish between accountability mechanisms based on the spatial relationship between actors.[24] Their concept of accountability is particularly helpful for our purposes for two reasons. Firstly, they emphasize that what matters in practice are *de facto* constraints on governments and not just *de jure* rules, which may not reflect what happens in reality.[25] Secondly, their threefold categorization of accountability is useful for thinking about societal constraints on governments. In the classical political science literature, we find mainly two subtypes of accountability: vertical (constraints from below) as emphasized for instance by Schmitter; and horizontal accountability (constraints among equals), which is at the heart of O'Donnell's ideas about accountability.[26] Which sub-type of accountability those constraints exercised by civil society actors belong to has been contested. O'Donnell argues that "various social agents and demands" exercise a type of vertical accountability linking the state to society.[27] Schmitter conceives of them originally in the realm of horizontal accountability, but later proposes a third type of accountability mechanism ("oblique" in his words).[28] Such calls have become louder in recent years.[29] In order to reflect that non-state actors have an important intermediary role and support both voters (vertical) and legislators (horizontal) through the provision of information (media) and sanctions (civil society protest), Lührmann et al. label such forces as diagonal accountability. This distinction is helpful here, because the actions of civil society are highly relevant for resistance to democratic erosion.

Building on this framework, we argue that three accountability mechanisms can impose costs on incumbents, and thus prevent or halt democratic erosion. The first is *vertical accountability* – the exercise of political rights in free and fair elections and within political parties.[30] In this realm, the competition *between* parties in multi-party elections as well as *intra-party* competition may halt democratic erosion by replacing in office incumbents and their parties.

Secondly, *horizontal accountability* mechanisms are designed to protect against abuses of state power. These include controls by the judiciary and other independent institutions, and legislative oversight.[31] The legislature, in addition to enforcing accountability to the public and to the law, can also be a space for political elites to coordinate against a threat by one of them to aggrandize. When political elites fear institutional capture by rivals who might exclude them from power, they may defend democratic institutions because it is in their best interests to do so.

Finally, *diagonal accountability* refers to the ability of civil society actors and the media to constrain governments.[32] They can use a broad range of actions to challenge autocratization processes.[33] For example, journalists may uncover corrupt and undemocratic behaviour by state officials, and civil society actors can mobilize against such action through mass protests or other forms of citizen engagement.

We argue that such mechanisms could, at least sometimes, contain destabilizing forces and avert breakdown in three different ways. Firstly, government officials should take the potential of being sanctioned into account and refrain from democratic erosion in the first place, or stop such processes before sanctioning mechanisms kick in. This deterrence effect is difficult to observe, as accountability mechanisms should work to prevent erosion. Secondly, these officials may underestimate the strength of accountability mechanisms and be sanctioned for democratic erosion. Thirdly, incumbents engaged in democratic erosion may reverse their behaviour if their power vis-a-vis "accountability actors" changes over time. We use the shorthand term "accountability actors" to designate people, groups or organizations who, in a particular context, pressure and constrain the incumbent through either of the accountability mechanisms. Accountability actors may emerge on the political scene or become stronger with changes in the political context. For instance, strong economic growth may have enabled democratic erosion by boosting the incumbent's popular support and decreasing the cost of autocratization. If economic growth stops, the incumbent may face greater pressure from opposition parties and from civil society. We would expect erosion to stop after such a change in the political environment strengthened accountability pressures. In the second and third scenarios described here, accountability mechanisms may contribute to the end of democratic erosion even when they could not prevent its onset.

We use this framework to understand how erosion was halted in cases where incumbents' efforts to undermine democratic institutions initially caused autocratization but were then upended. We study within-case variation over time in order to identify some of the accountability-related factors that change the "costs" of democratic erosion to incumbents.

Accountability: constraints on the power to erode democracy?

Incumbents who seek to weaken the constraints set in place by democratic institutions are likely to face opposition from a range of diverse agents mentioned above. However, these need not be motivated only by a commitment to democracy and its institutions. Some who hold positions from which they can constrain the incumbent may also be concerned with their personal or their group's advancement. For example, judges may think the rule of law is important, but put their personal careers or the future of their institution first. Elected politicians similarly may not only seek to defend their ideological principles or realize their policy goals but may also want to ensure the continuity of their political careers. Voters, in turn, may prioritize partisan loyalties and economic outcomes, and hence tolerate power abuses.[34]

This multiplicity of interests and goals in practice complicates the realization of accountability pressures because it provides the incumbent with the possibility of dividing and co-opting potential opponents. Combining co-optation and repression, incumbents may successfully evade and undermine accountability – oversight and sanctions – and cause democratic erosion. Figure 1 illustrates this interactive process. Particularly in "low quality" democracies, where democratic institutions and supporting civil society structures are already weak (for example due to corruption or a repressive legal framework, or because civil society and media organizations are

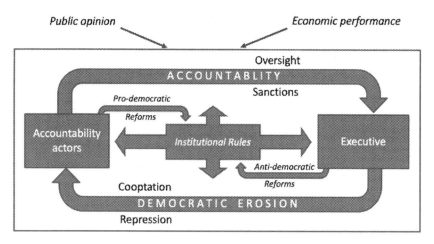

Figure 1. The interaction between the executive and accountability actors.

dependent on the state), it is relatively easy for incumbents to weaken accountability pressures by exploiting the diverse interests of accountability actors. As erosion advances, it will become even harder for accountability actors to gather information, to publicly voice criticism of the government, to coordinate their actions, and to compete in elections. Over time, incumbents can also use their position and powers to reform institutions (such as term limits or judicial checks) in ways that further weaken accountability pressures. As a result of these feedback mechanisms, democratic erosion is often a slippery slope.[35]

Nevertheless, our theoretical framework suggests two scenarios in which democratic erosion can be halted. The first is a miscalculation scenario, where attempts to evade accountability mechanisms eventually fail and are sanctioned. The second is a power balance mechanism, where incumbents who previously had the political power to neutralize accountability pressures lose some of their sway and become vulnerable to sanctioning. Both institutional rules and external factors may play a part in changing the power balance (see Figure 1). For example, evading accountability is likely to be easier for incumbents who enjoy strong popular support and a good economic record. High courts may be less willing to constrain popular incumbents who have a prospect of remaining in power.[36] Similarly, members of the ruling party may be less likely to oppose the incumbent when they expect him or her to stay in office.[37] Besides boosting public support for the incumbent, good economic performance may also make it easier for the government to co-opt elites, who are likely to disproportionately benefit from economic expansion. Because such contextual factors like economic growth can change considerably over time, they may account for why accountability mechanisms would not prevent erosion but could ultimately halt it. In what follows, we employ this framework to study the cases where democratic erosion happened but was halted before breakdown.

Research design and case selection

We conduct theory-building case studies with the aim of revealing how accountability mechanisms halted democratic erosion, even though they could not prevent its onset.

We therefore need cases where the outcome of interest is clearly present.[38] In order to identify such cases, we use the Episodes of Regime Transformation (ERT) data.[39] It permits the identification of all cases of autocratization of democracies in the period from 1990 to 2019 that were halted before breakdown. Autocratization is operationalized as a decline of more than 10% of the value in V-Dem's Electoral Democracy Index (EDI) over a year or an unbroken period of time.[40] The EDI reflects Dahl's polyarchy concept: universal suffrage, officials elected in free and fair elections, alternative sources of information and freedom of speech as well as freedom of association.[41] The index ranges from 0 to 1, with higher values indicating greater proximity to Dahl's concept of polyarchy.[42] We measure regime type using the Regimes of the World classification, which classifies those countries as democracies which somewhat fulfil Dahl's criteria.[43]

In total we find 61 episodes of autocratization of democracies since the end of the Cold War.[44] Thirty-six of them (59%) actually led to the breakdown of the democratic regime. Using the episode dates identified in the ERT, and qualitative sources, we classify another 14 episodes as still ongoing (23%).[45] Only in the remaining 11 cases (16%) did the autocratization episode halt before leading to democratic breakdown. Among these 11 cases of halted autocratization, we only find three unambiguous cases of democratic erosion driven primarily by incumbents who undermined democratic norms: Benin (2007–2012), Ecuador (2008–2010), and South Korea (2008–2016). In the other cases, we consider that autocratization was primarily the result of different challenges, such as ethnic and religious conflict, civil unrest, international involvement, or state capture.[46] We therefore do not select them as case studies.

Table 2 provides descriptive information about our three cases. In Benin, President Yayi Boni repeatedly attempted to punish and undermine the political opposition, while also trying to extend his term of office. In Ecuador, President Rafael Correa used his popularity to enhance his powers, undermine institutional oversight mechanisms, and weaken the opposition. South Korea had a substantially higher level of democracy prior to the onset of democratic erosion (EDI score of 0.86 compared to 0.71 for Benin and 0.76 for Ecuador). Nevertheless, President Park Geun-hye and her party violated citizens' rights to privacy, media freedom and administrative impartiality for electoral and financial gain. In the following, we provide a structured-focused comparison of democratic erosion in these cases and how it was eventually halted.[47]

Table 2. Selected cases of democratic erosion.

	EDI before	Drop in EDI	Democracy Age*	Context
Benin (2007–2012)	0.71	−0.13	15	President Boni curtails media and quality of elections and criminalizes opponents.
Ecuador (2008–2010)	0.76	−0.17	28	President Correa weakens checks and balances, undermines electoral opposition, pressures media and civil society.
South Korea (2008–2016)	0.86	−0.16	20	Government limits media and academic freedom, right to privacy and administrative impartiality.

Notes: EDI = V-Dem Electoral Democracy Index (0=not democratic; 1= fully democratic; see Coppedge et al., "V-Dem Dataset v10."); * Before onset of autocratization episode.

48 RESILIENCE OF DEMOCRACY

Empirical analysis

In the following, we analyse each case with a view to identifying the factors that helped to halt democratic erosion. We address the following questions in each case study:

- What did the executive do to undermine democracy?
- Why did accountability actors not prevent democratic erosion earlier?
- How did accountability actors manage to halt democratic erosion?
- What changed and helped to activate accountability?

We use academic and news sources to analyse the cases. We also discuss declines in the V-Dem component indices (Clean Elections, Freedom of Speech and Alternative Sources of Information, Freedom of Association) which form the Electoral Democracy Index and which therefore led to the episode being classified as democratic erosion. Finally, we summarize the empirical findings with a view to distilling hypotheses about how democratic erosion can be halted.

Benin (2007–2012)

What did the executive do to undermine democracy?

In 2006, the year before democratic erosion began, Benin had an EDI score of 0.71. By 2012, it had dropped to 0.59. Yayi Boni came to power in 2006 as an independent candidate promising change and economic revival, in a context where the political class had been discredited due economic stagnation.[48] His proposal to reform the constitution met with strong opposition, resulting in the formation of an opposition coalition in 2009.[49] They accused Boni of corruption and launched a legislative impeachment procedure in 2010, which failed because the opposition did not have the necessary majority.[50] Faced with an electoral challenge, Boni resorted to manipulating electoral rolls in the run-up to the 2011 presidential election. Through the creation of a digital voter registry, the government excluded hundreds of thousands of voters residing in opposition strongholds.[51] This was reflected in a large drop in the Clean Elections Index. In addition, there were delays in elections, particularly the 2013 municipal elections, which were only held in 2016.[52]

Boni won re-election in 2011, and the opposition led a wave of protests.[53] In his second term, he started to criminalize his opponents, undermining political freedoms and the rule of law.[54] Patrice Talon – a wealthy businessman and former ally of the president – was arrested because of alleged assassination and coup attempts targeting the president, and the government ignored court orders against his detention.[55] Thus, Benin registered minor declines in the Freedom of Association and Alternative Sources of Information Indices.

Why did accountability actors not prevent democratic erosion earlier?

Despite forming an electoral coalition for the 2011 presidential elections, the opposition became fragmented again thereafter. Meanwhile the media lacked the autonomy and the professionalism to constrain the government even before Boni's presidency.[56] Although civil society actors, notably public sector unions and members of the judiciary, voiced opposition and successfully mobilized, their actions had a limited capacity to constrain the government. Banégas attributes this to a failure of collective

RESILIENCE OF DEMOCRACY 49

action and a lack of credible leadership in a context where most in the opposition had, at some point or other, been associated with the regime.[57]

How did accountability actors manage to halt democratic erosion?

The legislative and municipal elections in 2015 were considered free and fair, because the opposition parties in parliament forged a new electoral code establishing an independent electoral commission and revising the controversial digital voter registry.[58] The mobilization of civil society to support and legitimize the electoral process also contributed to the success of these elections.[59] The opposition won a majority of seats in the legislature. The president declared he would not seek a third term, supporting the candidacy of his prime minister instead.[60]

What changed and helped to activate accountability?

The government's political appointments to the courts, its punishment of individual judges, and its push for constitutional changes that would allow for a third presidential term, led to broad-based popular mobilizations in 2013 and a general strike in 2014.[61] Boni's attempts to nationalize and control major sources of economic rent, most notably the cotton exports and the black market for smuggled oil, fuelled factional rifts inside the ruling coalition, particularly with the powerful cotton magnate Talon, while also causing economic disruption and instability.[62] These miscalculations by the government, the related economic troubles and corruption scandals, combined with the efforts of the judiciary,[63] of civil society and of parliamentary elites to protect the country's constitution and secure a free and fair electoral process, culminated in defeats for Boni in the 2015 parliamentary and the 2016 presidential elections.

Benin's democracy survived this democratic erosion episode, but by 2019 it was again in distress due to the new President Patrice Talon's aggrandizement and repressive policies.[64]

Ecuador (2008–2010)

What did the executive do to undermine democracy?

In 2007, the year before democratic erosion began, Ecuador had an EDI score of 0.76. By 2010 it had dropped to 0.59. Rafael Correa was elected president in 2006 following a long period of crisis and political instability that led voters to reject the country's political parties.[65] Correa launched a constitutional process after his election. To be able to disband the sitting congress and elect a constituent assembly, he maneuvered to have a number of legislators and judges impeached.[66] The resulting constitution established a framework with vast executive powers and weak independent checks on the president's powers.[67] Correa used these powers and his persistent popularity to establish hegemony over the country's political institutions and civil society. From 2007 onwards, the Alternative Sources of Information, Freedom of Assembly, and Clean Elections measures all registered decline. Through a constitutional referendum held in 2011, Correa expanded his influence over judicial appointments and placed new restrictions on private media.[68] After winning a large majority of the seats in the legislature in the 2013 elections, Correa was able to further increase his powers, for example by creating a supervisory body allowing him to sanction opposition media, and eliminating term limits for the president.[69]

Why did accountability actors not prevent democratic erosion earlier?

Despite the fact that Correa's actions and growing powers undermined the rule of law and fair political competition, his popularity remained high throughout these years thanks to economic growth and high public investment and spending financed by a large inflow of oil rents. Meanwhile Correa's growing formal powers, his political influence over the judiciary and the bureaucracy, and the support of the ruling party in the legislature weakened horizontal accountability.[70] Finally, important civil society organizations like unions and indigenous organizations were divided and co-opted,[71] while independent media and opposition activists were weakened through legal sanctions, criminalization, and personal attacks by the President.[72]

How did accountability actors manage to halt democratic erosion?

As falling oil prices dragged the country into an economic slowdown and Correa's popularity started falling, large and sustained mobilizations erupted in 2015. Although the presidential term limit had been abolished via a constitutional amendment approved in the legislature, Correa decided not to run in the 2017 election.[73] But he did not intend to give up his political influence and wanted his vice president and close friend Jorge Glas to succeed him in the presidency. As Glas was very unpopular due to his involvement in corruption, Correa had to endorse Lenin Moreno, vice president in his previous administration.[74] Glas was placed on the ticket as vice-president.

A few months after being narrowly elected, Moreno brought corruption charges against the vice president and other Correa appointments in the judiciary and the comptroller's office. This led to a split in the party (which was taken over by Moreno) and criminal investigations against many from the Correa group, including Correa himself, who was abroad at the time and eventually became unable to return to Ecuador due to criminal charges.[75] Correa later received a prison sentence.[76]

What changed and triggered accountability mechanisms?

The worsening economic prospects of the country, the sustained civil society mobilization against corruption and against the re-election of Correa, and the public's rejection of Glas – whose corruption had become irrefutable once the Odebrecht investigation[77] was made public by American and Brazilian prosecutors – brought on Correa's demise. Moreno's decision to turn against Correa was likely motivated, at least in part, by political calculations. Moreno faced a debt crisis compounded by shrinking rent revenues and sought to strengthen his position by distancing himself from Correa.[78]

Correa's exit from office and the Moreno government's reversal of some of Correa's institutional reforms stopped the process of democratic erosion. While some of Ecuador's democracy scores improved after the government's break with Correa, the Moreno government continued to use a plebiscitarian style and extensive executive discretion.[79]

South Korea (2008–2016)

What did the executive do to undermine democracy?

In 2007, the year before democratic erosion began, South Korea was classified as a liberal democracy with an EDI score of 0.86. By 2016, South Korea's EDI score had dropped to 0.7. V-Dem indicators show adverse change in how free and fair South

Korea's elections were as well as in press freedoms (media censorship, harassment of journalists, and media manipulation) and freedom of academic and cultural expression. The drop in the press freedom indicators largely reflects a surveillance scandal that surfaced in 2010. The government allegedly used intelligence agencies and an "ethics commission" to illegally monitor citizens – in particular, journalists – and influence public media.[80] Furthermore, ahead of the 2012 elections, the National Intelligence Service secretly posted comments in online forums favouring the candidate of the ruling party – Park Geun-hye.[81] She is the daughter of late President Park Chung-hee, who acceded to power in a military coup in 1963. She won the elections and was later involved in a major corruption scheme involving abuse of power, state funds and undue pressure on journalists.[82] Her government also excluded thousands of artists from government support programmes for political reasons.[83]

Why did accountability actors not prevent democratic erosion earlier?

Democratic erosion in South Korea was relatively mild. It was mainly caused by the ruling party using state resources illegitimately to limit press freedom and give an advantage to the ruling party in online discussions. Since these were mainly clandestine activities, those perpetuating them possibly thought they could evade sanction. Indeed, there were no electoral sanctions in the 2012 elections for several reasons. Firstly, the information about the involvement of the intelligence agency in the electoral process was disputed publicly by a leading police officer shortly before the election, leading voters to be "confused" about what to believe before election day.[84] This might have been aided by a highly restrictive campaign environment in South Korea, which does not allow ordinary citizens to talk about their preferred candidate.[85] Secondly, the opposition did not unite early enough behind one candidate.[86] Due to both factors, the 2012 election could not halt democratic erosion. However, after the election, the prosecution found evidence of the involvement of the intelligence service in the election campaign.[87]

How did accountability actors manage to halt democratic erosion?

In fall 2016, public prosecutors uncovered President Park Geun-hye's involvement in corruption, and media reports about the scandal sparked mass protests calling for her removal. According to Shin and Moon "[i]n the eyes of much of the public, [Park Geun-hye] stood condemned as a figure who had violated democratic principles and regressed toward practices that smacked of the country's authoritarian past".[88] In 2017, pressure from mass protests forced South Korea's parliament to impeach Park Geun-hye, and in April 2018 she was sentenced to jail for 24 years on corruption charges.[89]

What changed and helped to activate accountability?

The corruption scandal swayed popular opinion against the President.[90] The decisive action of both the legislature and the judiciary is an indication for the strength of South Korean institutions of horizontal accountability, which were not affected severely by democratic erosion. However, observers agree that the country's political parties and parliament initially hesitated and only pursued the impeachment process as a result of the mass protests.[91] Thus, popular protest played an important role in ensuring accountability.

Discussion

In the theory section, we discussed three mechanisms that could halt democratic erosion: (1) vertical accountability, (2) diagonal accountability, and (3) horizontal accountability. Vertical accountability refers to pressures coming from competition between parties and inside ruling parties. Diagonal accountability involves pressures exerted by independent media and civil society activities such as protests. Finally, horizontal accountability refers to legislative and judicial checks on executive power. Table 3 summarizes to what extent these mechanisms were relevant for halting democratic erosion in the three cases studied.

Using structured-focused comparisons of three rare cases where democratic erosion was halted, we can advance hypotheses to explain how democratic erosion stops. Table 3 shows that all accountability mechanisms could play a role in halting democratic erosion. Diagonal accountability – and in particular pressure from civil society – was important in all cases. While protests and civil society pressures are by themselves not sufficient to halt democratic erosion, they might be necessary for other accountability mechanisms to be effective. To have an incentive to check on the incumbent, and to successfully sanction incumbents either electorally (vertical accountability) or through institutional checks and balances (horizontal accountability), elites must often be pressured by civil society mobilization.

All civil society mobilizations may not be equally effective in triggering accountability mechanisms, however. In the absence of a cause that is widely perceived to be legitimate, incumbents may succeed in marginalizing and criminalizing anti-government protests. This does not imply that if grievances are widespread and severe enough, democratic erosion will always be halted. Whether or not an accumulation of grievances and related mobilizations trigger accountability partly has to do with the strategy of the opposition.[92] The political strength of the incumbent, for example the extent to which the ruling coalition is cohesive, can also affect the outcome.

The role of mass mobilizations in triggering or supporting vertical and horizontal accountability mechanisms gives a clue as to how accountability actors could halt democratic erosion, even though they were unable to prevent its onset. When low economic performance or corruption scandals – contextual factors we highlighted in the theory section – reduced support for the government, the opposition obtained opportunities to sanction incumbents. In Ecuador as well as Benin, economic crisis and disruption weakened the incumbent's support. In South Korea, the President

Table 3. Mechanisms resolving episodes of democratic erosion.

	Vertical accountability		Diagonal accountability		Horizontal accountability	
	Defection inside ruling party	Electoral competition between parties	Media	Civil Society/ Protest	Parliament	Judiciary
Benin (2007–2012)		x		x	x	x
Ecuador (2008–2010)	x		(x)	x		(x)
South Korea (2008–2016)			x	x	x	x

Note: A "x" marks primary importance of this factor; a "(x)" secondary importance and no mark implies a low relevance.

was at the centre of a major corruption and power abuse scandal. Corruption allegations affected the incumbent's support in Benin and Ecuador as well.

Our cases show that the institutional framework was also a dynamic factor. Sometimes, accountability actors successfully changed the rules in their favour. In Benin, a new electoral law became a turning point. But even where the rules did not change, their political impact could change over time. This was the case with presidential term limits. Although they were present at the beginning of the term, they only became a constraint for incumbents as their term limit was approaching. At that point, the constitutional limit provided a common cause for different accountability actors to mobilize and coordinate around.

The role of the contextual factors identified above were not identical in all our cases, however. These served as "triggers" for accountability mechanisms in Benin and Ecuador, but not in South Korea. In Benin and Ecuador, whose democratic institutions were not strong to begin with, democratic erosion could be halted only thanks to a shift in the political power balance between the government and its opposition, which allowed the latter to activate the mechanisms of accountability that the incumbent had thus far successfully neutralized. In South Korea, where democratic institutions were much stronger to begin with, accountability mechanisms worked even in the absence of such a shift and despite the fact that the incumbent obtained re-election. This was thanks to judicial independence and the legislature's ability to impeach the president, and to civil society pressure.

The above leads us to three observations concerning how and why democratic erosion processes may be halted, even after having caused significant democratic erosion. Firstly, in "high-quality" democracies where incumbents attempt to evade accountability by abusing power covertly, accountability mechanisms may fail to prevent abuses and yet eventually sanction them. Secondly, in relatively "low-quality" democracies where a weaker institutional environment allows incumbents to openly evade accountability using co-optation and repression, incumbents may nevertheless be sanctioned when a decline in their popular support (usually caused by economic downturns and corruption scandals) strengthens accountability actors by boosting and focusing the latter's efforts to sanction the incumbent. Thirdly, in either case, accountability actors may need to work together to successfully sanction incumbents. In particular, broad-based civil society mobilization may be needed to trigger and/or complement actions by political elites who try to constrain incumbents through institutions of horizontal accountability or at the ballot box.

Based on these observations, two hypotheses may be advanced. Firstly, accountability mechanisms are more likely to halt democratic erosion if the popularity of the incumbent decreases substantively (for example, due to economic crisis or corruption scandals) and/or if the incumbent is approaching the end of their constitutionally allowed term. Secondly, broad-based anti-government mass mobilization can enhance the probability that opposition emerges or strengthens in legislatures or within ruling parties, helping to constrain the incumbent and halt democratic erosion.

Conclusions

Our article presents an analysis of three systematically selected episodes of democratic erosion that were halted before democratic breakdown (Benin 2007–2012, Ecuador

54 RESILIENCE OF DEMOCRACY

2008–2010 and South Korea 2008–2016). Based on our study of the role of three accountability mechanisms – vertical, horizontal, and diagonal – in these cases, we highlight two dynamics that could address the puzzle of why accountability actors helped to halt autocratization even though they could not prevent it. Firstly, contextual factors affecting the incumbent's popularity, such as economic performance or corruption scandals, as well as an approaching term of office limit, may change the balance of power between the incumbent and accountability actors, setting sanctions in motion. Secondly, for democratic erosion to be halted, civil society mobilizations (diagonal accountability pressures) against the government may be needed to trigger or support other accountability mechanisms. In all our cases, multiple accountability mechanisms involving pressure from the public and from political elites worked together to avert further democratic decline.

Our study focused on "positive" cases, where democratic erosion was halted before complete breakdown, and was not designed to test the hypotheses mentioned above. Future studies with theory-testing research designs are needed to assess the extent to which the hypotheses we propose are sustained beyond our cases. The fact that staunch opposition from civil society was able to help halt democratic erosion in the cases we studied but failed to do so in others – such as Turkey or Venezuela – calls for further investigation of the conditions under which such mobilizations may serve as triggers for accountability mechanisms.

Notes

1. Bermeo, "On Democratic Backsliding."
2. Lührmann et al., "Constraining Governments" and Schedler, Diamond, and Plattner, "The Self-Restraining State."
3. Lührmann and Lindberg, "Third Wave."
4. Ibid.
5. Coppedge et al., "V-Dem Dataset v10."
6. We use "high quality" and "low quality" democracy in reference to the debate on the quality of democracy, embracing the notion that a high quality democracy is a system where the different procedural and substantive elements considered essential to modern democracy are all present, balancing and complementing each other, while "low-quality" democracies are weak on at least some of these dimensions. See Diamond and Morlino, "The Quality of Democracy," pp. 22,30.
7. Lührmann and Lindberg, "Third Wave" and Waldner and Lust, "Unwelcome Change."
8. Bermeo, "On Democratic Backsliding."
9. Ibid.
10. Lührmann and Lindberg, "Third Wave."
11. Although the rule of law is not an explicitly necessary condition for polyarchy according to Dahl's definition, the de-facto protection of individual civil and political rights is closely related to the rule of law, understood here in the "minimal" sense as a body of law that meets certain procedural and formal criteria for its creation and enforcement (See Morlino, "Two 'Rules of Law,'" 48–9). As Morlino notes, the extent to which civil and political rights are enforced is a key indicator when assessing democratic quality.
12. Lührmann, Tanneberg and Lindberg, "Regimes of the World."
13. Bermeo, "On Democratic Backsliding."
14. Lührmann and Lindberg, "Third Wave" and Cassani and Tomini, "Revisiting Concepts."
15. Waldner and Lust, "Unwelcome Change."
16. Lührmann and Lindberg, "Third Wave."
17. Lipset, "Social Requisites of Democracy;" Cheibub et al. "Makes Democracies Endure."
18. Boix, "Democracy and Redistribution."
19. Dahl, *Polyarchy* and Beissinger, "Ethnicity and Democracy."

RESILIENCE OF DEMOCRACY 55

20. Linz, "Perils of Presidentialism"; Lijphardt, "Consociational Democracy"; Norris, *Driving Democracy;* Sartori, *Parties and Party Systems.*
21. Linz, *Crisis, Breakdown and Reequlibration.*
22. Dahl, *Polyarchy*, 141.
23. Przeworski, *Democracy and the Market*, 10.
24. See Lindberg, "Mapping Accountability." Schmitter (in "Ambiguous Virtues," 52–54) acknowledges that the spatial distinction is the most common one, but also proposes a temporal distinction in relation to policy and electoral cycles.
25. Lührmann et al., "Constraining Governments," 3.
26. Schmitter, "Ambiguous Virtues," 53; O'Donnell, "Horizontal Accountability."
27. O'Donnell, "A Response," 68.
28. Schmitter, "The limits," 60; Schmitter, "Ambiguous Virtues," 53.
29. Goetz and Jenkins, "Hybrid Forms of Accountability"; Malena and Forster, "Social Accountability."
30. Schedler, Diamond, and Plattner, "The Self-Restraining State."
31. O'Donnell, "Horizontal Accountability."
32. Goetz and Jenkins, "Hybrid Forms."
33. For excellent overviews of such actions, see Grimes, "Contingencies of Societal Accountability" and Malena and Forster, "Social Accountability."
34. Achen and Bartels, *Democracy for Realists*; Graham and Svolik, "Democracy in America?"
35. Linz, Crisis, *Breakdown and Reequilibration.*
36. Helmke, *Courts Under Constraints*; Chavez, Ferejohn, and Weingast, "Theory of Independent Judiciary."
37. McKie, "Presidential Term Limit Contravention."
38. Mahoney and Goertz. "A Tale," 239.
39. Edgell et al., "Episodes of Regime Transformation," based on V10 of the V-Dem data (Coppedge et al., "V-Dem Dataset v10").
40. Replicating our analysis using the Liberal Democracy Index (LDI) rather than the EDI leads to a similar set of cases with some differences, which we discuss in the Appendix.
41. Dahl, *Polyarchy.*
42. Autocratization episodes may start with a relatively small decline in the EDI (0.01) and end with an increase in the EDI (greater than 0.02) or four years of stagnation in the EDI – fluctuations of at most 0.01. For details, see Lührmann and Lindberg, "Third Wave," 7.
43. Lührmann, Tannenberg, and Lindberg, "Regimes of the World."
44. In two cases – Turkey (2007–2011) and Turkey (2013–2019), and Venezuela (1999–2001) and Venezuela (2003–2019) – we consider two episodes of autocratization to be part of a single process. Thus, the episode in Turkey (2007–2011) is considered to have ended in breakdown, even though democracy only broke down during the later episode (2013–2019).
45. Either these episodes had 2019 as the ending year or, even though the coding rule suggested that the autocratization episode ended in 2017 or 2018, we were not able to identify a significant change or resolution that would lead us to consider the episode as having really ended.
46. Autocratization was related primarily to international conflict (Georgia 2006–2010), a coup attempt (Venezuela 1992), ethnic conflict (North Macedonia 2000, Bosnia and Herzegovina 2013–2015), communal violence (India 2002–2010), or gang violence and crime (Honduras 1998–2006) in other cases. In Moldova (2012–2018) we consider that autocratization was largely driven by an oligarch's attempt to capture the state. Finally, although Mali (1997–1998) comes up as an episode of autocratization that halted before breakdown, we could not identify democratic erosion there. The episode seems to have been driven by fluctuations in the EDI in the immediate aftermath of the transition to democracy.
47. George and Bennett, *Case Studies.*
48. Mayrargue, "Boni, un Président Inattendu?"
49. Souaré, "The 2011 Presidential Election," 74.
50. *Reuters*, "Benin Parliament Rejects Impeachment," August 20, 2010. https://www.reuters.com/article/benin-politics/head-of-benin-parliament-rejects-impeachment-request-idUSLDE67J1MV20100820.
51. Souaré, "The 2011 Presidential Election," 85.
52. Laleyè, "The Waiting Game."

56 RESILIENCE OF DEMOCRACY

53. Jeune Afrique, "Présidentielle Béninoise," February 22, 2011. https://www.jeuneafrique.com/182274/politique/pr-sidentielle-b-ninoise-pol-mique-autour-de-la-lepi/.
54. Banégas, "Benin: Challenges for Democracy," 449–50.
55. Ibid., 455.
56. Ibid., 451–2.
57. Ibid., 453.
58. EISA, "The Conduct of the 26 April 2015 National Assembly Election: A Test of the Capacity of the Political Leadership to Build a Consensus," July 2015. https://www.eisa.org/epp-benin.php.
59. Ibid.
60. Tyson Roberts, "Here's Why Benin's Election Was a Step Forward for African Democratic Consolidation. and Why It Wasn't.", March 22, 2016. https://www.washingtonpost.com/news/monkey-cage/wp/2016/03/22/heres-why-benins-election-was-a-step-forward-for-african-democratic-consolidation-and-why-it-wasnt/
61. Laleyè, "The Waiting Game," 8.
62. Banégas, "Benin: Challenges for Democracy," 454–6.
63. Ibid., 452.
64. Duerksen, Mark, "The Testing of Benin's Democracy," Africa Center for Strategic Studies, May 29, 2019. https://africacenter.org/spotlight/the-testing-of-benin-democracy/.
65. Conaghan, "Ecuador," 262–4.
66. Ibid., 271.
67. Polga Hecimovich, "La Presidencia del Ejecutivo Unitario," 109.
68. Polga-Hecimovich, "Estabilidad Institucional," 144.
69. Basabe-Serrano and Martínez, "Ecuador: Menos Democracia"; de la Torre and Ortiz Lemos, "Populist Polarization."
70. Polga Hecimovich, "La Presidencia del Ejecutivo Unitario."
71. Martínez Novo, "Collaborations and Estrangements."
72. Basabe-Serrano and Martínez, "Ecuador: Menos Democracia," 155–7.
73. de la Torre, "Ecuador after Correa," 80.
74. Labarthe and Saint-Upéry, "Leninismo versus Correísmo," 39.
75. Ibid.
76. León Cabrera, "Ecuador's Former President Convicted," April 7, 2020. https://www.nytimes.com/2020/04/07/world/americas/ecuador-correa-corruption-verdict.html
77. Odebrecht is a Brazilian construction giant, which was systematically bribing officials to obtain public sector contracts across Latin America and the Caribbean. An investigation by the US Department of Justice unearthed ample evidence of corruption across the region. See Shiel and Chavkin. "Bribery Division: What is Odebrecht? Who is Involved?" June 25, 2019. https://www.icij.org/investigations/bribery-division/bribery-division-what-is-odebrecht-who-is-involved/.
78. Labarthe and Saint-Upéry, "Leninismo versus Correísmo," 34.
79. Burbano de Lara and de la Torre, "The Pushback."
80. *New York Times*, "South Korea Scandal," April 9, 2012. https://www.nytimes.com/2012/04/10/world/asia/government-spying-charges-complicate-korean-vote.html.
81. ho and Kim, "Procedural justice," 1185. BBC News, "South Korea's Spy Agency Admits Trying to Influence 2012 Poll," August 4, 2017. https://www.bbc.com/news/world-asia-40824793.
82. Hyun-Soo Lim, "A Closer Look."
83. *New York Times*, "6 Ex-Officials in South Korea Are Sentenced for Blacklisting Artists," July 27, 2017. https://www.nytimes.com/2017/07/27/world/asia/south-korea-park-aides-artists-blacklist.html.
84. Cho and Kim, "Procedural Justice and Perceived Electoral Integrity," 1186. "Prosecutors Detail Attempt to Sway South Korean Election", November 21, 2013. https://www.nytimes.com/2013/11/22/world/asia/prosecutors-detail-bid-to-sway-south-korean-election.html
85. Cho and Kim, "Procedural Justice and Perceived Electoral Integrity," 1187. Fish, "Internet censorship."
86. Kim, "The 2012 Parliamentary and Presidential Elections", 20.
87. *New York Times*, "Investigators Raid Agency of Military in South Korea," October 22, 2013. https://www.nytimes.com/2013/10/23/world/asia/south-korean-military-agencys-headquarters-raided-in-growing-scandal.html.

88. "South Korea After Impeachment," 119.
89. BBC News, "South Korea's Ex-Leader Jailed". April 6, 2018. https://www.bbc.com/news/world-asia-43666134
90. A Gallup poll showed an approval rating of only 5% for the President in early November 2016. https://www.reuters.com/article/us-southkorea-politics-poll-idUSKBN12Z04Y.
91. Shin and Moon, "South Korea After Impeachment," 130; Turner et al. "Making Integrity Institutions Work," 980.
92. Gamboa, "Opposition at the Margins" and Cleary and Öztürk, "Opposition Strategies."

Acknowledgement

We thank Ana Good God, Ana Laura Ferrari and Sandra Grahn for their skillful research assistance and participants at the Berlin Democracy Conference (11/2019) and the APSA conference (2020) as well as Staffan I. Lindberg and Wolfgang Merkel for their helpful feedback on an early version of this article. We thank the anonymous reviewers for their thoughtful suggestions that have helped improve the article, and Katherine Stuart and Marcin Ślarzyński for their careful reading and corrections.

Disclosure statement

No potential conflict of interest was reported by the author(s).

Funding

This research was supported by the Swedish Research Council [Vetenskapsrådet] [grant number 2018-016114], PI: Anna Lührmann and European Research Council [H2020 European Research Council], grant 724191, PI: Staffan I. Lindberg, V-Dem Institute, University of Gothenburg, Sweden as well as by internal grants from the Office of the Vice-Chancellor, the Dean of the Department of Social Sciences, and the Department of Political Science at the University of Gothenburg.

ORCID

Melis G. Laebens ⓘ http://orcid.org/0000-0003-2023-9177
Anna Lührmann ⓘ http://orcid.org/0000-0003-4258-1088

Bibliography

Achen, Christopher H., and Larry M. Bartels. *Democracy for Realists*. Princeton: Princeton University Press, 2017.
Banégas, Richard. "Benin: Challenges for Democracy." *African Affairs* 113, no. 452 (2014): 449–459. doi:10.1093/afraf/adu043.

Basabe-Serrano, Santiago, and Julián Martínez. "Ecuador: Cada Vez Menos Democracia, Cada Vez Más Autoritarismo … con Elecciones." *Revista de Ciencia Política (Santiago)* 34, no. 1 (2014): 145–170. doi:10.4067/S0718-090X2014000100007.

Beissinger, Mark R. "A New Look at Ethnicity and Democratization." *Journal of Democracy* 19, no. 3 (2008): 85–97. doi:10.1353/jod.0.0017.

Boix, Carles. *Democracy and Redistribution.* Cambridge, UK: Cambridge University Press, 2003.

Cassani, Andrea, and Luca Tomini. "Reversing Regimes and Concepts: From Democratization to Autocratization." *European Political Science* 19 (2020): 272–287. doi:10.1057/s41304-018-0168-5.

Chavez, Rebecca Bill, John A. Ferejohn, and Barry R. Weingast. "A Theory of the Politically Independent Judiciary." In *Courts in Latin America*, edited by G. Helmke, and J. Ríos-Figueroa, 219–247. Cambridge, UK: Cambridge University Press, 2011.

Cheibub, Jose Antonio, Adam Przeworski, Fernando Papaterra Limongi Neto, and Michael M. Alvarez. "What Makes Democracies Endure?" *Journal of Democracy* 7, no. 1 (1996): 39–55. doi:10.1353/jod.1996.0016.

Cho, Youngho, and Yong Cheol Kim. "Procedural Justice and Perceived Electoral Integrity: The Case of Korea's 2012 Presidential Election." *Democratization* 23, no. 7 (2016): 1180–1197. doi:10.1080/13510347.2015.1063616.

Cleary, Matthew R., and Aykut Öztürk. "When Does Backsliding Lead to Breakdown? Uncertainty and Opposition Strategies in Democracies at Risk." *Perspectives on Politics*, 1–17. doi:10.1017/S1537592720003667.

Conaghan, Catherine M. "Ecuador: Rafael Correa and the Citizen's Revolution." In *The Resurgence of the Latin American Left*, edited by S. Levitsky, and K. M. Roberts, 260–282. Baltimore: Johns Hopkins University Press, 2011.

Coppedge, Michael, John Gerring, Carl Henrik Knutsen, Staffan I. Lindberg, Jan Teorell, David Altman, Michael Bernhard, et al. "V-Dem [Country–Year/Country–Date] Dataset v10." Varieties of Democracy (V-Dem) Project. 2020. doi:10.23696/vdemds20.

Dahl, Robert Alan. *Polyarchy: Participation and Opposition.* New Haven: Yale University Press, 1971.

Diamond, Larry, and Leonardo Morlino. "The Quality of Democracy: An Overview." *Journal of Democracy* 15, no. 4 (2004): 20–31. doi:10.1353/jod.2004.0060.

Edgell, Amanda B., Seraphine F. Maerz, Laura Maxwell, Richard Morgan, Juraj Medzihorsky, Matthew C. Wilson, Vanessa Boese, et al. Episodes of Regime Transformation Dataset, v1.0, 2020. https://www.v-dem.net/en/data/data/ert-dataset/.

Fish, Eric S. "Is Internet Censorship Compatible with Democracy? Legal Restrictions of Online Speech in South Korea." *Asia-Pacific Journal on Human Rights and the Law* 10, no. 2 (2009): 43–96. doi:10.1163/138819010X12647506166519.

Gamboa, Laura. "Opposition at the Margins: Strategies against the Erosion of Democracy in Colombia and Venezuela." *Comparative Politics* 49, no. 4 (2017): 457–477. doi:10.5129/001041517821273044.

George, Alexander L., and Andrew Bennet. *Case Studies and Theory Development in the Social Sciences.* Cambridge, MA: MIT Press, 2004.

Goetz, Anne Marie, and Rob Jenkins. "Hybrid Forms of Accountability: Citizen Engagement in Institutions of Public-Sector Oversight in India." *Public Management Review* 3, no. 3 (2001): 363–383. doi:10.1080/14616670110051957.

Graham, Matthew H., and Milan W. Svolik. "Democracy in America? Partisanship, Polarization, and the Robustness of Support for Democracy in the United States." *American Political Science Review* 114, no. 2 (2020): 392–409. doi:10.1017/S0003055420000052.

Grimes, Marcia. "The Contingencies of Societal Accountability: Examining the Link Between Civil Society and Good Government." *Studies in Comparative International Development* 48, no. 4 (2013): 380–402.

Helmke, Gretchen. *Courts Under Constraints: Judges, Generals, and Presidents in Argentina.* Cambridge, UK: Cambridge University Press, 2005.

Hyun-Soo Lim. "A Closer Look at the Korean Constitutional Court's Ruling on Park Geun-hye's Impeachment." May 18, 2017. *Yale Journal of International Law.* https://www.yjil.yale.edu/a-closer-look-at-the-korean-constitutional-courts-ruling-on-park-geun-hyes-impeachment/.

Kaltwasser, Cristóbal Rovira. "The Ambivalence of Populism: Threat and Corrective for Democracy." *Democratization* 19, no. 2 (2012): 184–208. doi:10.1080/13510347.2011.572619.

Kaufman, Robert R., and Stephan Haggard. "Democratic Decline in the United States: What Can We Learn from Middle-Income Backsliding?" *Perspectives on Politics* 17, no. 2 (2019): 417–432. doi:10.1017/S1537592718003377.

Kim, Youngmi. "The 2012 Parliamentary and Presidential Elections in South Korea." *Electoral Studies* 34 (2014): 326–330. doi:10.1016/j.electstud.2013.08.013.

Labarthe, Sunniva, and Marc Saint-Upéry. "Leninismo versus correísmo: la «tercera vuelta» en Ecuador." *Nueva Sociedad* 272 (2017): 29-42. https://nuso.org/articulo/leninismo-versus-correismo-la-tercera-vuelta-en-ecuador/.

Laleyè, Francis Adébola. "Benin Elections: The Waiting Game." ECOWAS Peace and Security Report 11 (2014). https://issafrica.org/research/west-africa-report/benin-elections-the-waiting-game.

de Lara, Felipe Burbano, and Carlos de la Torre. "The Pushback Against Populism: Why Ecuador's Referendums Backfired." *Journal of Democracy* 31, no. 2 (2020): 69–80. doi:10.1353/jod.2020.0022.

Lijphart, Arend. "Consociational Democracy." *World Politics* 21, no. 2 (1969): 207–225. doi:10.2307/2009820.

Lindberg, Staffan I. "Mapping Accountability: Core Concept and Subtypes." *International Review of Administrative Sciences* 79, no. 2 (2013): 202–206. doi:10.1177/0020852313477761.

Linz, Juan J. *Crisis, Breakdown & Reequilibration.* Baltimore: Johns Hopkins University Press, 1978.

Linz, Juan J. "The Perils of Presidentialism." *Journal of Democracy* 1, no. 1 (1990): 51–69.

Lipset, Seymour. "The Social Prerequisites for Democracy Revisited. Economic Development and Political Legitimacy." *American Sociological Review* 59 (1959): 1–22.

Lührmann, Anna, and Staffan I. Lindberg. "A Third Wave of Autocratization Is Here: What Is New About It?" *Democratization* 26, no. 7 (2019): 1095–1113. doi:10.1080/13510347.2019.1582029.

Lührmann, Anna, Kyle Marquardt, and Valeriya Mechkova. "Constraining Governments: New Indices of Vertical, Horizontal and Diagonal Accountability." *American Political Science Review* 114, no. 3 (2020): 811–820. doi:10.1017/S0003055420000222.

Lührmann, Anna, Marcus Tannenberg, and Staffan I. Lindberg. "Regimes of the World (RoW): Opening New Avenues for the Comparative Study of Political Regimes." *Politics & Governance* 6, no. 1 (2018). doi:10.17645/pag.v6i1.1214.

Mahoney, James, and Gary Goertz. "A Tale of Two Cultures: Contrasting Quantitative and Qualitative Research." *Political Analysis* 14, no. 3 (2006): 227–249. doi:10.1093/pan/mpj017.

Malena, Carmen, and Reiner Forster. "Social Accountability: An Introduction to the Concept and Emerging Practicoe." World Bank Working Papers 31042 (2004). https://documents.worldbank.org/en/publication/documents-reports/documentdetail/327691468779445304/social-accountability-an-introduction-to-the-concept-and-emerging-practice.

Martínez Novo, Carmen. "Intellectuals, NGOs and Social Movements Under the Correa Regime: Collaborations and Estrangements." In *Assessing the Left Turn in Ecuador*, edited by F. Sánchez, and S. Pachano, 137–162. London: Pelgrave Macmillan, 2020.

Mayrargue, Cédric. "Yayi Boni, un président inattendu ?" *Politique Africaine* 102 (2006): 155–172. doi:10.3917/polaf.102.0155.

McKie, Kristin. "Presidential Term Limit Contravention: Abolish, Extend, Fail, or Respect?" *Comparative Political Studies* 52, no. 10 (2019): 1500–1534. doi:10.1177/0010414019830737.

Morlino, Leonardo. "The Two 'Rules of Law' Between Transition to and Quality of Democracy." In *Rule of Law and Democracy: Inquiries into Internal and External Issues*, edited by L. Morlino, and G. Palombella, 39–63. Leiden: Brill, 2010.

Norris, Pippa. *Driving Democracy. Do Power-Sharing Institutions Work.* Cambridge, UK: Cambridge University Press, 2008.

O'Donnell, Guillermo A. "Horizontal Accountability in New Democracies." *Journal of Democracy* 9, no. 3 (1998): 112–126. doi:10.1353/jod.1998.0051.

O'Donnell, Guillermo A. "A Response to my Commentator." In *The Self-Restraining State: Power and Acountability in New Democracies*, edited by A. Schedler, L. Diamond, and M. Plattner, 68–71. Boulder: Lynne Rienner Publishers, 1999.

Pemstein, Daniel, Kyle L. Marquardt, Eitan Tzelgov, Yi-ting Wang, Juraj Medzihorsky, Joshua Krusell, Farhad Miri, and Johannes von Römer. *The V-Dem Measurement Model: Latent Variable Analysis for Cross-National and Cross-Temporal Expert-Coded Data.* V-Dem Working Paper No. 21. 4th ed.. University of Gothenburg: Varieties of Democracy Institute, 2019.

Polga-Hecimovich, John. "Ecuador: Estabilidad Institucional y la Consolidación de Poder de Rafael Correa." *Revista de Ciencia Política (Santiago)* 33, no. 1 (2013): 135–160. doi:10.4067/S0718-090X2013000100007.

Polga-Hecimovich, John. "La Presidencia del Ejecutivo Unitario de Rafael Correa." *Revista Latinoamericana de Política Comparada* 15 (2019): 99–122.

Przeworski, Adam. *Democracy and the Market.* Cambridge, UK: Cambridge University Press, 1991.

Sartori, Giovanni. *Parties and Party Systems: A Framework for Analysis.* Colchester, UK: ECPR Press, 2005 [1976].

Schedler, Andreas, Larry Jay Diamond, and Marc F. Plattner, eds. *The Self-Restraining State: Power and Accountability in New Democracies.* Boulder: Lynne Rienner Publishers, 1999.

Schmitter, Philippe C. "The Limits of Horizontal Accountability." In *The Self-Restraining State: Power and Acountability in New Democracies,* edited by A. Schedler, L. Diamond, and M. Plattner, 59–62. Boulder: Lynne Rienner Publishers, 1999.

Schmitter, Philippe C. "The Ambiguous Virtues of Accountability." *Journal of Democracy* 15, no. 4 (2004): 47–60. doi:10.1353/jod.2004.0073.

Shin, Gi-Wook, and Rennie J. Moon. "South Korea After Impeachment." *Journal of Democracy* 28, no. 4 (2017): 117–131. doi:10.1353/jod.2017.0072.

Slater, Dan. "Democratic Careening." *World Politics* 65, no. 4 (2013): 729–763. doi:10.1017/S0043887113000233.

Souaré, Issaka K. "The 2011 Presidential Election in Benin: Explaining the Success of One of Two Firsts." *Journal of African Elections* 10, no. 2 (2011): 73–92.

de la Torre, Carlos, and Andrés Ortiz Lemos. "Populist Polarization and the Slow Death of Democracy in Ecuador." *Democratization* 23, no. 2 (2016): 221–241. doi:10.1080/13510347.2015.1058784.

de la Torre, Carlos. "Latin America's Shifting Politics: Ecuador After Correa." *Journal of Democracy* 29, no. 4 (2018): 77–88. doi:10.1353/jod.2018.0064.

Turner, Mark, Seung-Ho Kwon, and Michael O'Donnell. "Making Integrity Institutions Work in South Korea." *Asian Survey* 58, no. 5 (2018): 898–919. doi:10.1525/as.2018.58.5.898.

Waldner, David, and Ellen Lust. "Unwelcome Change: Coming to Terms with Democratic Backsliding." *Annual Review of Political Science* 21 (2018): 93–113. doi:10.1146/annurev-polisci-050517-114628.

Pernicious polarization, autocratization and opposition strategies

Murat Somer, Jennifer L. McCoy and Russell E. Luke

ABSTRACT

"Pernicious polarization" – the division of society into mutually distrustful Us versus Them camps in which political identity becomes a social identity – fosters autocratization by incentivizing citizens and political actors alike to endorse non-democratic action. An exploratory analysis of new V-Dem data on polarization indeed shows the negative relationship between the *level of* political polarization and liberal democracy ratings. How can pernicious polarization be avoided or reversed once present? By drawing on an endogenous explanation of polarization, where the decisions and actions of both opposition actors and incumbents contribute to its evolution, we focus on the question of what democratic opposition actors can do to stop or reverse pernicious polarization. Based on insights from examples across the world and deductive theory-building, along with illustrative cases, we offer a typology of potential opposition goals, strategies and tools, and then analyse how these may affect polarization and in turn democratic quality at early and late stages. We identify goals as either *generative* or *preservative*, and we argue that "active-depolarizing" and "transformative-repolarizing" strategies are more promising than "passive-depolarizing" and "reciprocal polarizing" strategies to improve a country's resilience to autocratizing pressures. The specific tools employed to pursue these goals and strategies are also crucial, though the effectiveness of available institutional accountability and mobilizational tools will change as the process of polarization advances. The emerging literatıres on opposition strategies to democratize electoral autocracies and to improve the resilience of democracies should incorporate their impact on polarization as a critical intervening variable.

Introduction

Severe polarization fosters "autocratization",[1] by which we mean the gradual erosion of democratic quality in democracies and the democratic elements of electoral authoritarian regimes. While temporary upsurges of polarization limited to politics may be part and parcel of politics and may even help democratization, as argued by a large body of research, "pernicious polarization" – the division of society into mutually distrustful

---

Supplemental data for this article can be accessed at https://doi.org/10.7910/DVN/J16BPJ.

Us versus Them camps in which political identity becomes a social identity – has negative consequences for democracies and for democratization in autocracies. A society locked into pernicious polarization views politics to be in an exceptional state, in which each side views the other political camp and their supporters as a threat to the nation or their way of life and considers extraordinary and forceful policies as legitimate to defend its interests.[2] Under such conditions, citizens and political actors alike have incentives to endorse non-democratic actions to gain or keep power, and to prevent or remove their opponents from power.[3]

The editors of this special issue define democratic resilience as the capacity of a democracy to recover or preserve the "same or a similar level of democratic quality when facing challenges" of illiberalism and authoritarianism. Similarly, democratic capacity could be defined as the capacity of a democracy to improve its democratic quality and of an electoral autocracy to adopt more democratic features. We focus on the resilience of a democracy to withstand, and the capacity of an electoral autocracy to overcome, one particular challenge: sustained severe polarization. We argue that democratic resilience must include capacities to prevent or reverse pernicious polarization that erodes democracies and strengthens autocrats. We thus add a focus on this missing link to the emerging literature on opposition strategies during democratic erosion[4] and on ending electoral autocracies.[5] Our contribution is the first to delineate the strategies open to opposition actors to avoid reciprocating the harmful aspects of polarizing politics and instead to mobilize voters around democracy-enhancing depolarizing or repolarizing strategies. Oppositions include social movements as well as parties where intra-movement and intra-party politics can be fierce. Hence, opposition resilience comprises both the ability to choose the right strategies and to cooperate around *a* common strategy.

The article first provides a theoretical overview of the autocratizing consequences of polarization. We explain our conceptualization of polarization as a *process* and a *condition* or state of pernicious polarization. We argue that the process of deepening polarization is primarily driven by political actors deliberately employing polarizing politics to achieve their aims. We thus offer an endogenous and agentic explanation of polarization and autocratization, but we acknowledge that polarization can be facilitated by exogenous factors such as economic, institutional, and informational environments, preexisting social-political cleavages, and historical memory. A large-N exploratory analysis supports our argument that the severity, i.e. level of polarization, is mostly responsible for the negative consequences for democracy. This raises the question of what pro-democratic opposition actors can do to prevent their polities from reaching this level, or to reduce polarization to lesser levels once it does.

The bulk of the article then turns to an analytical framework of potential opposition strategies to address processes of polarization and respond to polarizing incumbents in ways that may enhance democratic resilience and potential for democratization. We discuss heuristic examples from across the world selected with a view to illustrate these strategies and our theoretical propositions, rather than offer a systematic comparative case analysis, which is beyond the scope of this article.[6]

The endogenous nature of polarization and negative consequences for democracy

As we have elaborated elsewhere, unlike many contemporary analyses that treat polarization as a given in a society or caused by exogenous factors such as economic or demographic structural change, our political and relational explanation argues that, given the opportunities created by these exogenous and facilitating factors and preexisting cleavages in a society, polarization episodes are initiated by political entrepreneurs who choose polarizing strategies to further their political aims.[7] Many of these aims may *a priori* be authoritarian, and polarizing politics may be employed as a deliberately chosen instrument to change power balances and make room for autocratization; however, we do not assume that every political actor who uses polarizing tactics is a would-be authoritarian. Rather we maintain that increasing polarization incentivizes autocratization regardless of initial actor aims.

We conceptualize polarization as both a *process* of simplifying politics, and a *condition* in which an equilibrium of severe political polarization is eventually reached where neither side has the incentive to move to a depolarizing strategy, short of exogenous shocks or the rise of new actors and innovative political realignments. The very game of polarization transforms the actors through two main mechanisms. First, it increasingly induces both citizens and political actors to see politics as a battlefield between rival blocs, each posing an existential threat to the other, which renders them willing to endorse and undertake extraordinary, usually democracy-eroding or autocracy-endorsing, political acts. Second, polarization by its very nature advantages the most extreme or radical voices within each camp – extreme in their willingness to antagonize rivals and ignore democratic decorum – over potential bridge-builders or de-polarizing centrists. Hence, severe polarization changes actor incentives and even fosters internal transformations within both the incumbent and opposition groups in an authoritarian direction. Often unintentionally, "democratic" oppositions also contribute to pernicious polarization through their own actions and reactions.

Considering this, and due to the fact that polarizing politics is a major item in the toolkit of intentionally autocratizing actors, democratic oppositions necessarily *must* develop strategies in response to polarization, and their other anti-authoritarian polices need to be rethought with respect to their impact on polarization. Precisely because we provide an endogenous explanation of polarization, agency comes into play and the strategies chosen by political and social actors to initiate or respond to polarizing politics will determine its outcomes.

Empirical relationship between polarization and democratic quality

A lack of cross-national quantitative measures of polarization has made it difficult to empirically test the different theoretical positions regarding how polarization affects democratic quality. New data from the Varieties of Democracy project is a major improvement as it allows for a robust examination across polities.[8] Similar to our conceptualization of pernicious polarization, this new measure, termed "political polarization", asks "Is society polarized into antagonistic, political camps?"[9] Crucially, it captures "the extent to which political differences affect social relationships beyond political discussions", thereby encapsulating affective polarization that can turn pernicious.[10] While theoretical contributions focusing on the political aspects of issue or party polarization are divided over the constructive – e.g. by inducing party system institutionalization – and destructive – e.g. by undermining compromise – roles of polarization in democracies, studies of affective polarization emphasize the latter.[11] Accordingly, we argue that polarization is more likely to turn pernicious when it

64 RESILIENCE OF DEMOCRACY

permeates society, creating mutually distrustful societal camps who increasingly view one another through a Manichaean lens.[12]

To examine this relationship, we perform a series of relatively straightforward analyses of three interrelated hypotheses:

H_1: Increased polarization decreases the quality of liberal democracy in a state.

H_2: An increased *rate* of polarization disproportionately decreases the quality of liberal democracy in a state.

H_3: The *level* of polarization disproportionately decreases the quality of liberal democracy in a state.

While the goal of H_1 is straightforward, H_2 and H_3 aim to unpack how and when polarization undermines democracy – whether the rate of change or the level of polarization matters more. A spike of polarization, tested by H_2, can often happen around election years, and is more likely to include cases of temporary polarization with neutral or potentially positive effects on democracy. Even if the rate of change is quite large, this type of polarization may be short lived or otherwise not spill into social relations. Yet, as the *level* of polarization rises, however gradually, it is more likely to affect social relations. Hence, we can expect it to damage democratic quality to a greater degree.

To test these hypotheses, we perform a series of linear regression analyses, with fixed effects on both the year and the country, on the period from 1900 to 2019.[13] We also lag the polarization measure at 1, 2, and 5 year intervals to examine the delayed effect of polarization on democratic quality – the effects of polarization may be delayed or otherwise manifest primarily around election years. At the expense of efficiency, the fixed effects approach is theoretically most appropriate as we are primarily concerned with the "within" estimator for each country – the effect of polarization on democratic quality. Moreover, in pursuit of the most parsimonious model, it allows us to eschew an unwieldy number of country-specific factors such as level of development, that cause systematic heteroskedasticity by relegating their influence to the country-specific error term.[14] Also including fixed effects terms for each year, we can more easily account for global trends to and away from democracy, i.e. democratic waves, without including imprecise, time-specific measures such as the global mean value of liberal democracy.[15]

We assume that the effect of polarization is consistent across groups and across time. To make this assumption, we exclude those country-year observations that are categorized as "closed autocracies" in the Regimes of the World typology, as politics under a closed dictatorship operate under a different set of rules and incentives.[16] Also excluded from analysis are those states with less than 30 observation years.[17] Democratic quality is measured with the V-Dem measure for liberal democracy, where 1 denotes the most liberal democracy and 0 the least. Polarization is standardized to a 0–1 scale from its original 0–4 scale, such that higher values on this scale denote higher levels of polarization.

Table 1 presents the results of the tests for H_1. The observed effect of polarization on liberal democracy is negative and statistically significant for each of the periods examined.[18] The effect appears to diminish in influence the further from the analysis year, but it remains substantial nonetheless.

To test H_2, we subset the data to identify periods of what we term rapid polarization, based on rate of change: periods where polarization increased by at least 10% (0.1 units

Table 1. Effect of Political Polarization on Liberal Democracy: 1900–2019.

	Analysis Year	One Year Lag	Two Year Lag	Five Year Lag
Political Polarization	−0.420**			
	(0.061)			
Political Polarization		−0.415**		
		(0.062)		
Political Polarization			−0.391**	
			(0.062)	
Political Polarization				−0.305**
				(0.057)
Constant	0.333**	0.334**	0.347**	0.291**
	(0.044)	(0.044)	(0.047)	(0.047)
N	6,192	6,161	6,120	5,973
Number of States	119	119	119	119
Number of Years	119	118	117	114
Adjusted R^2	0.573	0.572	0.565	0.539

Note: Coefficient estimates are linear regression estimates with state and year fixed effects. Outcome variable is V-Dem liberal democracy score. "Lag" refers to temporal lags of political polarization measure. Robust standard errors in parentheses. $**p < 0.01$, $*p < 0.05$.

on the polarization scale) in 5 or less years, where there were two or more years of increased polarization, and where there were no declines in polarization greater than 0.01 units.[19] We then compared the effect of polarization on democratic quality during periods of rapid polarization and all other cases. The effect on democratic quality remained negative and statistically significant for both groups, but the difference between the two was not statistically significant. Thus, we cannot conclude that periods of rapid polarization are any more damaging to democratic quality than other periods of increased polarization.[20]

Lastly, we examined the effect of polarization on democratic quality at different levels of polarization in H_3. We argue that periods of sustained severe polarization exert a distinct and more negative effect on democratic quality over other periods of polarization. We subset the data using different thresholds of polarization. These are labelled Elevated, Heightened, and Severe. Elevated uses the mean value of 0.456, Heightened uses the top quartile of 0.566, and Severe uses the top 5% of all cases – 0.722. This threshold for Severe polarization allows us to examine the most extreme cases of polarization, and roughly corresponds to a response of 4, "Supporters of opposing political camps generally interact in a hostile manner", in the original V-Dem scale. Each category is coded such that polarization is sustained over a period of at least five years with no declines greater than 0.01.[21]

The results of each model indicate a negative, statistically significant, relationship of polarization on democratic quality; the full regression tables for each model are located in Appendix B. Table 2 presents the difference coefficients between the models for each elevated, heightened, and severe polarization.[22] For periods of both elevated and heightened polarization, there is no observable difference between the effect of polarization within these periods, and all other cases. In line with our expectations, the effect of polarization on democratic quality is shown to be more damaging under periods of severe polarization, for the analysis year and single year lag, than all other periods. In none of these periods is there a statistically significant difference between polarizing periods lagged 2 or 5 years on democratic quality, so these results are excluded for ease of presentation. These results provide suggestive evidence that the periods of sustained severe polarization, our primary

Table 2: Difference Coefficients between Periods of Elevated, Heightened, and Severe Polarization, and All Other Cases: 1900–2019.

	Elevated Polarization		Heightened Polarization		Severe Polarization	
	Analysis Year	One Year Lag	Analysis Year	One Year Lag	Analysis Year	One Year Lag
Difference Coefficient	−0.167		−0.032		−0.640*	
	(0.122)		(0.153)		(0.284)	
Difference Coefficient		−0.165		0.009		−0.654*
		(0.119)		(0.154)		(0.326)
Constant	0.307**	0.303**	0.314**	0.314**	0.324**	0.326**
	(0.048)	(0.048)	(0.046)	(0.046)	(0.047)	(0.046)
N	6,192	6,161	6,192	6,161	6,192	6,161
Number of States	119	119	119	119	119	119
Number of Years	119	118	119	118	119	118
Adjusted R^2	0.576	0.576	0.577	0.577	0.575	0.573

Note: Coefficient estimates are the result of interaction term between political polarization and period indicators. Outcome variable is V-Dem liberal democracy score. Robust standard errors in parentheses. $**p < 0.01$, $*p < 0.05$.

focus, pose a distinct threat to democratic quality in democracies and electoral autocracies above the baseline threat of polarization.

Opposition dilemmas and challenge

Our endogenous explanation of polarization posits that agency is critical to the development of polarization, and the long-term ideological-programmatic goals as well as the strategies chosen by political and social actors to initiate or respond to polarizing politics will determine its outcomes. In this article, we do not offer an explanation of how and why oppositions choose one strategy over another. Instead, we offer a framework with two broad opposition goals and four different strategies that oppositions may adopt to respond to polarizing incumbents[23] with democracy-eroding behaviours. We theorize about the potential consequences of each for polarization and, in turn, democratic quality. We argue that some anti-authoritarian policies, even though ethically acceptable and feasible in early stages, will not be recommendable at later stages precisely because we expect them to reinforce polarization and thus backfire, or because they have already been disarmed by severe polarization. Polarization is thus always an intervening variable and strategies to reciprocate, avoid, reduce or transform it are choices for actors with consequences for both polarization and democracy.

We also argue that the timing of each strategy and the practical instruments with which it is implemented affect the outcomes. Democratic oppositions aiming to prevent or reverse autocratization have two basic sets of instruments to hold accountable a democracy-eroding incumbent: legal-institutional forms of vertical, horizontal and diagonal accountability, and extra- or unconstitutional mechanisms.[24] The severity of the polarization and the length of time it has been sustained at high levels will shape the opportunity structures of opposition groups and the effectiveness of their choice of instruments and strategies. At early stages, before polarization has progressed significantly, oppositions often retain significant institutional leverage in the form of horizontal accountability mechanisms – judiciaries, legislatures, bureaucracies, as well as vertical and societal mobilizational capacity from organized political and civil societies.[25] They are likely to have a large toolkit to choose from to prevent polarization from deepening.

At later stages of polarization, however, the toolkit is smaller as the institutions themselves become politicized and organizational capacity reduced. In contexts of severe, sustained polarization, incumbents are motivated to ignore horizontal-institutional accountability mechanisms seen as disloyal to them, discrediting them as politically biased, elitist or antagonistic in the eyes of their constituencies. Alternatively, if incumbents have managed to gain influence over accountability mechanisms by populating them with loyalists, oppositions will not accept them as legitimate. Simultaneously, the vertical and "diagonal"[26] accountability mechanisms become divided and weakened based on partisanship. For example, pro-incumbent media and popular contentious movements are mobilized against critical media and anti-incumbent popular protests with an Us vs. Them logic.[27] Anti-incumbent electoral coalitions can divide over whether to participate in unfair elections controlled by pro-incumbent election authorities.[28] In other words, no matter whether the opposition is motivated by principle or self-interest, polarization undermines its ability to constrain the incumbent's actions by appealing to the normal democratic accountability mechanisms.

Choices of polarization strategies and tools

The crucial decision pro-democratic oppositions need to make is not merely to choose between engaging in or avoiding polarizing politics – the former risks deepening the downward spiral and the latter risks demotivating or fragmenting opposition supporters and legitimizing incumbent actions.[29] Instead, oppositions should consider various long-term ideological and programmatic goals, repolarizing and depolarizing strategies, and the instruments with which to implement them.

Table 3 presents the basic choices of programmatic goals and strategies for political oppositions along with the predicted outcomes for polarization and democracy. We discuss each and give illustrative case examples below.

Table 3. Opposition Goals, Strategies, and Outcomes.

Goals	Counter-polarization Strategies	Expected Polarization Outcomes	Expected Democratic Outcomes
PRESERVATIVE (restore status quo ante)	REACTIVE Reciprocal Polarization (using same axis of polarization)	Deepening Pernicious polarization	Government dysfunction or paralysis or Creeping authoritarianism under Incumbent or Democratic collapse, return of old elites
	Passive depolarization (fails to confront or change axis of polarization)	Suspended elite polarization	Creeping authoritarianism under Incumbent Or Weakened democratization
GENERATIVE (a new social contract)	PROACTIVE Transformative repolarization (changes axis of polarization)	Pro-democratic axis of polarization. Reduced polarization if and when successful inclusive reforms are in place.	Slows or reverses autocratization
	Active depolarization (establish cross-cutting ties)	Polarization contained	Slows or reverses autocratization especially at local levels

We start by assuming that oppositions to polarizing and autocratizing incumbents seek to gain power, but that they do so with different goals about using that power. The first are those groups who wish to restore the status quo ante, to return to the prior set of political arrangements and rules and to reincorporate political (and social) actors who were excluded by the polarizing incumbent. We call this a *preservative* goal. The second goal characterizes those groups who wish to create a new social contract, or bring some fundamental change to the polity, economy or social relationships. We call this a *generative* goal. The actors pursuing a preservative goal can be expected to choose one of two reactive counter-polarization strategies, while those pursuing a generative goal can be expected to choose one of two proactive counter-polarization strategies.

Reactive counter-polarization strategies

Reactive counter-polarization strategies are aimed at restoring the status quo ante – either returning displaced elites to power in a backlash to a new group achieving electoral gains, or mobilizing the society against an unscrupulous incumbent. Comparative case examples indicate two versions: reciprocal polarization and passive depolarization.

Reciprocal polarization

A reciprocal polarization strategy engages in the same divisive discourse and tactics as the incumbent, contributing to an action-reaction cycle that ends up reinforcing the cleavages already politicized by the incumbent and deepening the affective partisan polarization characterized among the partisan camps. At earlier stages of polarization-cum-autocratization, when legal-constitutional mechanisms of accountability still retain their independence and before societies polarize in their very perceptions of such institutions, courts or oversight agencies including the media may serve to contain abuses by a polarizing executive and prevent pernicious polarization. For example, the constitutional impeachment of Indonesian president Abdurrahman Wahid in 2001 for corruption prevented more contentious politics erupting in the wake of his unilateral decision-making and failure to respect power-sharing agreements.[30]

In contrast, at later stages with sustained, severe levels of polarization, public perceptions of those same legal-constitutional accountability institutions become polarized – opposition groups view them as necessary mechanisms of oversight and accountability, while pro-incumbent supporters view them as sinister political attacks on the incumbent. For example, the Turkish opposition tried to block the governing AKP party's rise, among other strategies, through social mobilization in the form of massive anti-Islamist protests in 2007, and legal-constitutional tools such as media and judicial investigations into allegations of illegal party finances involving religious charities and a Constitutional Court case to de-register the party for its anti-secularism in 2008.[31] Since the main axis of these opposition mobilizations was the defense of secularism against the party's "religious retrogression" (*irtica*), they ended up "projecting their disdain for [the party] onto [its] supporters as well".[32] Hence, pro-incumbent pious Turks who felt disdained closed ranks behind the AKP. Further, as could be expected from the high level of political polarization – which rose from 3,09 in 2002 when the party came to power to 3.17 in 2005 and 3.68 (out of 4) in 2008, the court cases were seen as legal-institutional accountability at work by opposition supporters and as malicious political attacks by incumbent supporters.

In a polarized context, parties are often tempted to engage in an ultimately self-defeating tit-for-tat strategy out of indignation or pressured by their angered bases. The battle over the procedures for life-time judicial appointments in the U.S. Senate between 2013–17 is an example of both sides engaging in a tit-for-tat strategy that ultimately terminated the filibuster and cloture norm providing for bipartisanship in the appointment process. The result was the majority party could now make Supreme Court and federal judgeship appointments by a simple majority vote, excluding the minority party and raising the perception of an increasingly politicized and ideological judiciary. Thus, not only was the perceived impartiality of an important accountability institution reduced, but elections became an even higher-stakes affair to elect the party that would control future judicial nominations.

A second set of practical instruments includes the use of extra-constitutional mechanisms to oust or obstruct an autocratizing polarizer, including illegitimate impeachment procedures, violent mass protests, general strikes, military coups, and appeals to foreign interventions such as sanctions or military invasions. The Venezuelan opposition repeatedly resorted to such tools attempting to remove a polarizing incumbent without success. A coup attempt, a general strike, a military sit-in, massive protests, and a legislative election boycott, along with the legal instrument of a recall referendum, all failed to unseat President Hugo Chavez early in his tenure.[33] Instead, these elite failures fragmented the opposition and demoralized its supporters, while strengthening the incumbent's hold on power.

More advanced stages of democratic erosion or autocratization present special dilemmas for oppositions. In this context, an autocratizing incumbent may have been able to politicize accountability institutions by placing their own loyalists in key institutions, from electoral to judicial to security agencies. The polarized perceptions of these institutions are thus the reverse of the context of still-independent institutions; now, autocratizing incumbents use loyal institutions to burnish their pseudo-democratic credentials in the eyes of their supporters and the world, while oppositions distrust such institutions and must be creative in devising their anti-authoritarian strategies.

Passive depolarization

A passive depolarizing strategy refrains from participation in polarization, without questioning or trying to shift the axis of existing polarization. It seeks to defuse the conflict and mitigate abusive behaviour from within the system. It may be a normative choice to oppose polarization as many people realize the dangers of severe polarization for democracy and coexistence. Alternatively, it may be a strategy out of weakness, to improve political prospects. This strategy appeals to the centre based on existing axes of politics, or seeks a *modus vivendi* with rivals without trying to transform politics in ways addressing long-term polarizing issues. In the inter-war era, for example, many European democracies fell to authoritarianism among other reasons because indecisive centrist parties failed to counter fascist rivals who exploited left-right polarization and fear of communism.

Two variants of elite depolarization through cooperative agreements carry their own risks. First, elite depolarization can be achieved when opposition forces join in power-sharing agreements with autocratic incumbents, whether for personal gain or with the aim of changing the system "from within". Such strategies are unlikely to depolarize either society or politics in the long run, however, if the junior partner feels marginalized, democratizing agreements are not implemented or their supporters feel sold out. Instead, such a successful cooptation strategy may simply strengthen the hegemonic leader, as happened for example multiple times in Kenya and Zimbabwe.[34]

A second variant of passive avoidance depolarization is a pacted transition to democracy that produces an apparent elite consensus without addressing the underlying grievances fuelling the polarization. Such elite consensus-seeking efforts accompanying democratic transition may actually mask persistent underlying societal polarization that will later reemerge to threaten democratic resilience. For example, the 1989 transition in Chile brought the centre-left coalition Concertacion to power for two decades with an agreement to continue the Pinochet-era market approach to economic policy and to postpone transitional justice for human rights abuses committed by General Pinochet's regime. Polarization dropped immediately and continued low until 2006, when student protests began against the privatization of education and continued over the next decade. Polarization spiked in 2018–19 and widespread protests erupted over the persistent inequality, privatization of health and education, and Pinochet-era constitution still in place.[35]

A more recent example of elite consensus papering over underlying divisions is Tunisia since the popular upheaval – "the revolution" – for democracy and social justice ended a decades-long dictatorship in 2011. There, political parties with fiery rhetoric and deeply polarized over the Islamism-secularism fault line and questions of transitional justice have remarkably managed to avoid backsliding by compromising on a series of national unity coalition governments of Islamist and secularist parties.[36] This enabled the country to transition to parliamentary democracy with a new democratic constitution, which has so far proved itself stable. However, these passively depolarizing compromises postponed resolving the polarizing socioeconomic troubles and ideological divisions, instead of achieving broad-based and elite consensus on inclusive solutions. This has led to public disillusionment with democracy and the absence of any "effective opposition" and real programmatic differences across parties,[37] raising concerns over the long-term stability of Tunisian democracy.

Impact on polarization and democratic outcomes

Reactive strategies, even to prevent democratic erosion, risk deepening polarization and moving to a pernicious equilibrium. Reciprocal counter-polarization in particular can backfire: it may mobilize the opposition's supporters but also cause the incumbent's supporters to close ranks to defend "Ours against Theirs". Denigration and demonization of the incumbent and their supporters also inhibits the ability of a democratic opposition to attract allies from among disaffected incumbent supporters if needed to protest growing violations of democratic norms. This Manichean discourse strengthens tribalism and affective polarization and the simplification of politics makes the two camps more rigid, with less communication and even less fluid movement between them. The resulting perceptions of a zero-sum game lock both sides into a downward spiral of pernicious polarization.

At a minimum, pernicious polarization generates government paralysis and dysfunction. Further, to the extent that oppositions employ extra-institutional mechanisms to attempt the immediate removal of the incumbent before the end of the term, the opposition risks delegitimating itself and providing the incumbent a rationale to use repressive measures against it.[38] Alternatively, successful extra-constitutional ousters of polarizing elected leaders may lead to outright democratic collapse, as happened when the military intervened to remove polarizing incumbents in Thailand in 2014 or Egypt in 2013, which may serve to depolarize society in the short-term, but at the cost of killing democracy.

The risk of passive depolarizing politics is that it may fail to mobilize the opposition's own base enough to defeat the incumbent in elections, and it may be seen as too soft and legitimizing the incumbent's divisive and antidemocratic behaviour. Elite depolarizations through power-sharing agreements or concessions that fail to deliver political gains, risk fragmenting the opposition through internal rivalries, demoralization, or apathy. Withdrawal from engagement, including election boycotts, is also likely to strengthen an autocratizing incumbent.

Proactive counter-polarization strategies

wProactive counter-polarization strategies seek to change the axis of polarization. The polarizing variety seeks to change the axis of polarization away from the Manichean line emphasized by the polarizing incumbent and towards one that is more flexible and programmatic, such as those based on democratic or social justice principles. In this sense, it repolarizes with the goal of generating fundamental change, re-simplifying politics based on a stark choice between the proponents and opponents of such change, for example a renewed social contract that addresses underlying grievances that gave rise to severe polarization in the first place. The depolarizing variety seeks to dismantle the reinforcing cleavages resulting from the simplified politics of Us vs. Them polarization, and actively seeks through social and political action to construct cross-cutting ties more amenable to pluralist democracy. We call these two strategies *transformative repolarization* and *active depolarization*.

Once again, a proactive strategy can only succeed if supported by appropriate practices. Choice of practical instruments for proactive counter-polarization strategies include the previously discussed legal-constitutional and extra-constitutional institutional and mobilization mechanisms. Their effectiveness and impact also vary by the severity of polarization and democratic erosion. What differentiates successful proactive counter-polarization strategies, however, is their degree of innovation. Innovation in communication tools, campaign strategies and alliances with social movements and civic organization, recruitment methods, use of emotion and symbols, and narratives are key to proactive counter-polarization strategies.

A major challenge for innovation, for example, is to learn how to utilize the power of protest movements to improve electoral prospects rather than antagonize incumbent supporters and deepen polarization. Between 2012 and 2017, for instance, the Russian opposition is argued to have learned how to transform "reactive electoral mobilizations" (protesting the corruption of elections) to "proactive" ones, as a source of candidate recruitment and synergy to win elections.[39] Less successful counter-polarization strategies rely on older mechanisms such as patronage politics to regain power, continuity in leadership rather than generational change, separation of political society and mobilization from civil society and social mobilization, and an inability to create a narrative and a vision for a hopeful future.[40]

72   RESILIENCE OF DEMOCRACY

Transformative repolarization
For the more advanced stages of polarization and autocratization, the political challenge that democratic oppositions face may be to find the organizational and discursive ways to rebundle and redefine cleavages and politics along a new axis of polarization based on a pro-democratic programme. That is, democratic oppositions may sometimes have to respond through polarizing politics of their own, but they need to find a different axis of polarization based on a programme that can have democratizing consequences. In this way, oppositions can "de-fang" the power of the Us vs Them wedge magnified by the incumbent, reestablish the balance of power with would-be autocrats on a new axis, and mobilize a winning majority of the electorate on a democratizing agenda. They create a binary choice about democracy or justice by denouncing on principle, but not necessarily vilifying and excluding the "Other".

South Korea provides one example of, at least initially, successful transformative polarizing politics. The period between 2014 and 2016 was a major period of political polarization and civic mobilization, when South Korea's political polarization score jumped by 19% and 14% in 2016 alone. Yet, the same period was one of "near miss" for the country's consolidated liberal democracy, when democratic backsliding was stopped and gave way to democratic recovery through peaceful change of government.[41]

The opposition's initial response to a period of democratic backsliding under the conservative government from 2008–2016 was a reactive counter-polarization strategy, including a boycott of the parliament's opening and anti-government rallies in 2008, and labour strikes in 2010–11. Over time, however, the opposition moved to proactive counter-polarization strategies, which broadened the backlash against creeping authoritarianism. President Park's impeachment in 2016 in the wake of the Choi-gate corruption scandal was the product of an alliance between opposition parties and softliners within her own party. It was also a result of pressure from daily "candlelight" peaceful social protests remarkable for the diversity of their participants and "the ingenuity expressed in protest methods", supported by civil society and media.[42] The innovative methods and messaging about the need for executive accountability reflected a proactive strategy of transformative repolarization around a pro-democratic policy. Soon thereafter, Democratic Party leader Moo Jae-in won the presidency with a reformist-democratizing agenda, which led to changes that recovered the country's liberal democracy score to 0.80.

Active depolarizing strategies
Active depolarizing strategies attempt to mobilize a winning majority by redefining politics alongside new plural axes of polarization that devitalize the cleavages politicized by the incumbent and, in this way, depolarize politics. It consciously defuses the divisions, emphasizes cross-cutting ties, and seeks to unify the electorate with new political frames, campaign methods, actors and organizations. Successful examples include the 2019 opposition victories of crucial Istanbul and Budapest mayorships in Turkey and Hungary.

As we discussed above, until recently, the Turkish opposition forces tried to curb the incumbent Justice and Development Party (AKP)'s "populist-authoritarian" rise and creeping authoritarianism with reciprocal polarizing responses on the same religious-secular axis that brought the AKP and Erdoğan to power in the first place.[43] The opposition CHP's campaigns in 2019 local elections represented a shift to active-depolarizing politics, and the first electoral victory for the opposition in more than a decade, with the partial exception of June 2015 elections. It formed new electoral alliances to overcome organizational and ideological fragmentation and focused on redefining politics based on positive, service-oriented and non-ideological messages, low-profile campaign techniques such as door-to-door voter visits, and a simplification of voter choices with binaries such as hope-fear, love-hate, and democracy-authoritarianism.[44]

Perhaps the most notable innovation was the CHP campaign manual called "The Book of Radical Love". The strategy was focused on defusing polarization through new and cross-cutting axes of politics, and responding to the politics of hate and resentment with "love".[45] Furthermore, the book's author argued: "The real divide in Turkey is not between secularism and Islam or between Turks and Kurds, but between rich and poor. If you want people to break out of their echo chambers, focus on poverty".[46] Hence, this opposition strategy also displayed precursors of an emerging "transformative" strategy aiming to redefine politics based on an axis of social class and economic development. Arguably, the strategy may not have worked in Istanbul elections without the support of a strong grassroots organization built up in recent years that successfully mobilized and communicated with voters and defended ballot boxes, despite Erdoğan's attempts to reverse the election results.[47] Finally, the Turkish opposition parties have struggled to achieve unity around a "democracy-authoritarianism cleavage" and to coordinate their candidate selections.[48]

In Hungary, a similar movement towards active depolarization strategies in the 2019 mayoral elections in Hungary may suggest a pattern of local level success and a learning process at work. A highly fractious opposition ranging from the far right Jobbik to the progressive youth movement of Liberal Momentum and the traditional Socialist Party finally agreed to present unified mayoral slates based on primary elections for the 2019 mayoral elections. The Budapest candidate ran and won on a platform of representing the people against the seat of power, a pro-Europe and green agenda, and a willingness to work in a partnership with the national government.[49]

Impact on polarization dynamics and democratic outcomes

The transformative repolarizing strategy is perhaps the most difficult to carry out. Yet we expect that this strategy holds particular promise for reversing severe polarization that has facilitated serious autocratization, as long as it creates a binary choice over democracy or justice, without demonizing the "Other". Otherwise the logic of polarization will kick in again, including perceptions of the "Other" as an existential threat and enemy to be eliminated, tempting both sides to violate democratic norms to gain or retain power.

Here, mobilization around programmatic ideas rather than identities is key. Mobilizing against the incumbent by vilifying the incumbent and their supporters based on their values, attitudes and identities may make people feel excluded based on socioeconomic or cultural background; in contrast, providing a binary choice based on principles and policies, such as democracy vs authoritarianism, hope vs fear, justice vs impunity can open the tent to disaffected incumbent supporters while energizing opposition supporters around a positive vision of the future.

The risks of such a strategy include voters' fear that repolarization around a transformative agenda will be too radical to be a winning electoral strategy and instead allow an autocratizing incumbent to remain in place. For example, in the 2020 Democratic primary in the United States, a frequently repeated rationale for voters to eventually coalesce around the "safe", centrist and depolarizing campaign of Joe Biden over the more transformative Warren and Sanders campaigns was that the Biden approach presented the best prospect to defeat Donald Trump, even if it did not promise to address the underlying racial and income inequalities, or political and economic structural features that helped to give rise the polarizing presidency of Trump in the first place. A related risk is that if a transformative repolarizing strategy proves successful, the winning coalition could be tempted to resort to the "revanchist" and Manichean divisive discourse of pernicious polarization, or that supporters of the losing incumbent feel excluded and become alienated or engage in obstructionist politics.[50]

We posit, however, that innovative tools and practices can overcome these risks. Rather than conceding a nationalist message to populist polarizers, for example, transformative repolarizers could elaborate a civic nationalism to counter ethnonationalist narratives.[51] Refusing to vilify supporters of the polarizing incumbent, and countering the narrative rather than responding to personal insults or amplifying specific lies and disinformation can also help to defuse the Us vs. Them binary fuelled by deliberate provocation and disinformation.[52] Creating new alliances between social movement and civic resistance, and political parties and campaigns can reinforce a transformative campaign by providing a visionary platform of real change. The 2019 presidential victory of a little-known female politician over right-wing populist rivals in Slovakia exemplifies the successful use of such strategies: Caputova built on a powerful civic resistance movement enraged at a corruption-inspired murder of a journalist to marry her anti-corruption message with messages of inclusion and a refusal to engage in the reciprocating discourse of denigration and disinformation from her populist rivals.[53]

The risk of active depolarizing politics is similar to the risks of passive depolarization: it may fail to energize and excite the opposition's own base sufficiently to defeat the incumbent, and it may be seen as too soft and legitimizing the incumbent's divisive and antidemocratic behaviour. Such a failure will strengthen the polarizing incumbent's hand and demoralize the opposition, leaving the polarization dynamic with one "pole" and likely resulting in further autocratization.

If active depolarization is successful in the early stages of polarization, it may contain polarization at tolerable levels and even return a country to the cross-cutting ties of a pluralism. But if leaders do not address underlying grievances and cleavages, divisions are likely to resurge at some point in the future.

At later stages of polarization and autocratization, successful active depolarization is likely to occur first at the local or legislative level. Democratic outcomes then depend on the subsequent steps by both opposition and incumbent. An opposition can overreach, such as happened with the Venezuelan successful unity campaign in the 2015 National Assembly elections in which they won a super-majority. The Assembly leadership immediately reverted to the Manichean discourse of reciprocal polarization, taking down the portraits of Hugo Chavez and thus symbolically excluding his supporters, and promising to remove President Nicolas Maduro from office through a recall referendum or other means within six months. Maduro reacted by suppressing the Assembly's authority through Supreme Court rulings, eventually usurping its authority almost completely as well as suppressing the legal-institutional mechanism of a recall referendum, moving the country to authoritarianism. Alternatively, the incumbent

RESILIENCE OF DEMOCRACY 75

may recognize the victory of the opposition as happened in the 2019 Istanbul and Budapest mayoral opposition upsets, but then prevent them from carrying out their innovative strategies, blocking the democratizing moment.[54]

Conclusions

Our prior work theorized how deepening Us vs. Them polarization produces incentives for democratic erosion among both incumbent and opposition political groups as they react to growing perceptions of a zero-sum game, existential threat from the opposing camp, and politics as a state of exception requiring extraordinary, democracy-erodingactions. In this article, we present exploratory empirical analysis using new V-Dem data that supports our general proposition that polarization is associated with deterioration in democratic quality, including democratic elements of electoral authoritarian regimes, and that sustained severe levels of polarization have the most deleterious effects. Because we view polarization as an endogenous factor, we argue that agency and learning matter, and the wilful strategic decisions and actions by both incumbents and oppositions will together shape the unfolding of the polarization process and its effect on a democracy. Particularly because polarizing politics is a common strategy of intentionally autocratizing actors, we argue that democratic resilience must include capacities, including learning from other cases in the world, to prevent or reverse pernicious polarization. We therefore analyse polarization as an intervening variable or condition between opposition anti-authoritarian strategies and democratic outcomes.

Our focus on opposition strategies sets out a theoretical framework linking the choice of preservative vs. generative ideological-programmatic goals and reactive vs. proactive counter-polarization strategies with their expected impact on polarization dynamics and democratic outcomes. Drawing on our deductive framework and heuristic-empirical examples, we posit that reactive counter-polarization strategies, often associated with preservative ideological-programmatic goals to restore the *status quo ante*, are most likely to deepen and entrench pernicious polarization, and in turn, to damage democratic quality. If it is successful at removing the incumbent but using extra-constitutional means, it could actually kill democracy. Likewise, passively avoiding polarization through withdrawal or through elite cooperative mechanisms could depolarize the country at the elite level, but if that cooperation is done on an unequal basis or fails to address underlying grievances, the outcome could actually strengthen the autocratizing incumbent or simply suspend polarization until it resurges in the future.

In contrast, the proactive counter-polarization strategies tackle the dominant axis of pernicious polarization head-on, seeking to create a new pro-democratic axis in a transformative repolarizing strategy, or to defuse that dominant axis by (re)creating cross-cutting ties in a plural polarization. We expect these strategies to more effectively reduce pernicious polarization and reverse autocratization trends, particularly if the opposition actors use innovation in their strategies and practices. Creating new electoral coalitions and crafting messages that may either unify and actively depolarize, or repolarize around a transformative pro-democracy agenda, can succeed in challenging the incumbent party as long as elections retain some element of uncertain outcomes. Examples such as the 2019 municipal elections in Istanbul and Budapest suggest that even seemingly unassailable incumbents concede when faced with well-

76   RESILIENCE OF DEMOCRACY

organized oppositions and decisive defeat. We thus view transformative repolarization and active depolarization, contingent on contextual factors, as the most promising and democratizing strategies for opposition forces.

Notes

1. For an insightful discussion of the concept, see Lührmann and Lindberg, "A Third Wave of Autocratization."
2. McCoy and Somer, "Toward a Theory of Pernicious Polarization"; McCoy, Rahman, and Somer, "Polarization and Global Crisis."
3. Svolik, "Polarization versus Democracy"; Levitsky and Ziblatt, *How Democracies Die*; McCoy and Somer, "Toward a Theory of Pernicious Polarization."
4. See, for example, Yarwood, "The Power of Protest"; Gamboa, "Opposition at the Margins"; Ginsburg and Huq, "Democracy's Near Misses"; Kuisz and Wigura, "The Pushback against Populism"; Laebens and Lührmann, "What Stops Democratic Erosion?"
5. For example, Bunce and Wolchik, "Defeating Dictators"; Chenoweth and Lewis, "Unpacking Nonviolent Campaigns" Geddes, Wright, and Frantz, "Autocratic Breakdown"; Teorell and Wahman, "Institutional Stepping Stones"; Esen and Gumuscu, "Killing Competitive Authoritarianism"; Gorokhovskaia, "What It Takes to Win"; Ufen, "Opposition in Transition"; Wuthrich and Ingleby, "The Pushback against Populism."
6. See Przeworski, *Democracy and the Market,* and Bates et al. *Analytic Narratives* for employing empirical cases this way.
7. McCoy and Somer, "Special Issue on Polarized Polities."
8. Coppedge et al. *Varieties of Democracy Project.*
9. Ibid, 211.
10. Iyengar and Westwood, "Fear and Loathing"; Iyengar et al., "Consequences of Affective Polarization."
11. to capture polarization both longitudinally and cross-sectionally, including states from the Global South, and can be commended for featuring large numbers of cross-checking and complementary questions. It correlates in a statistically significant manner – at the $\alpha = 0.05$ level – with previously used measures of "range of consultation" and "respect counterarguments" from V-Dem – $\rho = -0.339$ and -0.267 respectively.
12. McCoy, Rahman, and Somer, "Global Crisis of Democracy"; McCoy and Somer, "Pernicious Polarization."
13. Future research will examine the impact of polarization during different periods, specifically post 1975 and 1994, to illuminate any differential effects.
14. Kmenta, "Elements of Econometrics."
15. Samuel P. Huntington. *The Third Wave.*
16. Bueno de Mesquita et al., *The Logic of Political Survival*; Svolik, *The Politics of Authoritarian Rule.*
17. States with fewer than 30 observation years are excluded to ensure proper functioning of country-specific error calculations. States excluded are Bahrain, Barbados, Bosnia & Herzegovina, France, Honduras, Iceland, Kazakhstan, Malaysia, Mozambique, Nepal, New Zealand, Oman, Serbia, Singapore, Slovakia, Somaliland, Switzerland, Syria, Timor-Leste, and Turkmenistan.
18. Critical value for these analyses is $\alpha = 0.05$.
19. This is analogous to Croissant's (2019) characterization of periods of democratic backsliding. We also used an alternative coding scheme dropping the requirement of 2 or more years of increased polarization. The results were not substantively different. However, a single year increase of polarization of at least 0.1 may be due to extraordinary events and otherwise is not within the scope of our conceptualization of rapid polarization. The results of this analysis are available upon request.
20. Full results of this analysis are presented in Appendix B, Tables 4, 5, and 6, and Figure 3.
21. Mean value here refers to the mean political polarization value for all observations excluding closed autocracies. Descriptive statistics for all variables are located in the appendix. For reference, the Severe category includes periods such as Chile from 1975–1984, Hungary

from 2015–2019, and Turkey from 2013–2019, among others (561 country-year observations).

22. This denotes the inclusion of an interaction term between political polarization and the period indicator. Significant results indicate a statistically significant difference in the impact of polarization on democratic quality between periods.

23. We use "Incumbent" to refer to either the individual holding office or the party or administration in office throughout the text.

24. Laebens and Luhrmann, "What Stops Democratic Erosion?"; Gamboa, "Opposition at the Margins"; Slater, "Democratic Careening."

25. McCoy and Somer, "Pernicious Polarization"; Gamboa , "Opposition at the Margins."

26. Media and civil society, Laebens and Lührmann, "What Stops Democratic Erosion?"

27. See Mietzner, "Sources of Resistance," for a discussion of Indonesian civil society divided and weakened by polarization and an illiberal incumbent.

28. See Pantoulas and McCoy, "An Unstable Equilibrium," for a discussion of the Venezuela opposition divisions in the face of the Maduro-controlled electoral institutions in Venezuela.

29. McCoy and Somer, "Pernicious Polarization."

30. Slater and Arugay, "Polarizing Figures."

31. Somer, "Moderate Islam and Secularist Opposition"; Somer, "Turkey: The Slippery Slope."

32. Wuthrich and Ingleby, "Pushback against Populism," 32–3.

33. McCoy and Diez, *International Mediation in Venezuela.*

34. Khadiagala, "Ethnic Polarization in Kenya"; Lebas and Munemo, "Elite Conflict, Compromise and Enduring Authoritarianism."

35. https://www.nytimes.com/2019/11/03/world/americas/chile-protests.html

36. Brumberg and Sale, "Tunisia's Endless Transition."

37. Grewal and Hamid, "The Dark Side of Consensus."

38. Gamboa, "Opposition at the Margins."

39. Gorokhovskaia, "What It Takes to Win"; McAdam and Tarrow, "Ballots and Barricades".

40. See William Galston's discussion of the weaknesses of liberalism that include an overemphasis on individualism at the expense of belonging and tribal communities, the burdens of personal responsibility that can give rise to desire for savior-leaders, and incrementalism and stability over visionary change in "The Enduring Vulnerability of Liberal Democracy".

41. Ginsburg and Huq, "Near Misses"; Laebens and Luhrmann, "What Stops Democratic Erosion."

42. Croissant, "Beating Backsliding?"

43. Somer, "Slippery Slope"; Sözen, "Competition in a Populist Authoritarian Regimee."

44. Esen and Sebnem, "Killing Competitive Authoritarianism Softly."

45. Wuthrich and Ingleby, "Pushback Against Populism," 25.

46. Partisi, "Book of Radical Love," 35.

47. Ashdown, "A Motorcycle-Riding Leftist."

48. Selçuk and Hekimci, "Rise of the Democracy – Authoritarianism Cleavage."

49. https://www.theguardian.com/world/2019/oct/13/opposition-parties-candidate-wins-budapest-mayoral-race; https://www.euronews.com/2019/11/04/the-new-mayor-of-budapest-gergerly-karacsony-talks-about-the-changes-in-hungary-s-politica

50. This might have contributed to the recent policies of South Korean government after successfully impeaching the previous president and winning elections. Shin, "South Korea's Democratic Decay."

51. Fish and Abrams, "The Polarization Paradox"; Galston, "Enduring Vulnerability."

52. Bandeira et al., "Disinformation in Democracies."

53. Xiao, "How to Defeat a Populist".

54. For example, Erdogan prohibited the new Istanbul mayor from raising funds to fight the Covid-19 pandemic in Spring of 2020.

Acknowledgements

We wish to thank the comments of the guest editors and two anonymous reviewers, and research assistance from Juan Gómez, Ozlem Tuncel Gurlek, Nimendra Mawalagedara at GSU and Ecem

Ersözlü and Fazıl Alp Akış at Koç University. Research by Jennifer McCoy was supported by the Institute of Advanced Studies, Central European University, Budapest.

Disclosure statement

No potential conflict of interest was reported by the author(s).

Bibliography

Ashdown, Nick. "A Motorcycle-Riding Leftist Feminist Is Coming for Erdogan." *Foreign Policy*, May 1.

Bandeira, Luiza, Donara Barojan, Roberta Braga, Jose Luis Peñarredonda, and Maria Fernanda Pérez Argüello. *Disinformation in Democracies: Strengthening Digital Resilience in Latin America*. Washington, DC: The Atlantic Council, 2019.

Bates, Robert H., Avner Greif, Margaret Levi, Jean-Laurent Rosenthal, and Barry R. Weingast. *Analytic Narratives*. Princeton: Princeton University Press, 1998.

Brumberg, Daniel, and Maryam Ben Salem. "Tunisia's Endless Transition?" *Journal of Democracy* 31, no. 2 (2020): 110–124.

Bueno de Mesquita, Bruce, Alastair Smith, Randolph M. Siverson, and James D. Morrow. *The Logic of Political Survival*. Cambridge: MIT Press, 2003.

Bunce, Valerie J., and Sharon L. Wolchik. "Defeating Dictators: Electoral Change and Stability in Competitive Authoritarian Regimes." *World Politics* 62, no. 1 (2009): 43–86.

Carothers, Thomas, and Andrew Donahue. *Democracies Divided: The Global Challenge of Political Polarization*. Washington, DC: Brookings Institution Press, 2019.

Chenoweth, Erica, and Orion A. Lewis. "Unpacking Nonviolent Campaigns: Introducing the NAVCO 2.0 Dataset." *Journal of Peace Research* 50, no. 3 (2013): 415–423.

Coppedge, Michael, et al. "V-Dem [Country–Year/Country–Date] Dataset v10." *Varieties of Democracy (V-Dem) Project*, 2020. https://www.v-dem.net/media/filer_public/28/14/28140582-43d6-4940-948f-a2df84a31893/v-dem_codebook_v10.pdf.

Croissant, Aurel. "Beating Backsliding? Episodes and Outcomes of Democratic Backsliding in Asia-Pacific in the Period 1950 to 2018." Heidelberg University, 2019. https://www.uni- Eaton heidelberg.de/md/politik/personal/croissant/s/croissant__2020__beating_backsliding.pdf.

Esen, Berk, and Sebnem Gumuscu. "Killing Competitive Authoritarianism Softly: The 2019 Local Elections in Turkey." *South European Society and Politics* 24, no. 3 (2019): 317–342.

Fish, M. Steven, and Neil Abrams. "The Polarization Paradox." *Journal of Democracy* 2 (2020): 182–185.

Galston, William. "The Enduring Vulnerability of Liberal Democracy." *Journal of Democracy* 3 (2020): 8–24.

Gamboa, Laura. "Opposition at the Margins: Strategies Against the Erosion of Democracy in Colombia and Venezuela." *Comparative Politics* 49, no. 4 (2017): 457–477.

Geddes, Barbara, Joseph Wright, and Erica Frantz. "Autocratic Breakdown and Regime Transitions: A New Data Set." *Perspectives on Politics* 12, no. 2 (2014): 313–331.

Ginsburg, Tom, and Aziz Huq. "Democracy's Near Misses." *Journal of Democracy* 29, no. 4 (2018): 16–30.

Gorokhovskaia, Yana. "What It Takes to Win When the Game Is Rigged: The Evolution of Opposition Electoral Strategies in Moscow, 2012–2017." *Democratization* 26, no. 6 (2019): 975–992.

Handlin, Samuel. *State Crisis in Fragile Democracies: Polarization and Political Regimes in South America*. Cambridge: Cambridge University Press, 2017.

Huntington, Samuel P. *The Third Wave: Democratization in the Later 20th Century*. Norman: University of Oklahoma Press, 1991.

Iyengar, Shanto, Yphtach Lelkes, and Matthew Levendusky. "The Origins and Consequences of Affective Polarization in the United States." *Annual Review of Political Science* 22, no. 1 (2019): 129–146.

Iyengar, Shanto, and Sean J. Westwood. "Fear and Loathing Across Party Lines: New Evidence on Group Polarization." *American Journal of Political Science* 59, no. 3 (2015): 690.

Khadiagala, Gilbert M. "Persistent Ethnic Polarization in Kenya." In *Democracies Divided: The Global Challenge of Political Polarization*, edited by Tom Carothers, and Andrew O'Donohue, 38–64. Washington, DC: Brookings Institution Press, 2019.

Kmenta, Jan. *Elements of Econometrics*. 2nd ed. New York: Macmillan, 1971.

Kuisz, Jarosław, and Karolina Wigura. "The Pushback against Populism: Reclaiming the Politics of Emotion." *Journal of Democracy* 31, no. 2 (2020): 41–53.

Laebens, Melis G., and Anna Lührmann. "What Stops Democratic Erosion? The Role of Institutions of Accountability." Paper presented at "Berlin Democracy Conference," Berlin. https://gupea.ub.gu.se/bitstream/2077/64508/1/gupea_2077_64508_1.pdf, 2019.

LeBas, Adrienne, and Ngonidzashe Munemo. "Elite Conflict, Compromise, and Enduring Authoritarianism: Polarization in Zimbabwe, 1980–2008." *The ANNALS of the American Academy of Political and Social Science* 681, no. 1 (2019): 209–226. doi:10.1177/0002716218813897.

Levitsky, Steven, and Daniel Ziblatt. *How Democracies Die*. New York: Crown, 2018.

Lührmann, Anna, and Staffan I. Lindberg. "A Third Wave of Autocratization Is Here: What Is New About It?" *Democratization* 26, no. 7 (2019): 1095–1113.

Lührmann, Anna, et al. "Democracy Facing Global Challenges: V-Dem Annual Democracy Report 2019." V-Dem Institute, May 2019. https://www.v-dem.net/media/filer_public/99/de/99dedd73-f8bc-484c-8b91-44ba601b6e6b/v-dem_democracy_report_2019.pdf.

McAdam, Doug, and Sidney Tarrow. "Ballots and Barricades: On the Reciprocal Relationship between Elections and Social Movements." *Perspectives on Politics* 8, no. 2 (2010): 529–42.

McCoy, Jennifer, and Francisco Diez. *International Mediation in Venezuela*. Washington, D.C: United States Institute of Peace, 2011.

McCoy, Jennifer, Tahmina Rahman, and Murat Somer. "Polarization and the Global Crisis of Democracy: Common Patterns, Dynamics, and Pernicious Consequences for Democratic Polities." *American Behavioral Scientist* 62, no. 1 (2018): 16–42.

Jennifer McCoy and Murat Somer, eds. "Polarizing Polities: A Global Threat to Democracy." Special Volume in *The Annals of the American Academy of Political and Social Science* 61, no. 1 (2019).

McCoy, Jennifer, and Murat Somer. "Toward a Theory of Pernicious Polarization and How It Harms Democracies: Comparative Evidence and Possible Remedies." *The ANNALS of the American Academy of Political and Social Science* 681, no. 1 (2019): 234–71.

Mietzner, Marcus. "Sources of Resistance to Democratic Decline: Indonesian Civil Society and Its Trials." *Democratization* 0, no. 0 (July 24, 2020): 1–18.

Pantoulas, Dimitris, and Jennifer McCoy. "Venezuela: an Unstable Equilibrium." *Revista de Ciencias Políticas* 32, no. 2 (2019): 391–408.

Partisi, Cumhuriyet Halk. *Book of Radical Love (within-Party Educational Material)*, 2019. http://dijitalmecmua.chp.org.tr/CHPRadikal%20SevgiKitabiEng.pdf.

Pelke, Lars, and Aurel Croissant. "Conceptualizing and Measuring Autocratization Episodes." Working Paper, 2020.

Przeworski, Adam. *Democracy and the Market: Political and Economic Reforms in Eastern Europe and Latin America*. Cambridge: Cambridge University Press, 1991.

Selçuk, Orçun, and Dilara Hekimci. "The Rise of the Democracy – Authoritarianism Cleavage and Opposition Coordination in Turkey (2014–2019)." *Democratization* (2020): 1–19. doi:10.1080/13510347.2020.1803841.

Shin, Gi-Wook. "South Korea's Democratic Decay." *Journal of Democracy* 31, no. 3 (2020): 100–114.

Slater, Dan, and Aries A. Arugay. "Polarizing Figures: Executive Power and Institutional Conflict in Asian Democracies." *American Behavioral Scientist* 62, no. 1 (2018): 92–106.

Somer, Murat. "Moderate Islam and Secularist Opposition in Turkey: Implications for the World, Muslims and Secular Democracy." *Third World Quarterly* 28, no. 7 (2007): 1271–89.

Somer, Murat. "Turkey: The Slippery Slope from Reformist to Revolutionary Polarization and Democratic Breakdown." *The ANNALS of the American Academy of Political and Social Science* 681, no. 1 (2019): 42–61.

Sözen, Yunus. "Competition in a Populist Authoritarian Regime: The June 2018 Dual Elections in Turkey." *South European Society and Politics* 24, no. 3 (2019): 287–315.

Svolik, Milan W. *The Politics of Authoritarian Rule*. New York: Cambridge University Press, 2012.

Svolik, Milan W. "Polarization versus Democracy." *Journal of Democracy* 30, no. 3 (2019): 20–32.

Teorell, Jan, and Michael Wahman. "Institutional Stepping Stones for Democracy: How and Why Multipartyism Enhances Democratic Change." *Democratization* 25, no. 1 (2018): 78–97.

Ufen, Andreas. "Opposition in Transition: Pre-Electoral Coalitions and the 2018 Electoral Breakthrough in Malaysia." *Democratization* 27, no. 2 (2019): 167–84.

Wuthrich, F. Michael, and Melvyn Ingleby. "The Pushback Against Populism: Running on 'Radical Love' in Turkey." *Journal of Democracy* 31, no. 2 (2020): 24–40.

Xiao, Jenny. "How to Defeat Populism: Three Lessons from Slovakia." *Social Science Research Council* (blog), September 3, 2019. https://items.ssrc.org/democracy-papers/how-to-defeat-populism-three-lessons-from-slovakia/.

Yarwood, Janette. "The Struggle Over Term Limits in Africa: The Power of Protest." *Journal of Democracy* 27, no. 3 (2016): 51–60. https://muse.jhu.edu/article/623606/pdf.

Negative partisanship towards the populist radical right and democratic resilience in Western Europe

Carlos Meléndez and Cristóbal Rovira Kaltwasser

ABSTRACT
Democracy is under threat today and scholars agree that the main challenge is not sudden regime breakdown, but rather the gradual erosion of key institutions and norms because of growing public support to political forces with illiberal tendencies. In the case of Western Europe, the major threat comes from the populist radical right. Although it is true that the latter has been gaining votes in Western Europe, scholars have not analysed the extent to which a sizeable share of the electorate dislikes this party family. Nevertheless, recent studies reveal that it is important to consider both those who feel close to and those who reject political parties, i.e. positive and negative partisanship. To address this research gap, in this contribution we rely on original survey data for 10 Western European countries to examine negative partisanship towards the populist radical right. The empirical analysis reveals that a large section of the Western European electorate has an aversion to this party family and this finding should be seen as an important sign of democratic resilience. In fact, those who dislike the populist radical right are strong supporters of both democracy per se and the liberal democratic regime.

1. Introduction

Hardly a day goes by without reports in the press about the populist radical right (PRR) and the danger it constitutes for democracy. Although it is true that PRR forces do not reject democracy per se, there is little doubt that they maintain an ambivalent and difficult relationship with key elements of the liberal democratic regime.[1] Put in other words, PRR parties should not be thought of as bluntly authoritarian forces, but rather as actors that play by the democratic rules of the game to gradually subvert the liberal democratic regime from within. By promoting illiberal ideas, the PRR can set in motion a process of democratic erosion that in some cases might even lead to democratic breakdown.[2] This argument aligns with the editors of this special issue, who rightly point out that "the main contemporary challenge to democracy is not sudden regime breakdown in the form of military coups, but its gradual demise after illiberal or authoritarian-leaning political leaders come to power in elections."[3]

 Supplemental data for this article can be accessed at https://doi.org/10.1080/13510347.2021.1883002.

Not by chance, this party family continues to make headlines and an increasing number of academics and pundits alike warn about its consequences for democracy.[4] While we certainly share this cautionary note, we are of the opinion that current analyses tend to be one-sided as they only consider the increasing electoral support that the PRR gets, without examining in detail if there is an electoral ceiling for this party family. In this contribution we are interested in addressing this research gap, the extent to which there is a clear limit to the potential electoral growth of PRR parties in Western Europe. Put differently, by talking about the electoral ceiling of the PRR in Western Europe, we are interested in studying if this party family is reaching its maximum potential mobilization under the current political circumstances, which are marked indeed by the high saliency of the immigration topic.[5]

While it is obvious that no party family can expand its electoral support endlessly, this problem is particularly evident for the PRR as it develops ideas that are at odds with what it is normally considered socially acceptable in Western Europe. As Harteveld and Ivarsflaten[6] have recently indicated, even though the message of the PRR resonates with large segments of the Western European electorate, "many of these parties also raise normative concerns about discrimination and prejudice due to fascist or extremist legacies or contemporary rhetoric and symbols." Therefore, it is not far-fetched to suggest that PRR forces should have difficulties expanding their base of support beyond their core constituency, which is normally depicted as the "losers of globalization": workers (mainly men) who, because of the transformation of advanced economies, face a devaluation of their skillsets and feel that their social status is seriously under threat.[7]

With the aim of theoretically and empirically analysing the electoral ceiling of the PRR, in this contribution we bring to the fore the concept and measurement of positive and negative partisanship. Whereas the former alludes to the extent to which individuals have an enduring psychological attachment to a specific political party, the latter refers to the extent to which individuals have a stable psychological *repulsion* from a specific political party.[8] Studies on the combination of these two types of partisanship have been gaining preponderance in the United States,[9] a country marked by a bipartisan political system that shows increasing levels of affective polarization: the tendency of Democrats and Republicans to dislike and distrust one another.[10] Another interesting example is Brazil, although this is a case of a multiparty system that has become increasingly polarized between those who support and reject one specific party: the center-left Workers' Party.[11]

However, there are almost no systematic and cross-national analyses of negative partisanship in Western Europe.[12] This means that we do have knowledge about those who identify with the PRR, but do not know much about those who have an animosity towards this party family. Part of problem lies in the existence of limited empirical evidence on negative partisanship in Western Europe. Nevertheless, a recent public opinion study conducted by the Bertelsmann Foundation for the 2019 elections for the European Parliament included a set of survey items to measure both positive and negative partisanship.[13] In this paper, we analyse this data in detail. Among other issues, we show that given that an important section of the Western European electorate is at odds with the PRR, the latter has serious difficulties continuing to expand its base of support and therefore it is possible to argue that democracy in the region is in safe hands. However, we also argue that this optimistic interpretation hinges on the capacity to activate and mobilize negative partisanship towards the PRR, something that our empirical analysis reveals is only partially occurring today.

The rest of this contribution is structured as follows. In the next section, we shortly define PRR parties and show that the concept and measurement of positive and negative partisanship towards this party family helps to understand its electoral ceiling. Here we also provide descriptive data of these two types of partisanships for the different party families that are predominant in the Western European context. After this, we present empirical evidence about those who have a positive and negative identity with the PRR in Western Europe, putting emphasis on their ideological characteristics, democratic profile and sociodemographic attributes. To examine the political relevance of positive and negative partisanship, in this section we also present evidence on the impact of these two types of partisanship towards the PRR on turnout in Western Europe. Finally, we close by summarizing the main findings of this contribution and by providing ideas about the future research agenda on the link between positive and negative identities towards the PRR and democratic resilience in Western Europe and beyond.

2. Positive and negative partisanship towards the PRR in Western Europe

There is a considerable body of academic literature on the PRR, which is normally defined as a party family identified by three ideological attributes: authoritarianism, nativism and populism.[14] While authoritarianism alludes to the defense of a strictly ordered society and strong punishment of what is seen as deviant behaviour, nativism refers to the argument that states should be inhabited exclusively by members of the native group ("the nation") and that nonnatives ("alien") are threatening to the alleged homogeneity of the nation-state. Populism, in turn, should be thought of as a set of ideas characterized by the Manichean distinction between "the pure people" versus "the corrupt elite" and the defense of popular sovereignty by all means. By combining these three ideological tenets – authoritarianism, nativism and populism – this party family has been able not only to carve out a political space to the right of Conservative and Christian Democratic parties, but also to defy the post-war consensus on what democracy means and how it should work in Western Europe.[15]

Most scholars share the opinion that the appearance of the PRR represents a major challenge, particularly because of its subtle but nonetheless significant attack on key institutions and the norms of the liberal democratic regime that are inherent in post-war Europe.[16] In effect, the PRR is at odds with the protection of minority rights, the independence of the judiciary and the delegation of power to supranational institutions that monitor the proper functioning of the rule of law. This danger is reinforced by recent research showing that the PRR has over time not moderated its agenda, but rather radicalized many of its programmatic positions.[17] The increasing relevance of the PRR can be seen in the following graph, which shows the average of votes for PRR parties per decade as percentages across Western Europe.[18] According to this data, the PRR party family has been able to establish itself and expand its electoral appeal from 8.9% in the 1980s to 13.8% in the 2010s (Figure 1).

The very fact that the PRR has become entrenched in Western Europe not only calls into question the famous "freezing hypothesis" of Lipset and Rokkan, but also sparks a debate about the strength of democracy in the region. Although we agree with the

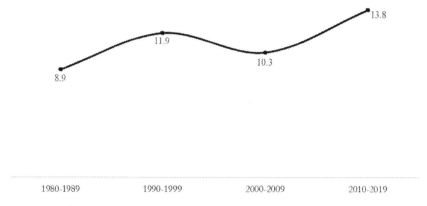

Figure 1. Support for Populist Radical Right Parties in Western Europe (average percentage per decade)

general idea that the PRR represents a major challenge to Western European democracy, extant research looks mainly at those who support the PRR and only marginally at those who reject it. By way of illustration, even though the recently published *Oxford Handbook of the Radical Right*[19] offers an excellent state of the art of the research on this topic, almost no space is given to the question about the limits to the electoral growth of the PRR. The only exception is the chapter by Nonna Mayer[20] on France, in which she devotes a couple of pages to argue that, despite Marine Le Pen's de-demonization strategy, there are clear barriers (e.g. education, gender and the relevance of the left-right cleavage) to the electoral expansion of the French PRR. Another interesting exception is the work of Ivarsflaten,[21] who has shown that the PRR struggles with an extremist reputation that constrains its electoral growth and this is why this party family pays increasing attention to issues other than immigration with the aim of developing a "reputational shield" to rebut charges of prejudice and adopt radical-right positions while retaining legitimacy.

The previous examples reveal that some scholars have done research that at least indirectly deals with the electoral ceiling of the PRR. However, to address this issue directly, we are of the opinion that it is crucial to take into account negative partisanship, a concept and measurement that has been gaining traction to paint a better picture of how voters relate to the political world today. For a long time, negative partisanship has been treated as the "forgotten side" of partisanship,[22] but given that citizens decreasingly identify with political parties, negative partisanship can be more powerful than its positive counterpart.[23] In line with previous research, we consider negative partisanship as a stable and systematic animadversion to a specific political party,[24] which has an independent psychological and sociological structure from its positive counterpart[25] and therefore can be particularly valuable when it comes to explaining political behaviour.[26] People's natural reflexes on building political boundaries can be expressed by perceiving themselves as members of an "ingroup" and/or members of an "out-group."[27] These perceived memberships can be understood as "instrumental partisanship" (i.e. to support parties based on an issue-agenda) or as "expressive partisanship" (i.e. to support parties based on emotional attachments associated to social affiliations like gender, religious or ethnic groups).[28] Positive and negative partisanships can imply instrumental reasoning and expressive connections towards specific political parties, but negative partisanships tend to be related to strong emotions like collective threat and defense of political identities. In this sense, the psychological micro-foundations of positive and negative partisanships are different: while the former is related to the positive feelings for the in-group, the latter is linked to negative evaluations of the out-group. This means that negative partisanship does not necessarily provide a psychological sense of belonging that positive partisanship does.[29] This argument stays in line with the classic work of Brewer[30] on the psychology of prejudice, who argues that one should not assume the existence of an automatic negative reciprocity between in-group and out-group distinctions. At the same time, negative information is received and processed differently than positive information: the former generates stronger reactions (e.g. anger) and heavier evaluations (e.g. persuading others not to support the disliked parties) than the latter.[31] In this sense, while an individual can endorse one political party, she can develop hostile feelings and actions for more than one. Actually, the literature of positive/negative partisanship in multiparty systems has warned that "every individual could hold only one positive party identification; however, he/she could have several negative party identifications."[32]

Nevertheless, as Mayer[33] has rightly pointed out, most studies on negative partisanship focus either on the United States[34] or on other similarly bipolar majority party systems.[35] This means that there is little theoretical discussion and empirical evidence about negative partisanship on stable multi-party systems, which are dominant in Western Europe.[36] To fill this research gap and generate evidence on the electoral ceiling of the PRR, in this contribution we utilize original data from an survey conducted by YouGov on behalf of the Bertelsmann Foundation in a single wave in January 2019 in the following ten Western Europe countries: Austria (1,984 cases), Denmark (1,973 cases), France (1,949 cases), Germany (1,995 cases), Greece (2,027 cases), Italy (1,952 cases), the Netherlands (1,924 cases), Spain (1,949 cases), Sweden (1,976 cases) and the United Kingdom (2,133 cases).[37] For the purpose of this study, we merged the country datasets in a single continental database of 19,862 observations.[38]

Two main options are available to measure positive and negative party identification. On the one hand, the group-identity approach classifies individuals based on their declared patterns of voting behaviour, i.e. by asking which parties individuals would definitively vote for or which ones would never vote for.[39] On the other hand, the feeling-thermometer/sympathies approach considers levels of proximity to the reference group.[40] We adopted the former since we conceptualize party identification as an enduring psychological attachment to a political party that conditions ingroup and outgroup references. Relying on previous research on negative partisanship[41] and adapting this to the European context marked by the coexistence of different electoral arenas, we operationalized positive and negative partisanships as a coherent behavioural intention, based on a battery of questions about the preferences of voters at three electoral levels: European Parliament, national parliament and regional parliament (in those countries where there are no regional parliaments, we asked instead about local elections). Multi-item scale of partisanships has advantages since it goes beyond measuring simple negative affect and it proxies more accurately identity-based measures of party identification.[42] In more concrete terms, we label respondents as positive partisans if they meet a demanding condition: if they *would definitively* vote for a candidate of the same party in each of the three elections asked. By contrast, we label respondents as negative partisans if they meet a similar exhaustive condition: if they *would definitively not* vote for a candidate of the same party in each of the three elections asked. We asked this set of questions for each relevant political party in each country under study. By employing this measurement, we are capturing hardcore (positive and negative) partisanships, which are the stronger, and, consequently, enduring kind of followers.[43]

Since we are interested in providing an analysis focused on the Western European electorate, we clustered positive and negative party identifiers – across countries – for each of the six different party families that are predominant in the region today: (1) populist radical right (PRR) parties, (2) Christian democratic and conservative parties, (3) liberal parties, (4) social democratic parties, (5) green parties, and (6) populist radical left (PRL) parties.[44] For example, if a Spanish respondent qualifies as a PSOE's positive partisan, she is grouped as being a positive partisan towards the social democratic party family, while if a Spanish respondent qualifies as a PSOE's negative partisan, she is grouped as being a negative partisan towards the social democratic party family. As expected for multiparty-systems,[45] positive partisanships are exclusive, while negative partisanships are not, i.e. individuals can hold multiple negative partisanships. The possibility of an individual holding one positive partisanship and multiple negative partisanships impedes conceiving a negative partisanship as the automatic bipolar counterpart of a positive one. Nevertheless, the low proportion of citizens with positive partisanship should not be confused with apathy or dealignment, since a big part of the electorate dislikes certain political parties. As Rose and Mishler have indicated, the process of cognitive mobilization that has occurred in advanced democracies encourages voters to behave as "knowledgeable sceptics," who are therefore "more likely to name a party they would never vote for than to identify positively with a party."[46]

Before presenting a detailed empirical analysis of those who have a positive and negative partisanship towards the PRR, we show descriptive data on the average number of positive and negative partisans towards each the six party families that are normally identified in the academic literature on Western Europe. This evidence is provided in Figure 2, from which two main points stand out. First, positive partisanship is much less widespread than negative partisanship. This is not a minor issue, because it implies that few citizens have a political party that they love, but most citizens do have aversion to certain political parties. In other words, many citizens do not opt first and foremost for the party to which they feel most attached but rather react against those parties that they most strongly oppose.

Second, it is quite clear that the PRR is the most peculiar party family of all those considered in the analysis: it is the one with the highest percentage of both positive partisanship (10.53%) and negative partisanship (52.59%). Even though many of the PRR parties are relatively new in Western Europe, they have been able to create an important number of loyal supporters as well as a large amount of detractors. This is probably related to the fact that the PRR continuously sparks heated debates on immigration and other topics, which fosters not only emotional reactions but also ideological polarization between those who belong and don't belong to the reference group.

What can we learn from this first piece of descriptive evidence on positive and negative partisanship in Western Europe? The very fact that, of all the party families considered, the PRR has the highest level of negative partisanship reveals that it generates strong feelings of rejection, and in consequence, it is not far-fetched to suggest that it

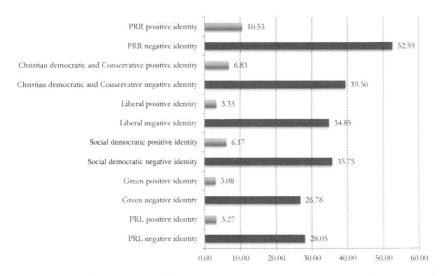

Figure 2. Positive and negative partisanship in Western European countries (in percentage)

has a clear electoral ceiling. On average, approximately half of the Western European electorate declares that will never support the PRR. There are good reasons to interpret this as a sign of democratic resilience. However, PRR negative partisans are electorally fragmented and we need to look at their sociopolitical characteristics. Therefore, to better substantiate if the high level of negative partisanship can be seen as a sign of democratic resilience, it is crucial to undertake a more fine-grained empirical analysis of the attributes of those who have both a positive and negative identity towards the PRR.

Before moving to the next section, it is important to clarify the very notion of democratic resilience. In line with the argument advanced by Boese et al.[47] in their contribution to this special issue, we define democratic resilience as the persistence of democratic institutions and practices, despite the existence of political forces that implicitly or explicitly attack the liberal democratic regime. In other words, democratic resilience means the ability to avoid the onset of autocratization as well as attempts of regime breakdown. Therefore, by exploring the ideological underpinnings of those who have positive and negative partisanship towards the PRR in Western Europe, we can examine if they have different values which are either supportive or contrary to democratic resilience.

3. The profile of citizens with positive and negative partisanship towards the PRR in Western Europe

The evidence presented above reveals that PRR parties in Western Europe are strongly rejected by approximately half of the electorate and strongly supported by a bit more than ten percent of the electorate. Are these two different constituencies with clear political and sociological backgrounds? To answer this question, we have built three profiles focused on the ideological characteristics, democratic preferences and sociodemographic attributes of those citizens who have positive and negative identities towards the PRR in Western Europe. Given that the construction of each these

88   RESILIENCE OF DEMOCRACY

three profiles deserves some clarification, we begin by discussing the measurement and method. After this we present the analysis and interpretation. Finally, we close this section with the examination of the impact of positive vis-à-vis negative partisanship towards the PRR on turnout.

3.1. Measurement and method

The survey data we employ in this contribution allows for the creation of three profiles that are useful for explaining the differences between those evincing positive and negative partisanships towards the PRR in Western Europe. The first profile considers ideological characteristics of voters and is articulated by the following variables: conventional ideological self-positioning (from extreme left, 1, to extreme right, 10), populist attitudes (8-item index based on Van Hauwaert and van Kessel[48]), attitudes towards European integration (one question asks for level of agreement with European Union integration), attitudes towards immigration (4-question index on tolerance of foreign immigrants in respondent's country; higher scores represent higher levels of disagreement with pro-immigration policies), left/right preferences in economic terms (4-question item, lower-scores represent pro-state preferences and higher scores represents pro-market preferences) and left/right preferences in moral terms (5-question item, lower scores represent liberal values and higher scores represent conservative values).[49]

The second profile alludes to the democratic preferences of citizens and it is composed of the following indicators, which were originally developed for the 2012 the European Social Survey[50]: relevance of electoral democracy (3-item index on the importance of free and fair elections, opposition's freedom to criticize government, and freedom to express one's political views), relevance of liberal democracy (3-item index on importance of courts in balancing power, protection of minorities' rights, and media's freedom to criticize government), relevance of direct democracy (2-item index on the importance of citizens' participation in issue-referendums and recall referendums) and relevance of social democracy (2-item index on the importance of the government taking actions to protect citizens from poverty and income inequality). In every case, higher scores represent more importance. Additionally, we included the classic question on support for democracy (5-level agreement scale on democracy as the most preferable form of government, where 1 represents strongly disagree and 5 represents strongly agree) and the question on satisfaction with democracy (0–10 scale of satisfaction, where 0 represents very dissatisfied and 10 very satisfied).[51]

The third and final profile deals with the socio-demographic attributes of citizens and it considers the following variables: gender, age, income and education level. Gender was coded as a dichotomic variable (1=female), and Age was coded as a continuous variable. Income was recoded in three levels of monthly income (less than 1,500 Euros, between 1,500 and 3,000 Euros, and more than 3,000 Euros) based on a question regarding gross household income after taxes, including wage, salaries, pensions, unemployment benefits, social care and rents. Education was codified and standardized in six levels, according to each country's educational system.

In order to assess the statistical effect of the ideological, democratic and socio-demographic profiles on positive and negative PRR identifiers, we performed binary logistic regressions, treating separately positive and negative partisanship towards the PRR as dependent variables (positive identifiers as 1, and the rest of the sample as 0; negative identifiers as 1, and the rest of the sample as 0), and the previously mentioned variables of the ideological, democratic and socio-demographic profiles as independent variables. We also employed the corresponding survey weights. Results are shown and interpreted in the next section.

3.2. Analysis and interpretation

As expected, Western European citizens with positive and negative identities towards the PRR are extremely different and constitute two contrary constituencies. Table 1 reports logistic coefficients considering both political identities as dependent variables (corresponding standard deviations are indicated in parenthesis and odds ratios between brackets). For each PRR partisanship, we performed two versions of logistic models with fixed-effects in order to control for potential country-effects. The first version (Full Model All) indicates a complete model in which we considered controls for every of the ten countries included in the analysis (Model 1 for PRR positive partisanship and Model 3 for PRR negative partisanship). In the second version (Full Model), as a robustness check, we excluded countries with no significant statistical relationship in the fixed-effect complete model since they might express outliers or cases that go against the direction of most of the observations (France and Denmark for PRR positive partisanship; Germany for PRR negative partisanship) (Model 2 for PRR positive partisanship and Model 4 for PRR negative partisanship).[52] We start by analysing PRR positive partisans based on the statistical findings (Model 1 and Model 2). The evidence reveals that PRR positive partisans are prone to position themselves as right-wingers, are attracted by populist appeals, can be seen as Eurosceptics and tend to be intolerant towards immigrants. It is worth indicating that left/right preferences in economic terms do not have a significant impact on holding a positive identity towards the PRR. Moreover, those with a positive PRR identity tend to be more conservative than liberal, although with a statistical significance level at 95% of confidence interval. This finding reinforces the argument made by several scholars who point out that support for the PRR is driven first and foremost by nativism.[53]

In terms of the democratic profile, the evidence shows that those who have a positive identity towards the PRR are not only at odds with the liberal dimension of democracy, but also in favour of the direct democratic dimension (Models 1 and 2). Giving more importance to the liberal dimension of democracy reduces the propensity for positive PPR identification, although the statistical significance reaches 95% of confidence interval in both models. Additionally, considering democracy as the most preferable regime decreases the propensity of being a positive PRR identifier (although its statistically significance is at the 95% of confidence interval in both models), and satisfaction with democracy does not condition PRR positive partisanship. In summary, PRR positive partisans' democratic profile is marked by the support for direct democratic mechanisms as well as the rejection of key liberal democratic institutions that seek to guarantee horizontal accountability. At the same time, PRR positive partisans are characterized by their objection to democratic support. When it comes to analysing those who have positive partisanship towards the PRR in Western Europe, neither satisfaction with democracy nor the social-democratic dimension is statistically significant. The latter point is interesting, since it connects to the growing literature on welfare chauvinism, which shows that the PRR does not develop a genuine social-

90   RESILIENCE OF DEMOCRACY

Table 1. Ideological, democratic and socio-demographic attributes as predictors for PRR positive and negative partisanships in Western Europe.

VARIABLES	(1) PRR positive partisanship Full Model All	(2) PRR positive partisanship Full Model	(3) PRR negative partisanship Full Model All	(4) PRR negative partisanship Full Model
Left/Right Self-positioning	0.287*** (0.015) [1.333]	0.307*** (0.017) [1.359]	−0.267*** (0.010) [0.766]	−0.264*** (0.011) [0.768]
Populism Index	0.282*** (0.060) [1.326]	0.290*** (0.067) [1.336]	−0.074* (0.039) [0.928]	−0.060
EU Index	−0.308*** (0.028) [0.735]	−0.316*** (0.032) [0.729]	0.265*** (0.020) [1.303]	0.253*** (0.021) [1.287]
Immigration Index	0.695*** (0.044) [2.003]	0.690*** (0.049) [1.994]	−0.687*** (0.028) [0.503]	−0.665*** (0.029) [0.514]
Liberal/Conservative Index	0.032** (0.015) [1.032]	0.032** (0.016) [1.032]	−0.111*** (0.010) [0.895]	−0.106*** (0.011) [0.900]
State/Market Index	0.002	0.002	−0.008	−0.012
Electoral Democracy	−0.041	−0.020	0.039** (0.019) [1.040]	0.043** (0.020) [1.044]
Liberal Democracy	−0.051** (0.024) [0.950]	−0.057** (0.026) [0.945]	0.075*** (0.018) [1.078]	0.072*** (0.019) [1.074]
Direct Democracy	0.087*** (0.020) [1.091]	0.098*** (0.023) [1.103]	−0.115*** (0.012) [0.891]	−0.111*** (0.013) [0.895]
Social Democracy	0.030* (0.018) [1.030]	0.019	0.038*** (0.013) [1.038]	0.036** (0.014) [1.037]
Democratic Support	−0.075** (0.034) [0.928]	−0.091** (0.038) [0.913]	0.182*** (0.026) [1.200]	0.174*** (0.027) [1.190]
Democratic Satisfaction	−0.011	−0.005	−0.023** (0.009) [0.978]	−0.029*** (0.010) [0.971]
Gender (1=Female)	−0.265*** (0.066) [0.767]	−0.223*** (0.074) [0.800]	0.163*** (0.044) [1.178]	0.136*** (0.047) [1.146]
Age	−0.000	−0.001	0.011*** (0.001) [1.011]	0.011*** (0.002) [1.011]
Income	−0.002	0.031	0.081** (0.032) [1.084]	0.090*** (0.033) [1.094]
Education	−0.085* (0.047) [0.918]	−0.053	0.092** (0.030) [1.096]	0.123*** (0.032) [1.131]
Austria_country_categoric	0.548*** (0.159) [1.729]	0.521*** (0.161) [1.685]	−0.811*** (0.095) [0.445]	−0.803*** (0.095) [0.448]
Denmark_country_categoric	−0.062		−0.606*** (0.102) [0.545]	−0.596*** (0.102) [0.551]

(Continued)

Table 1. Continued.

VARIABLES	(1) PRR positive partisanship Full Model All	(2) PRR positive partisanship Full Model	(3) PRR negative partisanship Full Model All	(4) PRR negative partisanship Full Model
France_country_categoric	0.206		−0.224**	−0.248**
			(0.098)	(0.098)
			[0.799]	[0.780]
Germany_country_categoric	0.918***	0.900***	0.101	
	(0.157)	(0.158)		
	[2.504]	[2.460]		
Greece_country_categoric	−1.607***	−1.646***	1.333***	1.279***
	(0.223)	(0.226)	(0.098)	(0.098)
	[0.201]	[0.193]	[3.794]	[3.593]
Italy_country_categoric	0.942***	0.933***	0.211**	0.205**
	(0.153)	(0.154)	(0.098)	(0.097)
	[2.566]	[2.542]	[1.235]	[1.227]
Netherlands_count_categoric	0.548***	0.514***	0.473***	0.462***
	(0.164)	(0.166)	(0.098)	(0.098)
	[1.730]	[1.671]	[1.605]	[1.588]
Sweden_country_categoric	1.067***	0.988***	−0.654***	−0.657***
	(0.161)	(0.164)	(0.103)	(0.103)
	[2.905]	[2.687]	[0.520]	[0.518]
UK_country_categoric	−0.7368***	−0.785***	0.354***	0.331***
	(0.205)	(0.209)	(0.105)	(0.105)
	[0.479]	[0.456]	[1.425]	[1.393]
Constant	−6.2246***	−6.560***	1.395***	1.321***
	(0.410)	(0.454)	(0.258)	(0.273)
	[0.002]	[0.001]	[4.035]	[3.749]
Pseudo r-sqaured	0.308	0.321	0.308	0.301
Observations	14,040	11,426	14,040	12,586

Note: Numbers reported are logistic coefficients. When these are significant, standard errors are indicated in parenthesis, and odds ratios are calculated and presented in brackets. Spain is used as baseline in all models. The two Full Model All indicate complete models in which we considered controls for each of the ten countries included in the analysis (Models 1 and 3). The respective two Full Models exclude countries with no significant statistical relationship in the fixed-effect complete model (France and Denmark for PRR positive partisanship in Model 2, and Germany for PRR negative partisanship in Model 4).
*** $p < 0.01$, ** $p < 0.05$, * $p < 0.1$.

democratic agenda but rather promotes the defense of generous social rights only for the native population.[54]

Regarding the socio-demographic profile, the propensity of being a PRR positive partisan is higher among men and decreases with education levels (although only in the Full Model and at the 90% of confidence interval). Neither income nor age condition PRR positive partisanship. This information about the socio-demographic profile of those who can be seen as PRR positive partisans stays in line with much of the extant research on this topic, which demonstrates that those who support the PRR are not predominantly "economic losers" in an objective sense, but rather individuals who at the subjective level feel left behind because of ongoing cultural and economic transformation that negatively affect their social status.[55] Last but not least, it is worth indicating, that overall, these three profiles – ideological, democratic, and socio-demographic – explain 30 percent of the general variation of PRR positive partisanship when controlling by country effects, and 32 percent of the same variation when excluding countries with no significant statistical relationship in the fixed-effect complete model (i.e. France and Denmark).

We proceeded similarly in order to explain the ideological, democratic and socio-demographic profile of PRR negative partisans (Model 3 and Model 4). Let's start with the ideological profile. Self-positioning to the left, having preferences for European integration, being tolerant towards immigration and embracing liberal values increase the propensity of being a PRR negative identifier. Interestingly, populist attitudes bear a negative effect on having negative partisanship towards the PRR only at the 90% of confidence interval in the Full Model All.

When considering the democratic profile, those with a negative identity towards the PRR are in favour of the electoral, liberal and social-democratic dimensions of democracy, while they also tend to reject the direct democratic dimensions. At the same time, PRR negative identifiers tend to be dissatisfied with democracy but to support it as the most preferable regime. Given that negative PRR identifiers are prone to support democracy as the most preferable regime despite the fact that they are dissatisfied with it, they can be classified as "critical citizens": voters who are in favour of the democracy but disappointed with the way democracy is working in practice.[56]

Regarding the socio-demographic profile, the propensity to be labelled as PRR negative identifier increases among women. It is positively associated with age, income, and education. When comparing the socio-demographic profile for the two profiles, it becomes clear that negative party identification towards the PRR is not simply the bipolar opposite of positive partisanship towards the PRR. Overall, these three profiles (ideological, democratic, and socio-demographic) explain 30% of the general variation of PRR positive partisans. Moreover, the fact that statistical relations comparing Full Model All and Full Model – for positive and negative partisanships – are similar gives us more confidence about the robustness of the findings.

What can we learn from this evidence about the different profiles of those who have positive and negative partisanship towards the PRR in Western Europe? The logistic regressions provided lend support for our expectation that PRR positive and negative identifiers should be thought of as constituencies with very different ideological, democratic and socio-demographic backgrounds. Even though both constituencies are not complete opposites, they are very distinctive in key issues, which have important consequences for the prospects of liberal democracy in Western Europe. On the one hand, PRR positive identifiers are inclined to the right-wing populist camp, are at odds with both European integration and immigration, are inclined to socially conservative values, endorse an illiberal understanding of democracy, and do not support democracy as the most preferable political regime. On the other hand, PRR negative identifiers are inclined to the left-wing camp, are in favour of both European integration and immigration, show preferences for the electoral, liberal and social-democratic dimensions of democracy, are at odds with the direct democratic model, and are supportive of the democratic regime despite their dissatisfaction with it. The finding that PRR positive partisans in Western Europe are averse to the liberal democratic regime and that tend to object democracy as preferable regime is in line with a significant body of literature that empirically assesses the characteristic of PRR voters.[57] However, the empirical evidence about those exhibiting a negative identity towards the PRR is quite novel, since we are able to demonstrate that in Western Europe there is a constituency of roughly half electorate that dislikes this party family and strongly supports liberal democracy despite its dissatisfaction with the ways in which the democratic regime is working. This is certainly a significant indicator of democratic resilience, because the ceiling for the PRR is related to the rejection of various of its core principles, such as anti-immigration, illiberalism and Euroscepticism, by a large part of the Western European electorate.

3.3. Analysing the impact of positive vis-à-vis negative partisanship towards the PRR on turnout

In the previous section we showed that citizens with positive and negative identities towards the PRR constitute two different constituencies, which each have their own views on what democracy means and how should it operate in Western Europe. The very fact that those who have an aversion towards the PRR have strong liberal-democratic credentials is good news for Western Europe, because it gives ground to think that there is a clear electoral ceiling for the PRR. However, to better examine the validity of this argument, we undertake an additional empirical test in this last section of the paper, namely, we explore the impact of having a positive versus a negative partisanship towards the PRR on declared turnout. By undertaking this additional analysis, we are able to see the extent to which positive and negative partisanship towards the PRR leads to the mobilization of the electorate. In theory, one can expect that not only those who like the PRR, but also that those who dislike the PRR would go to the polls: while the former should do this to support the party that they love, the latter should do this to avoid that the party that they hate becoming too strong.[58] The key question is, then, which type of partisanship has a stronger effect on turnout. Put shortly, the greater the impact of negative partisanship towards the PRR on turnout, the stronger the electoral ceiling for the PRR should be and therefore the safer democracy in Western Europe is.

It is worth emphasizing that the 2019 elections for the European Parliament are particularly interesting in this regard, since they reached the highest voter turnout in two decades: half of eligible voters casted their ballots.[59] To empirically analyse the impact of positive and negative partisanship towards the PRR on turnout, we performed binary logistic regression models – with fixed effects to control for potential country effects – considering responses about electoral participation in the upcoming European Parliament elections (1 = those who responded that they *will definitely vote* on those elections). We included ideological self-positioning and regular socio-demographic factors as control variables. The result of the analysis indicates that both PRR positive and negative partisanships are positively related to the intention to vote in the next elections, but the effect is stronger for those having a positive identity towards the PRR than for those having a negative identity towards the PRR (see Annex C, see supplemental data).

Figure 3 shows the predicted probabilities of a respondent's intention to vote in upcoming elections by PRR positive and negative partisanship, holding all covariates constant at their means or modes (see Models 5 and 6 in Annex C, see supplemental data). On the one hand, the probability of declaring to vote increases by nearly 9% between respondents who hold a PRR positive partisanship from those who do not hold it. On the other hand, the probability of declaring to vote increases by 4% between respondents who hold a PRR negative partisanship from those who do not hold it. Respondents who hold a PRR positive partisanship have a 83% predicted probability of voting in upcoming elections, while those who hold a PRR negative partisanship have a 76% of predicted probability of doing it.[60] Although both PRR positive and negative partisans are electorally mobilized, the level of mobilization among the latter

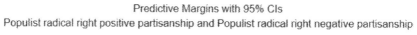
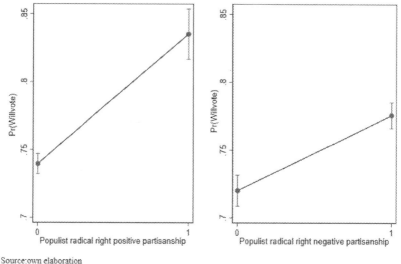

Figure 3. Predictive margins of intention to vote by populist radical right positive partisanship (left-hand panel) and populist radical right negative partisanship (right-hand panel)

group is lower. By contrast, PRR positive identifiers not only seem to be more prone to vote but it is also clear that they have one electoral option that find extremely attractive, the PRR. This means that the electoral ceiling for the PRR depends on the ability of existing political parties to raise awareness of the dangers that the PRR poses for the post-war consensus on what democracy means and how it should work in Western Europe, so that those eligible to vote actually end up going to the polls. In other words, the activation and mobilization of negative partisanship towards the PRR is crucial to strengthening the electoral ceiling for the PRR.

4. Conclusions

In this contribution we have brought to the fore the concept and measurement of negative partisanship, since they help us to understand that voters develop deep antipathies towards certain political parties. The empirical analysis reveals at least two interesting patterns. On the one hand, approximately 10 percent of the Western European electorate has a positive identity towards the PRR, and that group is distinguished by authoritarian and illiberal tendencies. On the other hand, approximately 50 percent of the Western European electorate has a negative identity towards the PRR, and that group is characterized by the defense of both immigration and European integration, as well as the promotion of the electoral, liberal and social-democratic dimensions of democracy.

This why we argue in this contribution that both the large amount of PRR negative identifiers and their democratic proclivities can be interpreted as a sign of democratic resilience in Western Europe. Nevertheless, the evidence also demonstrates that those who have a negative identity towards the PRR are less mobilized than those who have a positive identity towards the PRR. Part of the reason for this lies in the fact that those who dislike the PRR have very heterogenous electoral preferences (from PRL to conservative parties). This means that the effective politicization of PRR negative partisanship by the existing political parties depends on how they can overcome collective action problems in order to support a unique opposition towards the PRR. By looking at the empirical results presented above, one possibility of building a broad political coalition against the PRR could lie in the capacity of politicizing those issues that are relevant for those who dislike the PRR, namely support for immigration, liberal values, the European Union as well as electoral, liberal and social-democratic understandings of the democratic regime. The electoral ceiling of PRR parties depends then not only in their own (in)capacity to develop a "reputational shield" against accusations of racism and extremism,[61] but also from the ability of mainstream parties to mobilize all those who reject the PRR.

Given that studies on negative partisanship are still in their infancy in Western Europe, we would like to close this contribution by pointing out ideas for the future research agenda on negative partisanship towards the PRR and its impact on democratic resilience. Without the aim of providing a detailed discussion, we think that four ideas are particularly worth exploring. First, in this contribution we have developed a cross-national analysis, because this way it is easier to make an interpretation for Western Europe as a whole and also because the data employed comes from a survey that was done to study the positions of voters for the 2019 European Parliament election. However, there are good reasons to think that there are important differences between West European countries when it comes to studying negative partisanship towards the PRR. For instance, in a recent article Caramani and Manucci[62] have shown that the electoral performance of the PRR depends on the type of re-elaboration of countries' national past and their collective memories. Therefore, it would be interesting to analyse if the size of negative partisanship towards the PRR hinges on the types of collective memories that countries have developed over time.

Second, the analysis we offer here shows that both those having a positive identity as well as those having negative identity towards the PRR are mobilized, but the former seem to be more willing to participate in the elections than the latter. This finding suggests that the politicization of positive and negative partisanship towards the PRR is one factor among several that can influence the actual electoral ceiling of the PRR. Future research can explore other factors that can impact the raising or lowering of the electoral ceiling of the PRR, such as the actions of the PRR itself (e.g. its capacity to build a "reputational shield" to distance itself from extremism and racism) as well as contextual situations (e.g. economic downturns, immigration crises, etc.).

Third, the empirical study we offer here is focused on one single measure in time, and in consequence, we do not know how stable the size of both positive and negative partisanship towards the PRR are. To deal with this question, future studies should provide new empirical evidence on positive and negative partisanship towards the PRR and it would be particularly relevant to generate longitudinal data on this topic. Fourth and finally, the PRR is not exclusively a Western European phenomenon. This party family also exists in Eastern Europe and the rise of presidents such as Donald Trump in the United States and Jair Bolsonaro in Brazil demonstrates the PRR is becoming a global phenomenon with problematic consequences for democracy.[63] Therefore, scholars from other regions would do well to employ existing datasets or generate new ones to empirically assess not only the size of negative

Notes

1. Mudde, *Populist Radical Right Parties in Europe*; Mudde, "The Populist Radical Right"; Mudde, "Three Decades of Populist Radical Right Parties in Western Europe".
2. Mudde and Rovira Kaltwasser, *Populism*.
3. See introduction to this special issue, Lührmann and Merkel.
4. Mudde, *The Far Right Today*; Rydgren, *The Oxford Handbook of the Radical Right*; Wodak *The Politics of Fear*.
5. Dennison and Geddes, "A Rising Tide?".
6. Harteveld and Ivarsflaten, "Why Women Avoid the Radical Right".
7. Gidron and Hall, "The Politics of Social Status"; Mudde and Rovira Kaltwasser, "Studying Populism in Comparative Perspective"; Rydgren, *Class Politics and the Radical Right Right*.
8. Meléndez and Rovira Kaltwasser, "Political Identities".
9. Abramowitz and Webster, "The Rise of Negative Partisanship and Nationalization"; Abramowitz and Webster, "Negative Partisanship"; Medeiros and Noel, "The Forgotten Side of Partisanship"; Bankert, "Negative and Positive Partisanship".
10. Iyengar, Lelkes, Levendysky, Malhotra, and Westwood, "The Origins and Consequences of Affective Polarization".
11. Samuels and Zucco, *Partisans, Antipartisans, and Nonpartisans*.
12. A notable exceptions is Mayer "How Negative Partisanship Affects Voting Behavior in Europe".
13. Rovira Kaltwasser, Vehrkamp and Wratil, *Europe's Choice*.
14. Mudde, *Populist Radical Right Parties in Europe*.
15. Bale and Rovira Kaltwasser, *Riding the Populist Wave*.
16. Mudde, *The Far Right Today*; Rydgren, *The Oxford Handbook of the Radical Right*; Wodak, *The Politics of Fear*.
17. Akkerman, De Lange and Rooduijn, *Radical Right-Wing Populist Parties*;
18. A list of the parties included can be found in the appendix. The electoral data for the parties was collected from the ParlGov database (www.parlogov.org) and the European Journal of Political Research (ECPR) Political Data Yearbook.
19. Rydgren, *The Oxford Handbook of the Radical Right*.
20. Mayer, "The Radical Right in France".
21. Harteveld and Ivarsflaten, "Why Women Avoid the Radical Right"; Ivarsflaten, Blinder and Bjånesøy, "How and Why the Populist Radical Right Persuades Citizens".
22. Medeiros and Noel, "The Forgotten Side of Partisanship"; Samuels and Zucco, *Partisans, Antipartisans, and Nonpartisans*.
23. Baumeister et al., "Bad is Stronger than Good".
24. Meléndez and Rovira Kaltwasser, "Political Identities".
25. Medeiros and Noel, "The Forgotten Side of Partisanship"; Caruana et al., "The Power of the Dark Side".
26. Zhon et al., "Negational Categorization and Intergroup Behavior".
27. Huddy, "From Social to Political Identity".
28. Huddy et al. "Expressive Partisanship".
29. Bankert, "Negative and Positive Partisanship".
30. Brewer, "The Psychology of Prejudice".
31. Caruana et al., "The Power of the Dark Side".
32. Mayer, "Howe Negative Partisanship Affects Voting Behavior in Europe", 3.
33. Mayer, "How Negative Partisanship Affects Voting Behavior", 2.
34. Abramowitz and Webster, "The Rise of Negative Partisanship and Nationalization"; Abramowitz and Webster, "Negative Partisanship"; Iyengar et al., "The Origins and Consequences of Affective Polarization."
35. Caruana et al., "The Power of the Dark Side"; Medeiros and Noel, "The Forgotten Side of Partisanship".

36. Two notable exceptions are the work of Mayer, "How Negative Partisanship Affects Voting Behavior", and Spoon and Kanthak, "He's not my Prime Minister!".
37. More details about the survey data can be found in Rovira Kaltwasser, Vehrkamp and Wratil, *Europe's Choice.*
38. We are aware of the limitations of measuring party identifications in one point in time in order to tackle its temporal stability. However, previous research on negative partisanship by party families in Europe shows similar percentages of partisans' support and dislikes. See Mayer, "How Negative Partisanship Affects Voting Behavior".
39. Rose and Mishler, "Negative and Positive Party Identification"; Samuels and Zucco, *Partisans, Antipartisans, and Nonpartisans.*
40. Richardson, "European Party Loyalties Revisited."
41. Meléndez and Rovira Kaltwasser, "Political Identities".
42. Bankert, "Negative and Positive Partisanship".
43. To test this argument in detail, one would need longitudinal data, which unfortunately does not exist for Western Europe. However, it is not far-fetched to suggest that the more radical a political party becomes, the more polarization generates, thereby fostering positive and negative feelings that are not short-lived but rather enduring. Seen in this light, if PRR parties in Western Europe continue to radicalize, this can certainly reinforce negative partisanship against them.
44. We provide a list of the political parties included in each of these party families in Annex A, see supplemental data. It is worth noting that the survey data we use in this paper is for ten Western European countries, including the case of Greece, where one can find an extreme right party: Golden Dawn. We are aware that the academic literature makes the distinction between populist radical right parties and extreme right parties: while the former are nominally democratic, the latter are openly undemocratic. Nevertheless, we decided to include the case of Golden Dawn in our analysis of positive and negative partisanship towards the PRR, since this permit us to consider the Greek case study and therefore bring more variety to the research design.
45. Mayer, "How Negative Partisanship Affects Voting Behavior"; Caruana et al., "The Power of the Dark Side".
46. Rose and Mishler, "Negative and Positive Party Identification," 230–1.
47. Boese et al., "How Democracies Prevail".
48. Van Hauwaert and van Kessel, "Beyond Protest and Discontent".
49. We performed factorial analysis in order to build the corresponding indexes. We proceeded with orthogonal varimax rotation method. In the Populist Index, all items load heavily on the coalescing factor. The State/Market Index originally included 5 items, after factor analysis we dropped one item. The Conservative/Liberal Index originally included 5 items, and after factor analysis we dropped two items. The Immigration Index maintained their original item-compositions. The item-composition of the Populist Index and Immigration Index are based theoretically based on previous research (e.g. Meléndez and Rovira Kaltwasser, "Political identities", van Hauwaert and van Kessel, "Beyond protest and discontent"). State/Market and Conservative/Liberal indexes were modified empirically according to factor analysis results. We considered it appropriate to proceed by an exploratory technique in the latter cases, since the literature has employed diverse measurements to capture left-right preferences in economic and socio-cultural realms. For a detailed analysis of the items included in this ideological profile, see Annex A, see supplemental data.
50. Ferrín and Kriesi, *How Europeans View and Evaluate Democracy.*
51. We performed factorial analysis – orthogonal varimax rotation method – in order to build the corresponding indexes. All indexes kept their original item-composition. For a detailed analysis of the items included in this democratic profile, see Annex A, see supplemental data.
52. For fixed-effects models we arbitrarily took Spain as the reference case in order to control for potential country effects.
53. Ivarsflaten, "What Unites Right-wing Populists in Western Europe?"; Mudde, *Populist Radical Right Parties in Europe*; Mudde, "Three Decades of Populist Radical Right Parties"; Oesch, "Explaining Workers' Support"; van Hauwaert and van Kessel, "Beyond Protest and Discontent".

54. Akkerman, De Lange and Rooduijn, *Radical Right-Wing Populist Parties in Western Europe*; Häusermann, Picot and Geering, "Rethinking Party Politics and the Welfare State"; Schumacher and Van Kersbergen, "Do Mainstream Parties Adapt".
55. Gidron and Hall, "The Politics of Social Status"; Mudde and Rovira Kaltwasser, "Studying Populism in Comparative Perspective"; Rooduijn and Burgoon, "The Paradox of Well-being".
56. Dahlberg, Linde and Holmberg, "Democratic Discontent in Old and New Democracies"; Norris, *Democratic Deficit.*
57. Mudde, "The Populist Radical Right"; Mudde, "Three Decades of Populist Radical Right Parties in Western Europe".
58. Immerzeel and Pickup, "Populist Radical Right Parties Mobilizing 'the People'?".
59. Since 1979 turnout for the European Parliament elections has been steadily dropping, going from almost 62% in that year, down to a historic low of 42.6% in 2014. For more details on this, see Rovira Kaltwasser, Vehrkamp and Wratil, *Europe's Choice*, 8–9.
60. It is worth indicating that previous research has shown that results on questions about declared participation in elections tend to be inflated because of social desirability bias. This problem might be probably stronger for those with negative partisanship towards the PRR than for those with positive partisanship towards the PRR, since the latter do a have clear electoral preference (i.e. voting for the PRR), while the former have many different electoral preferences (i.e. voting for any party besides the PRR, including the option of abstaining or casting a blank/null vote). For more information about the social desirability bias in measuring turnout via surveys, see Jeffrey A. Karp and David Brockington, "Social Desirability and Response Validity", as well as, Allyson L. Hoolbrook and Jon A. Krosnick, "Social Desirability Bias in Voter Turnout Reports".
61. Harteveld and Ivarsflaten, "Why Women Avoid the Radical Right"; Ivarsflaten, Blinder and Bjånesøy, "How and Why the Populist Radical Right Persuades Citizens".
62. Caramani and Manucci, "National Past and Populism".
63. Mudde, *The Far Right Today.*

Disclosure statement

No potential conflict of interest was reported by the author(s).

Funding

This work was supported by Carlos Meléndez acknowledges support from the Centre for Social Conflict and Cohesion Studies (CONICYT/FONDAP/151330009) and Fondo Nacional de Desarrollo Científico y Tecnológico (FONDECYT Project 1161262). Cristóbal Rovira Kaltwasser acknowledges support from Fondo Nacional de Desarrollo Científico y Tecnológico (FONDECYT Project 1180020), the Centre for Social Conflict and Cohesion Studies - COES (ANID / FONDAP / 15130009) and the Observatory for Socioeconomic Transformations (ANID / PCI / Max Planck Institute for the Study of Societies / MPG190012).

References

Abramowitz, Alan, and Steven Webster. "The Rise of Negative Partisanship and Nationalization of U.S. Elections in the 21st Century." *Electoral Studies* 41 (2016): 12–22.

Abramowitz, Alan, and Steven Webster. "Negative Partisanship: Why Americans Dislike Parties but Behave Like Rabid Partisans." *Advances in Political Pyschology* 39, no. S1 (2018): 119–135.

Akkerman, Tjitske, Sarah de Lange, and Matthijs Rooduijn. eds. *Radical Right-Wing Populist Parties in Western Europe*. London: Routledge, 2016.

Bale, Tim, and Cristóbal Rovira Kaltwasser. eds. *Riding the Populist Wave: Europe's Mainstream Right in Crisis*. Cambridge: Cambridge University Press, 2021.

Bankert, Alexa. "Negative and Positive Partisanship in the 2016 U.S. Presidential Elections." *Political Behavior* (2020). https://doi.org/10.1007/s11109-020-09599-1

Bankert, Alexa, Leonie Huddy, and Martin Rosema. "Measuring Partisanship as Social Identity in Multi-Party Systems." *Political Behavior* 39 (2017): 103–132.

Baumeister, Roy, Ellen Bratslavsky, Catrin Finkenauer, and Kathleen D. Vohs. "Bad is Stronger Than Good." *Review of General Psychology* 5 (2001): 323–370.

Brewer, Marilynn. "The Psychology of Prejudice: Ingroup Love or Outgroup Hate?" *Journal of Social Issues* 55, no. 3 (1999): 429–444.

Boese, Vanessa A., Amanda B. Edgell, Sebastian Hellmeier, Seraphine F. Maerz, and Staffan Lindberg. "How Democracies Prevail: Democratic Resilience as a Two-Stage Process." *Democratization* (Forthcoming).

Caramani, Daniele, and Luca Manucci. "National Past and Populism: the re-Elaboration of Fascism and its Impact on Right-Wing Populism in Western Europe." *West European Politics* 42, no. 6 (2019): 1159–1187.

Caruana, Nicholas, R. Michel McGregor, and Laura B. Stephenson. "The Power of the Dark Side: Negative Partisanship and Political Behavior in Canada." *Canadian Journal of Political Science* 48, no. 3 (2014): 3–24.

Chen-Bo, Zhong, Katherine W. Philips, Geoffrey J. Leonardelli, and Adam D. Galinsky. "Negational Categorization and Intergroup Behavior." *Personality and Social Psychology Bulletin* 34 (2008): 793–806.

Dahlberg, Stefan, Jonas Linde, and Sören Holmberg. "Democratic Discontent in Old and New Democracies: Assessing the Importance of Democratic Input and Governmental Output." *Political Studies* 63, no. S1 (2015): 18–37.

Dennison, James, and Andrew Geddes. "A Rising Tide? The Salience of Immigration and the Rise of Anti-Immigration Political Parties in Western Europe." *The Political Quarterly* 90, no. 1 (2019): 107–116.

Ferrín, Mónica, and Hanspeter Kriesi. *How Europeans View and Evaluate Democracy*. Oxford: Oxford University Press, 2016.

Gidron, Noam, and Peter A. Hall. "The Politics of Social Status: Economic and Cultural Roots of the Populist Radical Right." *British Journal of Sociology* 68, no. S1 (2017): 57–84.

Greene, Steven. "Social Identity Theory and Party Identification." *Social Science Quarterly* 85, no. 1 (2004): 136–153.

Harteveld, Eelco, and Elisabeth Ivarsflaten. "Why Women Avoid the Radical Right: Internalized Norms and Party Reputations." *British Journal of Political Science* 48, no. 2 (2018): 369–384.

Häusermann, Silja, Georg Picot, and Dominik Geering. "Rethinking Party Politics and the Welfare State–Recent Advances in the Literature." *British Journal of Political Science* 43, no. 1 (2013): 221–240.

Hoolbrook, Allyson L., and Jon A. Krosnick. "Social Desirability Bias in Voter Turnout Reports: Tests Using the Item Count Technique." *Public Opinion Quarterly* 74, no. 1 (2010): 37–67.

Huddy, Leonie. "From Social to Political Identity: A Critical Examination of Social Identity Theory." *Political Psychology* 22, no. 1 (2001): 127–156.

Huddy, Leonie, Lilliana Mason, and Lene Aaroe. "Expressive Partisanship: Campaign Involvement, Political Emotions, and Partisan Identity." *American Political Science Review* 109, no. 1 (2015): 1–17.

Immerzeel, Tim, and Mark Pickup. "Populist Radical Right Parties Mobilizing 'the People'? The Role of Populist Radical Right Success in Voter Turnout." *Electoral Studies* 40 (2015): 347–360.

Ivarsflaten, Elisabeth. "What Unites Right-Wing Populists in Western Europe? Re-Examining Grievance Mobilization Models in Seven Successful Cases." *Comparative Political Studies* 41, no. 1 (2008): 3–23.

Ivarsflaten, Elisabeth, Scott Blinder, and Lise Bjånesøy. "How and Why the Populist Radical Right Persuades Citizens." In *The Oxford Handbook of Electoral Persuasion*, edited by Elizabeth Suhay, Bernard Grofman, and Alexander H. Trechsel, 815–838. Oxford: Oxford University Press, 2020.

Iyengar, Shanto, Yphtach Lelkes, Matthew Levendusky, Neil Malhotra, and Sean J. Westwood. "The Origins and Consequences of Affective Polarization in the United States." *Annual Review of Political Science* 22 (2019): 129–146.

Karp, Jeffrey A., and David Brockington. "Social Desirability and Response Validity: A Comparative Analysis of Overreporting Voter Turnout in Five Countries." *The Journal of Politics* 67, no. 3 (2005): 825–840.

Mayer, Nonna. "The Radical Right in France." In *The Oxford Handbook of the Radical Right*, edited by Jens Rydgren, 433–451. Oxford: Oxford University Press, 2018.

Mayer, Sabrina. "How Negative Partisanship Affects Voting Behavior in Europe: Evidence from an Analysis of 17 European Multi-Party Systems with Proportional Voting." *Research and Politics* 4, no. 1 (2017): 1–7.

Medeiros, Mike, and Alain Noël. "The Forgotten Side of Partisanship: Negative Party Identification in Four Anglo-American Democracies." *Comparative Political Studies* 47, no. 7 (2013): 1022–1046.

Meléndez, Carlos, and Cristóbal Rovira Kaltwasser. "Political Identities: The Missing Link in the Study of Populism." *Party Politics* 25, no. 4 (2019): 520–533.

Mudde, Cas. *Populist Radical Right Parties in Europe*. New York: Cambridge University Press, 2007.

Mudde, Cas. "The Populist Radical Right: A Pathological Normalcy." *West European Politics* 33, no. 6 (2010): 1167–1186.

Mudde, Cas. "Three Decades of Populist Radical Right Parties in Western Europe: So What?" *European Journal of Political Research* 52, no. 1 (2013): 1–19.

Mudde, Cas. *The Far Right Today*. London: Polity Press, 2019.

Mudde, Cas, and Cristóbal Rovira Kaltwasser. *Populism. A Very Short Introduction*. Oxford: Oxford University Press, 2017.

Mudde, Cas and Cristóbal Rovira Kaltwasser. "Studying Populism in Comparative Perspective: Reflections on the Contemporary and Future Research Agenda." *Comparative Political Studies* 51, no. 13 (2018): 1667–1693.

Müller, Jan-Werner. *What is Populism?* Philadelphia: Pennsylvania University Press, 2016.

Norris, Pipa. *Democratic Deficit: Critical Citizens Revisited*. Cambridge: Cambridge University Press, 2011.

Oesch, Daniel. "Explaining Workers' Support for Right-Wing Populist Parties in Western Europe: Evidence from Austria, Belgium, France, Norway, and Switzerland." *International Political Science Review* 29, no. 3 (2008): 349–373.

Richardson, Bradley. "European Party Loyalties Revisited." *American Political Science Review* 85, no. 3 (1991): 751–775.

Rose, Richard, and William Mishler. "Negative and Positive Party Identification in Post-Communist Countries." *Electoral Studies* 17, no. 2 (1998): 217–234.

Rovira Kaltwasser, Cristóbal, Robert Vehrkamp, and Christopher Wratil. *Europe's Choice. Populist Attitudes and Voting Intentions in the 2019 European Election*. Gütersloh: Bertelsmann Foundation, 2019.

Rooduijn, Matthijs, and Brian Burgoon. "The Paradox of Well-Being: Do Unfavorable Socioeconomic and Sociocultural Contexts Deepen or Dampen Radical Left and Right Voting Among the Less Well-Off?" *Comparative Political Studies* 51, no. 13 (2018): 1720–1753.

Rydgren, Jens. ed. *Class Politics and the Radical Right Right*. Abingdon: Routledge, 2013.

Rydgren, Jens. ed. *The Oxford Handbook of the Radical Right*. Oxford: Oxford University Press, 2018.

Samuels, David, and Cesar Zucco. *Partisans, Antipartisans, and Nonpartisans*. Cambridge: Cambridge University Press, 2018.

Schumacher, Gijs, and Kees van Kersbergen. "Do Mainstream Parties Adapt to the Welfare Chauvinism of Populist Parties?" *Party Politics* 22, no. 3 (2016): 300–312.

Spoon, Jae-Jae, and Kristin Kanthak. "He's not my Prime Minister! Negative Party Identification and Satisfaction with Democracy." *Journal of Elections, Public Opinion and Parties* 29, no. 4 (2019): 511–532.

Van Hauwaert, Steven, and Stijn van Kessel. "Beyond Protest and Discontent: a Cross-National Analysis of the Effect of Populist Attitudes and Issue Positions on Populist Party Support." *European Journal of Political Research* 57, no. 1 (2018): 68–92.

Wodak, Ruth. *The Politics of Fear. What Right-Wing Populist Discourses Mean.* London: Sage, 2015.

The supply and demand model of civic education: evidence from a field experiment in the Democratic Republic of Congo

Steven E. Finkel and Junghyun Lim

ABSTRACT
Can democratic orientations and political participation in fragile democracies be fostered through civic education? Early evaluation work reported generally positive effects, though recent work has been more skeptical, with some studies reporting negative impacts of civic education on political engagement through highlighting the poor performance of incumbents and ongoing political processes. In this article, we report the results of a field experiment using an encouragement design to assess the *Voter Opinion and Involvement through Civic Education* (VOICE) programme conducted in 2010-2011 in the Democratic Republic of Congo. We adapt Bratton and Mattes' (2007) "supply and demand" model of democratic support to the case of civic education, and derive hypotheses regarding expected impacts of *VOICE* on a series of democratic orientations and political participation. The results show that the *VOICE* programme had *negative* effects on support for the decentralization process and on individuals' satisfaction with democracy in the DRC, and *positive* effects on non-electoral participation as well as on democratic orientations such as knowledge, efficacy, and political tolerance. We suggest that this pattern of effects has positive normative implications, and that civic education programmes continue to have the potential to deepen democratic engagement and values, even in fragile or backsliding democratic settings.

Introduction

Can democratic orientations and political participation in fragile democracies be fostered through civic education? The importance of supportive democratic orientations for the consolidation and resilience of democratic regimes has long been noted by political scientists, with compelling cross-national evidence recently demonstrated by Claasen.[1] In this regard, international donors such as USAID, UNDP and the World Bank have devoted considerable resources over the past several decades to civic education programmes designed to promote democratic political culture and mobilize political participation.

Ⓑ Supplemental data for this article can be accessed https://doi.org/10.1080/13510347.2020.1843156.

Early evaluation work, in diverse settings in Africa, Latin America and Eastern Europe, reported generally positive effects of exposure to donor-sponsored adult civic education on political participation, and in some cases, impact on important orientations such as efficacy and political tolerance as well.[2] Recent work, however, has been more sceptical. Some studies report either null effects[3] or unintended *negative* impacts, with new information potentially exacerbating pre-existing resource-based disparities in participation[4] or depressing participation and political support by highlighting the poor performance of incumbents and ongoing political processes.[5]

In this article, we join this controversy by reporting the results of a field experiment from a 2011-2012 evaluation of a donor-sponsored civic education programme conducted in the Democratic Republic of Congo (DRC), a country ranked consistently in the lower tier of African democracies. The *Voter Opinion and Involvement through Civic Education* (VOICE) programme consisted of community workshops using a series of images ("*Boite à Images*") to stimulate discussion and awareness about an ongoing decentralization reform, and more generally about democracy and the role of the citizen in the democratic processes. We employed an "encouragement design" in eight villages where the *VOICE* workshops took place by randomly inviting a subset of individuals interviewed in baseline surveys to attend the events, and gauging the impact of encouragement, and of actual attendance at the workshop via an instrumental variable strategy, on changes in a series of democratic attitudes and behaviours over time.

The results show support for both sides of the civic education debate. We find substantial *negative* effects of the *VOICE* programme on support for the decentralization process as well as on individuals' satisfaction with democracy in the DRC: as individuals became aware of ideal democratic processes and the stalled implementation associated with the institutional reform, the less satisfied they were with the process and with current system performance more generally. At the same time, we find significant positive effects of the programme on non-electoral political participation, as well as on other important democratic orientations such as political efficacy, political tolerance, support for individual rights, and support for decentralization as a normative policy ideal. We explain this pattern by adapting Bratton and Mattes' "supply and demand" model of democratic support to the case of civic education.[6] We argue that in poorly functioning regimes the effects of civic education on *demand* for democratic governance are likely to diverge substantially from perceptions of current democratic *supply*. We suggest that this pattern of effects has positive normative implications, and that properly implemented civic education programmes continue to have the potential to deepen democratic engagement, values and, ultimately, political accountability, even in fragile or backsliding democratic settings.[7]

Literature review and the "Supply and Demand" model of civic education

Civic education programmes, designed to promote political knowledge, engagement, and democratic norms and values among ordinary citizens, have been an important component of democracy promotion among international donors in the post-Cold War period.[8] These programmes are usually conducted via partnerships between donors and civil society organizations, and encompass a variety of interventions designed, for example, to encourage voter participation, increase the ability of citizens to hold incumbent politicians accountable, promote the non-violent resolution of political disputes, and educate individuals about supportive democratic values such as political and social tolerance.[9]

The first assessments of whether civic education had attitudinal or behavioural impacts on the individuals who took part in the programmes' activities were conducted in the mid-to-late 1990s by Bratton *et al.* in Zambia,[10] and Finkel in the Dominican Republic, Poland, and South Africa.[11] Over the subsequent decade, USAID sponsored two larger-scale assessments in Kenya, the National Civic Education Programme (NCEP I) from 2001-2002, a nation-wide programme conducted during the run-up to the 2002 "democratic breakthrough" national elections,[12] and the similar Kenya NCEP II ("Uraia") programme conducted in the run-up to the disputed 2007 election that triggered massive ethnic violence in its wake.[13] Other work during this decade was undertaken in connection with programmes related to constitution-building and literacy in Uganda and Senegal.[14]

While these studies produced a range of findings, the overall pattern of results was optimistic regarding the potential of civic education to produce positive democratic outcomes. In the USAID-sponsored programmes evaluated by Finkel,[15] there were relatively strong effects on local-level participation, political knowledge and efficacy, and weaker, though detectable effects on democratic values, social trust, political tolerance, and support for democratic regimes.[16] The positive effects on participation were echoed in Kuenzi,[17] and virtually all of the studies found substantial effects on knowledge and often other indicators of civic competence and psychological engagement.[18] Even in the backsliding context of Kenya in 2007, civic education seemed able to promote resilience and support for democracy.[19]

Over the past decade, however, the number of evaluations of civic education interventions has increased markedly, with the evidence being much more mixed in terms of their effectiveness. Some studies have assessed the impact of civic education information campaigns on voting based on incumbent performance as opposed to ethnic or clientelistic grounds. Some report positive effects,[20] though others show null findings. Information provided to individuals about corrupt incumbents in settings ranging from India[21] to Benin[22] to Sao Tome and Principe seemed unable to spur public goods-oriented voting behaviour.[23]

Perhaps even more troubling are studies pointing to null or *negative* effects of civic information campaigns on social and political participation. To be sure, some positive effects of targeted mobilization and election-security programmes have been reported.[24] But many evaluations have produced the opposite. Chong *et al.*, for example, find that as voters exposed to corruption-oriented accountability information appeared to withdraw more generally from the electoral process, while Vincente similarly found that exposure to an anti-vote buying campaign decreased turnout[25]. Gottlieb shows that a civic education programme on democratic rights in Mali decreased turnout especially among women, thus exacerbating pre-existing gender disparities in political participation, while John and Sjoberg's evaluation of a Kenyan accountability programme produced lower intentions to turnout and contact representatives among individuals aligned with opposition parties. [26]

Further, civic education programmes outside of the electoral arena have also reported null or negative effects on participation. Lieberman *et al* find no effects of an information campaign designed to increase collective action related to the school system in Kenya.[27] Similarly, Sexton reports that participation in workshops related to democratic accountability and decentralization in Peru led to significant decreases among treated individuals in subsequent participatory budgeting activities, along with significant increases in support for civil unrest as a means for sanctioning poorly performing local governments.[28]

How can the divergent findings from these studies be explained? Certainly, early observational studies had limitations in terms of the causal identification of civic education treatments. But the recent advent of experimental methods in the field has nevertheless not produced scholarly consensus. Similarly, while recent work has been conducted more frequently in post-conflict settings as well as in electoral autocracies, conflicting findings have been reported in countries that are similar in terms of democratic development. We argue that at least a partial reconciliation of the findings of these literatures stems from the fact that civic education can have vastly different effects on what Bratton and Mattes term perceptions of the "supply" and "demand" for democracy in a particular context.[29] According to this model, democratic regimes are sustained through widespread public *demand* for democracy as a preferred form of government, along with the public's perception that the system is providing an adequate *supply* of democracy as well, i.e. institutions which enact laws, protect individual freedoms, and deliver public services effectively. We contend that civic education conducted in fragile, poorly functioning democratic contexts may increase individuals' demand for democracy while simultaneously decreasing their perceptions of democratic supply. That is, while civic education is designed to further positive support for democracy, democratic norms and values, or the "demand" for democratic governance, it may also have the effect of generating more acute perceptions of the regime's deficiencies in supplying effective, transparent, and impartial governance. Differential effects are to be expected then, depending on whether a particular study is assessing the impact of civic education on variables related to each of these dimensions of democratic political orientations.

Why should civic education interventions lead to these differing impacts? First, as individuals become generally more informed and politically aware as a result of civic education, they should naturally become more attuned to the objective deficiencies of the performance of the political system in poorly functioning regimes. And because cognitive awareness is also consistently related to support for democracy and political engagement,[30] we should therefore expect to observe differential effects of civic education on orientations related to democratic "demand" and "supply". Relatedly, as civic education induces positive changes in demand for democracy, this is likely to raise the standard or "reference point" that individuals use to gauge incumbent and regime performance[31]. This itself will then lead to greater discrepancies between perceived democratic ideals ("demand") and ongoing democratic practices ("supply"), especially in contexts with poor quality governance and weak democratic institutions.[32] Finally, these differential impacts are also plausibly related to the kinds of "good governance" civil society organizations which typically implement civic education programmes in emerging democracies; these groups " ... are often antagonistic toward governments that are perceived to be insufficiently democratic, insufficiently responsive to ordinary individuals, and hostile to democratic reforms".[33] Generating positive effects among individuals in support for democracy and democratic ideals, coupled with heightened awareness of the shortcomings of the regime in delivering democratic change, is precisely what these organizations attempt to accomplish through the delivery of civic education to average citizens.

We show the Supply and Demand model of the effects of democratic civic education in Figure 1. All of the dependent variables figure prominently in the decades-old rich literature on the relationship of public opinion and the stability of democratic regimes,[34] and all have been analysed as possible outcomes of civic education in previous evaluations as well.[35] The figure shows that exposure to civic education should have positive effects on two sets of indicators of "Democratic Demand": a set of *Civic Competence* variables, which includes knowledge, political efficacy, interest and civic skills; and a set of indicators for *Support for Democratic Values*, encompassing support for democracy as a political system and the rejection of non-democratic alternatives, as well as democratic values such as political tolerance, support for the non-violent resolution of conflict, and support for the exercise of democratic liberties.

At the same time, we predict a variable effect of civic education on indicators of Democratic Supply such as institutional trust and satisfaction with democracy, depending on the performance of the regime in delivering values political outcomes. In corruption-laden, clientelistic and ethnically fractured electoral autocracies and fledgling democratic regimes – such as the Democratic Republic of Congo (DRC), where this study takes place – we predict a *negative* effect of civic education on indicators of democratic supply.

The figure also depicts multiple alternative paths from exposure to civic education to participation, depending on the respective effects of democratic demand and supply on different forms of political action. It is likely that higher levels of perceived democratic supply should feed positively onto participation, especially on voting and other institutionalized forms of behaviour. This would suggest, then, a *negative* indirect effect of civic education exposure on participation via more negative overall perceptions of democratic supply. On the other hand, increases in democratic demand should also have positive effects on political engagement, which implies a *positive* indirect effect from civic education via more enhanced levels of political efficacy, knowledge, and support for democratic values.

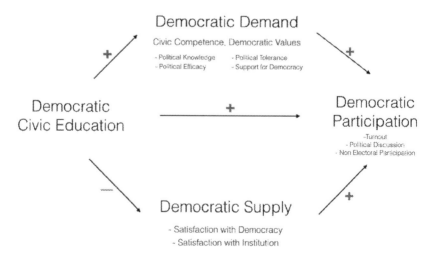

Figure 1. The Supply and Demand Model of democratic civic education.

Finally, civic education may also have direct effects on participation, over and above the indirect processes discussed thus far. In some cases, political mobilization is the ostensible purpose of the programme,[36] while in others it may be an ancillary part of the training that individuals receive from programmes providing other kinds of political information.

This model of the differential impacts of civic education on perceptions of democratic supply and democratic finds echoes in early evaluation work, for example, in Moehler's characterization of participation in Ugandan constitution-building workshops producing "distrustful democrats", that is, individuals with lower levels of institutional trust along with higher levels of political knowledge.[37] Finkel *et al.* similarly reported that civic education's effect on institutional trust was negative in late 1990s post-authoritarian Dominican Republic, where economic and political performance was extremely poor.[38] At the same time, they found positive effects of civic education on many of the indicators of democratic demand – political knowledge, efficacy, and awareness of individual rights, support for democratic values, and perceptions of civic competence.

These differential effects also resonate well with findings from more recent literature. Civic education programmes providing corruption and other performance-related information on incumbents highlight inadequacies in the supply of democracy, with concomitant withdrawal in many instances from engagement with the political process.[39] Similarly, programmes designed to promote knowledge and awareness about democratic norms and values invariably bring into focus the discrepancies between democratic ideals and the realities of current institutions and practices. As a result, these programmes produce positive effects on the former and negative effects on the latter, to the extent that the objective performance of the regime or political incumbents is poor.[40]

In sum, we derive the following hypotheses from the Supply and Demand Model of Democratic Civic Education, as they pertain to contexts with poor economic and political performance:

H1: Exposure to civic education will lead to negative impacts on indicators of Democratic Supply, such as trust in institutions and satisfaction with the contemporary democratic system.

H2: Exposure to civic education will lead to positive impacts on indicators of Democratic Demand related to both civic competence and support for democratic values.

H3: Exposure to civic education will lead to negative indirect effects on participation via its negative effects on perceptions of Democratic Supply (H3a), and positive indirect effects via its positive effects on Democratic Demand (H3b).

We assess each of these hypotheses in the context of the *VOICE* civic education programme on democracy and political decentralization implemented in the DRC between 2010-2011.

Decentralization, democratization and the *VOICE* civic education programme in the DRC

The country context

Despite the introduction of the country's first multiparty elections in 2006, democratization in the DRC has been very slow to take hold. The country's score on the widely-

108 RESILIENCE OF DEMOCRACY

used V-DEM Electoral Democracy indicator increased from .20 on a 0–1 scale before the 2006 election – reflecting a "closed" autocratic regime – to values in the .35–.40 range (.36 in 2001 at the time of our data collection) and a classification of "electoral autocracy" from 2007 onward. The country has been wracked by war, ethnic conflict and civil unrest nearly continuously since the onset of democratization, and its elections have been characterized by high levels of campaign-related violence, voter intimidation, vote-rigging and other kinds of electoral fraud.[41]

As part of the opening to democracy in 2006, the government of the DRC committed to a constitutionally mandated process of decentralization. This entailed the passage of a law on *Entites Territoriale Decentralise (ETD)*, creating 26 provinces from the existing 11 and more than 6000 subprovincial electoral constituencies from the existing 189, giving provinces more control over locally generated revenue, and establishing a fund for local development projects. The motivations behind decentralization, commonly advanced among international donors, were to bring greater accountability to existing governmental institutions, to reduce levels of economic and political inequality across different geographic regions, to enhance the inclusion of broader strata of Congolese civil society, and to provide greater input from communities into decisions related to economic development in their localities.[42]

Unfortunately, the decentralization process in the DRC advanced haphazardly, until ongoing political crises and tensions between various factions within the government effectively stalled formal implementation. At the time of our study, *de facto* changes regarding the creation of subnational administrative units and the establishment of local development funds had yet to take place.[43] There had been no further provincial elections since 2007, nor local elections that had been mandated in the *ETD*. In short, the decentralization process had been limited to formal designations of future territorial reforms, but, through mismanagement and political strife, did not extend to actual local development or political reforms, nor to changes in the revenue streams between the central, provincial and local levels of government.[44]

The civic education treatment

In this context, the international NGO International Foundation for Electoral Systems (IFES) designed and implemented the Voter Opinion and Involvement through Civic Education programme (*VOICE*) with the goal of improving the capacity of the Congolese people to participate effectively in the political process and the ongoing decentralization reforms. The *VOICE* programme consisted of a range of activities aimed at enabling ordinary citizens to better understand and engage the decentralization process and the political system more generally, motivating individuals to participate, and providing local community organizations with the capacity to implement civic and voter education campaigns. The central tool was the *Boîtes à Images* community workshop, in which facilitators used a series of "picture boxes" to illustrate aspects of decentralization and broader issues of political, economic, and democratic development to audiences of approximately 100 persons in villages throughout the country.

IFES specifically designed the use of images as a civic education delivery mechanism in order to convey messages in the DRC context, where World Bank figures indicates that adult literary reaches only 65%. These information sessions lasted roughly two hours and were conducted throughout 2010-2011 in four target provinces: Bandundu, Kantanga, Maniema, and South Kivu. Due to budget constraints, our study is limited to the *Boîtes à Images* sessions conducted during the summer of 2011 in Bandundu province.

The specific 13 *Boîtes à Images* were organized into more general "modules", corresponding to the different aspects of the civic education emphasized by the *VOICE* programmes. Two modules dominated the *Boîtes à Images* sessions under consideration here:

Module 1. Let's understand our new institutions: This module introduced concepts of decentralization in the DRC and the importance of participation in local elections and government; it explained decentralized institutions and decentralization law, the responsibilities of urban and municipal counsellors, and the responsibilities of sector and *chefferie* counsellors. Module 1's theme of understanding decentralization policy is illustrated in Figure 2a, which is Image #2 in the *Boîtes* sequence, "Decentralization in the Democratic Republic of the Congo". The figure shows the map of the 11 current provinces and a large arrow pointing to the envisioned 26 provinces (including Kinshasa) that would exist post-decentralization.

Module 2. Let's be a part of the new Congo: This module focused on the roles of the actors in the decentralization and political process (i.e. the election commission, politicians, political parties and opposition, judges, civil society), and explained the rationale for, and the benefits of democracy and active participation in civic life. Module 2's theme of political participation and civic engagement is exemplified in Figure 1b, which is Image #11, "The Role of the Citizen". This image depicts ordinary individuals engaging in various acts of political participation, including attending a community meeting, submitting a petition to an elected official, and participating in a peaceful demonstration.

The *Boîtes* sessions were designed to be highly participatory forums where active learning took place, as all of the images were accompanied by questions posed by facilitators to the audience in order to stimulate discussion and learning (e.g. "ask participants to share their experiences in participating in peaceful protests", "ask participants if they know how much revenue their entity mobilizes and what efforts have been made to develop their communities"). The discussion guide for facilitators of the *Boîtes* sessions can be found in Appendix A3.

Study design

We aim to identify the effects of exposure to the *VOICE* programme on individuals' attitudes towards democratic supply and demand as well as on political participation. We implement surveys before and after the *Boîtes* sessions to estimate the changes in individuals' attitudes between the pre- and post-treatment. The study was designed to produce a random sample of 140 individuals residing in each of eight villages where a *Boîtes à Images* event was to take place, for a total of 1120 respondents. We randomly selected eight different *groupements* in the Bandundu province of the DRC where we had knowledge that *Boîtes* events were to occur. One village was selected at random from each *groupement* as a research site, though logistical and travel difficulties made village substitutions necessary in four instances (See Table A1 in the appendix for selected villages).

Given that attendance at the *VOICE* workshops was voluntary, we could not randomly assign individuals to attend or to not attend the event. To overcome problems of self-selection bias, we implement an *encouragement design*.[45] We randomly selected

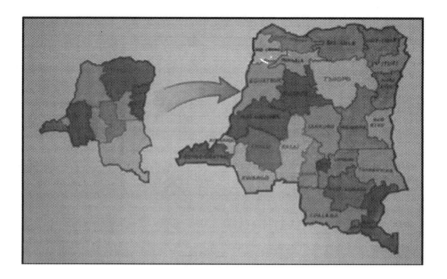

(a) Decentralization in the DRC

(b) The Role of the Citizen

Figure 2. Examples of the *VOICE* programme's *"Boîtes à Images"*.

100 of the 140 respondents in each research site and invited them at the end of the baseline interview to attend the upcoming *Boîtes à Images* event.[46] Because it is randomly assigned, the encouragement to attend a *Boîtes à Images* session is unrelated to all factors that are correlated with both exposure to the treatment (the *Boîtes* sessions) and our outcomes of interest. Provided that encouragement significantly increased the likelihood of attended the event – which in our case it did (see footnote 53) – it can be used as an instrument for exposure to the *Boîtes à Images* event and thus identifies the causal effect of exposure on outcomes of interest.

Random assignment worked satisfactorily in the field, producing treatment and control groups that were virtually identical aside from their being encouraged to attend the upcoming *Boîtes* information session. Nevertheless, we include pre-treatment levels of all dependent variables and other demographics in all our models to improve the precision of our estimates. Table 1 summarizes our research design.

Survey instrument and field work

We included in the survey instrument indicators related to democratic supply and demand, as well as for various modes of political participation. For perceived democratic supply, we asked the often-utilized question on the individual's satisfaction with democracy in the DRC, as well as a question on general support for the current decentralization process. For the civic competence component of democratic demand, we asked questions related to both general political knowledge and knowledge about decentralization, and political efficacy. For the democratic values component of demand, we included questions on political tolerance, support for the exercise of democratic rights, and support for decentralization as a normative policy ideal. For participation, we included questions relating to diverse forms of political participation, including a measure of intention to vote in possible future local elections, discussion of politics with others, and an index of non-institutionalized forms of participation consisting of community problem solving, protest, and registering a complaint about an injustice of violation of the individual's rights. We also include standard demographic and political variables, including gender, education, age, and media exposure. A list of the all the variables used, the exact question wording, and response categories can be found in the Appendix (A2), and descriptive statistics for all variables can be found in Table A2 in the same section.

The survey also included questions related to the individuals' attendance at the *Boîtes* events. In the post-workshop survey, all respondents were asked whether they had attended the workshops that had recently taken place in their communities. This introduces the potential for social desirability in reporting attendance to the events. To reduce measurement error in self-reported attendance, we introduced a specific recall measure to assess the validity of self-reports.[47] Participation of

Table 1. Summary of research design.

	Respondents per Site	Total Respondents
Research Sites (8 villages)	140	1120
Encouraged to Attend the VOICE: Treatment	100	800
Not Encouraged to Attend the VOICE: Control	40	320
Pre-treatment (Baseline) Survey	140	1120
Post - treatment Survey	140	1120

112   RESILIENCE OF DEMOCRACY

individuals who claimed to have attended a particular *Boîtes* event in our survey was verified by asking a specific question about the method of delivery of the *Boîtes à Images* session (i.e. a presentation and discussion about images). This resulted in an attendance rate of 77% among those in the treatment sample compared with the self-reported 87% attendance rate.

Baseline interviews were conducted between 8 June 2011 (Bulungu *Territorie*) and 23 July 2011 (Kusango Lunda *Territorie*). In each *territorie*, the baseline survey was conducted within the week prior to the *Boîtes à Images* session taking place in each village. Interviewers followed standard random route household interviewing pro-cedures. Detailed information about the respondent and how s/he could be recon-tacted in a future follow-up survey was collected. Following the *Boîtes* session, interviewers attempted to reinterview all respondents from the baseline wave. This proved highly successful, as BERCI achieved a remarkable 98% reinterview rate. Post-*Boîtes* interviews were conducted between 8 July 2011 and 4 September 2011; this period represented a time of between one and 26 days after the *Boîtes* session. The overall time between pre- and post-event interviews ranged from three to 39 days.

Estimation strategy

Our research design allows us to identify the effect of the random encouragement to attend the *Boîtes* sessions on all dependent variables ("Intent to Treat (ITT)"), as well as the effects of attending the workshops instrumented, as noted above, by the random encouragement (IV). The ITT provides an estimate of the effects of encour-agement itself to attend the *Boîtes* sessions on the change in individuals' attitudes:

$$\Delta DV_{v,i} = \beta_{0_{v,i}} + \beta_1 Encouragement_{v,i} + \beta_2 DV_{v,i,pre} + Z_{v,i}\tau + \varphi_v + \varepsilon_{v,i}$$

where v indexes village, and i indexes each respondent. β_0 represents the average change in each dependent variable for non-encouraged individuals, β_1 represents the additional changes in the dependent variable for individuals who were encouraged to attend the session. The equation also includes village fixed effects (φ_v) as well as the pre-treatment value of the dependent variable ($DV_{v,i,pre}$) in order to increase the pre-cision of the estimates.[48] Lastly, the model includes other demographics such as gender, age, and level of education ($Z_{v,i}\tau$) to address potential imbalance in our sample.

As discussed above, even though encouragement is randomly assigned, attendance at the *Boîtes* sessions is voluntary. Thus, ITT will generate a potentially biased estimate of the effects of attending the *Boîtes* sessions. To overcome this, we identify the causal effects of attendance at the *Boîtes* sessions using instrumental variables estimation. We use the random assignment of "encouragement" as an instrument that exogenously increases the attendance at the *Boîtes* sessions. The estimation equation is written as below

$$Attendance_{v,i} = \beta_{0_{v,i}} + \beta_1 Encouragement_{v,i} + Z_{v,i}\tau + \varphi_v + \varepsilon_{v,i} \ (First\ Stage)$$

$$\Delta DV_{v,i} = \beta_{0_{v,i}} + \beta_1 \widehat{Attendance}_{v,i} + \beta_2 DV_{v,i,pre} + Z_{v,i}\tau + \varphi_v + \varepsilon_{v,i} \ (Second\ Stage)$$

where v indexes villages, and i indexes individuals. The process identifies the Com-plier Average Causal Effect (CACE), that is, the effect of attendance on change in each of the dependent variables among individuals who attended the *Boîtes* session as the result of the randomized encouragement (β_1 in the Second Stage).

Lastly, in order to investigate the direct and indirect effects of civic education on political participation through perceived democratic supply and demand respectively (H3), we employ the widely-utilized approach to causal mediation analysis suggested by Imai et al.[49] The procedure decomposes the total effect from a treatment to an outcome into the "average causal mediation effect" (ACME) – that is, the portion resulting from the indirect effect of the treatment on the outcome through a specified mediator, and the remaining "average direct effect" (ADE), which represents both the direct causal effect of the treatment on the outcome as well as any effects from potentially unmeasured or unspecified mediators.

Results

We show the results from the estimation of equations (1) and (2) for *Democratic Supply* in Table 2. As can be seen, for both overall satisfaction with democracy and support for the ongoing decentralization process, the estimates for *VOICE* exposure are negative and statistically significant. The ITT effects show that individuals who were randomly encouraged to attend the workshops decreased on both outcomes, relative to those who were not encouraged to attend in the baseline survey, controlling for prior levels of each outcome and for standard demographic variables such as gender, age, education, and media exposure.

The IV estimates of the complier average causal effect (columns 2 and 4), are substantially larger than the corresponding ITT effects.[50] In standardized terms, the IV estimate of *Boîtes* attendance on satisfaction with democracy is nearly ½ of a standard deviation, while the corresponding IV effect on support for the current decentralization process is over ¾ of a standard deviation. This is strong evidence in support of H1: the *Boîtes* civic education workshops heightened individuals' *dissatisfaction* with the current supply of democratic outcomes, both in terms of the specific decentralization reform as well the overall democratization process in DRC.

Table 2. Effects of voice exposure on perceived democratic supply.

	Dependent Variable:			
	Satisfaction with Democracy		Support for Decentralization Process	
	ITT	IV	ITT	IV
Encouraged	—0.088*		—0.167***	
	(0.046)		(0.050)	
Attended		—0.397*		—0.803
		(0.214)		(0.272)
Male	—0.022	—0.012	0.064	0.082
	(0.044)	(0.045)	(0.047)	(0.053)
Age	0.003***	0.004**	—0.001	0.001
	(0.002)	(0.002)	(0.002)	(0.002)
Education	0.020	0.020	0.007	0.003
	(0.016)	(0.016)	(0.017)	(0.019)
Media	0.007	0.0004	0.065*	0.047
	(0.038)	(0.038)	(0.039)	(0.044)
Lagged DV	X	X	X	X
Village FE	X	X	X	X
Observations	1,047	1,047	1,025	1,025
Adjusted R^2	0.413	0.383	0.514	0.380
First Stage F		70.270***		59.320***

p<0.1*; p<0.05**; p<0.01***

114 RESILIENCE OF DEMOCRACY

Table 3. Effects of voice exposure on democratic demand: civic competence.

	Dependent variable:					
	General Knowledge		Decentralization Knowledge		Political Efficacy	
	ITT	IV	ITT	IV	ITT	IV
Encouraged	0.082		0.479***		0.338***	
	(0.058)		(0.086)		(0.064)	
Attended		0.363		2.209***		1.604***
		(0.256)		(0.404)		(0.338)
Male	0.024	0.017	0.242***	0.208**	0.326***	0.285***
	(0.055)	(0.055)	(0.082)	(0.084)	(0.061)	(0.068)
Age	0.003*	0.002	0.011***	0.006*	0.0001	—0.004
	(0.002)	(0.002)	(0.003)	(0.003)	(0.002)	(0.003)
Education	0.062***	0.064***	0.040	0.043	—0.034	—0.031
	(0.020)	(0.020)	(0.029)	(0.030)	(0.021)	(0.024)
Media	0.029	0.040	0.082	0.035	—0.061	—0.022
	(0.047)	(0.047)	(0.070)	(0.071)	(0.053)	(0.059)
Lagged DV	X	X	X	X	X	X
Village FE	X	X	X	X	X	X
Observations	1,003	1,003	1,092	1,092	1,052	1,052
Adjusted R^2	0.345	0.344	0.498	0.476	0.476	0.353
First Stage F		71.647***		70.532***		63.990***

Note: $p<0.1$*; $p<0.05$**; $p<0.01$***

The effects of encouragement and *Boîtes* attendance on outcomes related to *Democratic Demand*, on the other hand, are almost uniformly *positive*, both in terms of the Civic Competence dimension (Table 3) and on Democratic Values (Table 4). The effects on Civic Competence variables, in particular on specific knowledge of decentralization and on political efficacy were both highly significant and of very large substantive magnitude (with standard deviation changes of 1.66 and 1.42, respectively).

Table 4. Effects of VOICE exposure on democratic demand: values and norms.

	Dependent variable:					
	Decentralization Ideal		Tolerance		Right to Criticize	
	ITT	IV	ITT	IV	ITT	IV
Encouraged	0.155**		0.134**		0.104**	
	(0.064)		(0.064)		(0.046)	
Attended		0.772***		0.636**		0.475**
		(0.332)		(0.315)		(0.217)
Male	0.202***	0.185***	0.084	0.076	0.078*	0.059
	(0.061)	(0.063)	(0.061)	(0.063)	(0.043)	(0.045)
Age	0.001	—0.001	—0.005**	—0.007***	0.0003	—0.001
	(0.002)	(0.002)	(0.002)	(0.002)	(0.002)	(0.002)
Education	0.002	0.001	—0.052**	—0.053**	—0.029*	—0.027*
	(0.021)	(0.022)	(0.022)	(0.022)	(0.015)	(0.016)
Media	0.061	0.076	0.036	0.023	0.008	0.0004
	(0.052)	(0.053)	(0.052)	(0.053)	(0.037)	(0.039)
Lagged DV	X	X	X	X	X	X
Village FE	X	X	X	X	X	X
Observations	1,048	1,048	1,070	1,070	1,027	1,027
Adjusted R^2	0.527	0.495	0.516	0.485	0.464	0.420
First Stage F		57.412***		64.640***		67.012***

Note: $p<0.1$*; $p<0.05$**; $p<0.01$***

A similar pattern can be seen for the second *Demand* dimension of support for democratic values and norms, though the size of the effects is of somewhat smaller magnitude. Individuals who attended the *Boîtes* workshops (based on the exogenous push of the random encouragement) were substantially more likely to support the normative ideal of decentralization than the control group (standard deviation change of .72), and were more likely to endorse core democratic values such as extending political rights even to those espousing non-democratic principles (standard deviation change of .64) and supporting the rights of individuals to criticize the government (standard deviation change of .68). This is strong evidence in support of H2.

We present the effects of *VOICE* exposure on three measures of political participation in Table 5: discussing politics with others, expressing intention to vote in possible upcoming local elections, and engaging in non-electoral behaviours such as community action, protest, and the redress of personal injustices or grievances. The results show an interesting pattern, with the effects of civic education exposure on discussion and non-electoral participation being significant and positive, while its impact on turnout intention is insignificant and slightly negative in sign. The instrumental variable estimates for discussion and non-electoral behaviour are moderate in substantive magnitude, with the effect for discussion being nearly ½ of a standard deviation, and for non-electoral behaviour approximately ¼ of a standard deviation as well. The figure for non-electoral behaviour is notable in that the post-test took place no longer than one month after the *Boîtes* event, and thus there were not likely to be an abundance of opportunities for engaging in these actions in that limited a time frame.

The reasons for the null effect of exposure on turnout intention are not altogether clear. It may have been that, given the delays in scheduled local elections that had occurred in the recent past, individuals discounted the possibility of elections actually taking place. The negative effect is also consistent, however, with recent work

Table 5. Effects of VOICE exposure on democratic demand: values and norms.

	Dependent variable:					
	General Knowledge		Decentralization Knowledge		Political Efficacy	
	ITT	IV	ITT	IV	ITT	IV
Encouraged	0.082		0.479***		0.338***	
	(0.058)		(0.086)		(0.064)	
Attended		0.363		2.209***		1.604***
		(0.256)		(0.404)		(0.338)
Male	0.024	0.017	0.242***	0.208**	0.326***	0.285***
	(0.055)	(0.055)	(0.082)	(0.084)	(0.061)	(0.068)
Age	0.003*	0.002	0.011***	0.006*	0.0001	−0.004
	(0.002)	(0.002)	(0.003)	(0.003)	(0.002)	(0.003)
Education	0.062***	0.064***	0.040	0.043	−0.034	−0.031
	(0.020)	(0.020)	(0.029)	(0.030)	(0.021)	(0.024)
Media	0.029	0.040	−0.082	−0.035	−0.061	−0.022
	(0.047)	(0.047)	(0.070)	(0.071)	(0.053)	(0.059)
Lagged DV	X	X	X	X	X	X
Village FE	X	X	X	X	X	X
Observations	1,003	1,003	1,092	1,092	1,052	1,052
Adjusted R^2	0.345	0.344	0.498	0.476	0.476	0.353
First Stage F		71.647***		70.532***		63.990***

Note: $p<0.1$*; $p<0.05$**; $p<0.01$***

demonstrating a "deliberate disengagement" hypothesis, whereby new information about flawed political processes leads to voter withdrawal from behaviours such as turnout that would legitimate the political regime.[51] We explore the differential effects on turnout and the other forms of participation more thoroughly in the mediation analyses that follow in Tables 6 and 7.

Table 6 shows the mediated effects of *VOICE* civic education on participation via its effect on perceptions of Democratic Supply, using overall satisfaction with democracy as the mediator so as to minimize the complexity of the model. As can be seen, the effect of democratic satisfaction on all three forms of participation is positive and statistically significant, such that individuals who are more satisfied are more likely to express intention to turn out to vote and engage in other forms of passive (discussion) and active participation. In combination with the negative effect of *VOICE* exposure on democratic satisfaction (see Table 2), this produces a *negative* indirect effect on participation in all forms. This can be seen from the statistically significant Average Causal Mediation Effect (ACME) of approximately –.01 on each form of behaviour. This suggests that one effect of civic education is to depress participation by heightening individual's dissatisfaction with contemporaneous political processes and regime outputs. This pattern is consistent with H3a from the Supply and Demand model of Figure 1. It should be noted, however, that these indirect effects are modest in magnitude, explaining less than 15% of the total civic education effects in each of the three dependent variables.

We find partial support for H3b from the results in Table 7, which shows the indirect effects of *VOICE* exposure via Democratic Demand. Again, we select one indicator of Demand, political efficacy, for ease of presentation. Here the effects of efficacy on political discussion and non-electoral participation are positive and significant. Coupled with the positive effects of *VOICE* on efficacy as shown in Table 3, this process produces an overall positive and significant ACME for these two outcomes.

Table 6. Effects of VOICE exposure on political participation.

	Dependent variable:					
	Political Discussion		Non-Electoral Participation		Electoral Participation	
	ITT	IV	ITT	IV	ITT	IV
Encouraged	0.115**		0.074***		-0.059	
	(0.051)		(0.027)		(0.055)	
Attended		0.541**		0.341**		-0.328
		(0.248)		(0.134)		(0.308)
Male	0.267***	0.262***	0.079***	0.073***	0.065	0.073
	(0.049)	(0.050)	(0.025)	(0.028)	(0.051)	(0.053)
Age	0.005***	0.004**	0.003***	0.002**	0.001	0.002
	(0.002)	(0.002)	(0.001)	(0.001)	(0.002)	(0.002)
Education	0.024	0.025	-0.0003	-0.0002	0.044**	0.044**
	(0.017)	(0.018)	(0.009)	(0.010)	(0.018)	(0.019)
Media	0.080*	0.092**	0.068***	0.075***	-0.089**	-0.100
	(0.042)	(0.043)	(0.022)	(0.023)	(0.044)	(0.045)
Lagged DV	X	X	X	X	X	X
Village FE	X	X	X	X	X	X
Observations	1,092	1,092	1,092	1,092	911	911
Adjusted R^2	0.410	0.377	0.445	0.352	0.482	0.461
First Stage F		67.623***		69.460***		41.239***

Note: p<0.1*; p<0.05**; p<0.01***

Table 7. Effects of CE on participation: mediated through (perceived) democratic supply.

2nd Stage	Dependent variable:		
	Political Discussion	Non-Electoral Participation	Electoral Participation
Satisfied with	0.090**	0.081***	0.121***
Democracy	(0.035)	(0.018)	(0.036)
Encouraged	0.120**	0.084***	−0.053
	(0.052)	(0.027)	(0.055)
Male	0.245***	0.084***	0.061
	(0.050)	(0.025)	(0.051)
Age	0.005***	0.002**	0.002
	(0.002)	(0.001)	(0.002)
Education	0.027	0.002	0.047**
	(0.018)	(0.009)	(0.019)
Media	0.088**	0.065***	−0.090**
	(0.043)	(0.022)	(0.044)
Village FE	X	X	X
Lagged DV	X	X	X
ACME	−0.0088**	−0.0077**	−0.0127**
	[−0.02082 − −0.00003]	[−0.01670 − −0.00003]	[−0.0306 − −0.00001]
ADE	0.1188**	0.0807***	−0.0512
	[0.01665 − 0.2189]	[0.02775 − 0.1341]	[−0.1716 − 0.0550]
TE	0.1100**	0.07307***	−0.0639
	[0.00750 − 0.2120]	[0.02041 − 0.1259]	[−0.1802 − 0.0426]
Prop.Mediated	−0.0725	−0.10120	0.1413
Sensitivity Score	0.1	0.2	0.2
Observations	1,066	1,066	909

95% confidence intervals in square brackets estimated, 95% confidence intervals in square brackets estimated based on nonparametric bootstrap with 1000 resamples. Both mediation and outcome equations are estimated with OLS. p<0.1*; p<0.05**; p<0.01***

The mediated effect is also relatively large, explaining between 20 and 35% of the total effect of *VOICE* on the outcomes. In the case of intention to vote, however, the effect of efficacy is unexpectedly insignificant, rendering the indirect effect negligible and insignificant as well. Table 8.

Taken together, these analyses show that there were offsetting indirect effects linking *VOICE* exposure to subsequent political behaviour. The programme stimulated participation by generating more politically competent and aware individuals, but depressed participation by generating individuals who were more dissatisfied with current democratic supply. The processes resulted with, on balance, positive indirect effects in the case of political discussion and non-electoral or unconventional behaviours, and on balance negative indirect effects in the case of intention to vote. In all three cases, however, the direct effect of *VOICE* – positive for discussion and non-electoral actions, negative for turnout intentions – outweighed the indirect effects by a substantial amount. These direct effects may represent the effects of civic education exposure through as yet unobserved mediators. But we interpret at least some of these direct effects as the result of the direct mobilization messages contained in the *VOICE* programme as well. As can be seen in the *Boîte à Image* depicted in Figure 2b, the programme encouraged individuals to engage explicitly in the redress of grievances (illustration at the lower left of the figure) and to participate in collective action or protest on issues of importance (lower right).

118   RESILIENCE OF DEMOCRACY

Table 8. Effects of CE on participation: mediated through democratic demand (efficacy).

2nd Stage	Dependent variable:		
	Political Discussion	Non-Electoral Participation	Electoral Participation
Efficacy	0.114***	0.046***	0.017
	(0.025)	(0.013)	(0.026)
Encouraged	0.055	0.062**	−0.045
	(0.052)	(0.027)	(0.056)
Male	0.224***	0.066**	0.046
	(0.050)	(0.026)	(0.052)
Age	0.005***	0.003***	0.002
	(0.002)	(0.001)	(0.002)
Education	0.027	−0.001	0.044**
	(0.017)	(0.009)	(0.019)
Media	0.104**	0.065***	−0.087*
	(0.043)	(0.022)	(0.045)
Village FE	X	X	X
Lagged DV	X	X	X
ACME	0.0363***	0.0152***	0.0047
	[0.0207 - 0.0602]	[0.0059 - 0.0262]	[−0.0091 - 0.0211]
ADE	0.0566	0.0611**	−0.0421
	[−0.0492 - 0.1476]	[0.0093 - 0.1147]	[−0.1510 - 0.0700]
TE	0.0928*	0.0762***	−0.0373
	[0.0096 - 0.1866]	[0.0266 - 0.1300]	[−0.1495 - 0.0743]
Prop.Mediated	0.3473	0.1975	−0.0351
Sensitivity Score	0.1	0.2	0.2
Observations	1,071	1,071	906

95% confidence intervals in square brackets estimated, 95% confidence intervals in square brackets estimated based on nonparametric bootstrap with 1000 resamples. Both mediation and outcome equations are estimated with OLS. $p<0.1$*; $p<0.05$**; $p<0.01$***

Conclusion

We proposed a general Supply and Demand model of the effects of civic education in emerging democracies by adapting Bratton and Mattes' model of democratic support. We suggest that new information imparted in civic education programmes may successfully instil political knowledge, self-competence and support for democratic values and norms ("Demand"), while at the same time highlighting and deepening dissatisfaction with poorly functioning political institutions and regimes ("Supply"). We tested hypotheses derived from the model with the *VOICE* programme undertaken in the Democratic Republic of Congo in 2011-2012, which attempted to further citizen knowledge, support and engagement with the country's decentralization reforms and the democratization process.

Using an "encouragement design", we found consistent support for the model's hypotheses. Estimates of both ITT and IV models showed that the workshops led to increases on virtually all indicators of Democratic Demand – knowledge of decentralization, political efficacy, tolerance and support for the exercise of democratic rights – while leading to negative effects on indicators of Democratic Supply – satisfaction with democracy in the DRC and support for the ongoing decentralization process. These processes then differentially fed into subsequent political engagement. Civic education exposure had positive indirect effects on political discussion and non-electoral participation via increases in democratic demand, and these effects were partially offset by negative indirect effects on participation via decreases in perceived democratic supply. Finally, we found strong direct effects of *VOICE* workshop exposure on reported non-electoral participation and informal political discussion, though no corresponding increase was shown on intentions to vote in upcoming local elections.

The findings have important normative implications for the role of civic education in furthering democratic political culture. That civic education provides information to individuals about poorly functioning institutions is laudable, as there may be a limited amount of objective information available elsewhere on political performance in fragile democracies and electoral autocracies. The fact that this heightened awareness of deficiencies in institutional performance was accompanied by increases in supportive democratic values, norms and behaviours also provides a positive normative view on what civic education can accomplish. Gibson *et al.* asserted that "a democratic citizen is one who believes in individual liberty and who is politically tolerant, who holds a certain amount of distrust of political authority ... [and] who is obedient but nonetheless willing to assert rights against the state".[52] This is precisely what the *VOICE* programme appears to have accomplished in the Democratic Republic of Congo. Though democratic development depends on many factors, it is nevertheless plausible to assert that this increase in "distrusting democrats" [53] is likely to provide at least some incentive for elites in poorly performing contexts to increase the future supply of democracy to a citizenry that is more committed to democratic norms as well as more politically engaged.

The results also have more practical implications for the future design and implementation of civic education information campaigns in emerging and in backsliding democracies. Although negative effects of civic education on perceptions of democratic supply may be laudable in poorly-functioning democracies, it is also the case that no democracies are perfect, and civic education programmes need to be cognizant of modulating to some degree the discrepancy between democracy in theory and in practice. Programmes could also exploit the positive effects we reported on political discussion, by providing supplementary materials and explicit instructions to participants on how best to transmit the civic education messages to others in their social networks. And the relatively strong individual-level effects observed here indicate that the VOICE programme could serve as an example for future large-scale information campaigns, given its use of the kinds of active and participatory methodologies that previous work has identified as "best practices" for civic education.[54]

At the same time, much more needs to be done in future research. The present study has limitations, for example, in our reliance on measuring participation using self-reported as opposed to objective indicators, in our focus on relatively short-term effects of civic education exposure, and our inability to incorporate variation in implementation quality into the evaluation. More generally, though our supply and demand model has attempted to integrate previous work into a general theoretical framework, there are still important avenues left to explore. For example, we need to know much more about possible heterogenous effects of civic education for individuals with differing levels of political and social resources.[55] Moreover, future work should directly test the mechanisms which may lead to the differential impacts of civic education on democratic supply and demand. We suggested increased cognitive awareness and changes in the expectations or reference points with which individuals compare democratic ideals to ongoing democratic practices; others, for example, increases in voluntary association memberships or informal mobilization from family or friends, may also need to be considered in modelling the linkages between civic education, democratic orientations, and political engagement. Finally, it is likely that the micro-level impacts of civic education programmes depend on macro-level and contextual factors, such as the country's level of democracy or recent trajectory, few of which have been considered in previous work. In better-functioning democracies, the combination of demand and supply effects may differ considerably from the pattern found here in the Democratic Republic of Congo. As more research is done in different settings on all of these issues, a more comprehensive understanding may be achieved on how civic education and related information campaigns affect individuals in emerging democracies.

Notes

1. Classen, "Does Public Support Help Democracy Survive?"
2. Finkel,"Can Democracy be Taught?"; "The Impact of Adult Civic Education Programmes in Developing Democracies".
3. Lieberman *et al.*, "Does Information Lead to More Active Citizenship?"
4. Gottlieb, "Why Might Information Exacerbate the Gender Gap in Civic Participation?."
5. Chong *et al*, "Does Corruption Information Inspire the Right or Quash the Hope?"; Sexton, "The Long Road to Accountable Democracy."
6. Bratton and Mattes, "Learning About Democracy in Africa."
7. Mvukiyehe and Samii, "Promoting Democracy in Fragile States."
8. Azpuru *et al.*, "Trends in Democracy Assistance"; Moehler, "Democracy, Governance, and Randomized Development Assistance."
9. Many programmes have been conducted among primary and secondary students in the formal school systems of developing democracies; we focus in this article on non-formal civic education programmes aimed at adults.
10. Bratton *et al.*, "The Effects of Civic Education on Political Culture."
11. Finkel *et al.*, "Civic Education, Civil Society, and Political Mistrust in a Developing Democracy"; "Can Democracy Be Taught?"
12. Finkel and Smith, "Civic Education, Political Discussion."
13. Finkel, Horowitz, and Rojo-Mendoza, "Civic Education and Democratic Backsliding."
14. Moehler, *Distrusting Democrats*; Kuenzi, "Nonformal Education, Political Participation."
15. Finkel, "Can Democracy Be Taught?"
16. Finkel and Smith, "Civic Education, Political Discussion."
17. Kuenzi, "Nonformal Education, Political Participation."
18. Moehler, *Distrusting Democrats.*
19. Finkel, Horowitz, and Rojo-Mendoza, "Civic Education and Democratic Backsliding."
20. Gottlieb, "Greater Expectations: A Field Experiment."
21. Banerjee *et al.*,"Can Voters Be Primed to Choose Better Legislators?."
22. Keefer and Khemani, "Do Informed Citizens Receive More ... or Pay More?"
23. Vincente, "Is Vote Buying Effective?."
24. Gine and Mansuri, "Together We Will"; Collier and Vincente, "Votes and Violence"; Mvukiyehe and Samii, "Promoting Democracy in Fragile States."
25. Chong *et al.*, "Does Corruption Information Inspire?"; Vincente, "Is Vote Buying Effective?."
26. Gottlieb, "Why Might Information Exacerbate"; John and Sjoberg, "Partisan responses to democracy promotion."
27. Lieberman *et al.*,"Does Information Lead to More Active Citizenship?"
28. Sexton, "The Long Road to Accountable Democracy."
29. Bratton and Mattes, "Learning About Democracy in Africa."
30. Norris, *Democratic Deficit: Critical Citizens Revisited*; Milner, *Civic Literacy: How Informed Citizens.*
31. Gottlieb, "Greater Expectations: A Field Experiment."
32. Sexton, "The Long Road to Accountable Democracy: Evidence from a Field Experiment in Peru."
33. Finkel *et al.*, "Civic Education, Civil Society, and Political Mistrust in a Developing Democracy: The Case of the Dominican Republic," 1867-1868.

34. Almond and Verba, *The Civic Culture: Political Attitudes*; Claasen, "Does Public Support Help Democracy Survive?"; Gibson *et al.*, "Democratic Values and the Transformation of the Soviet Union"; Verba *et al.*, *Voice and Equality: Civic Voluntarism*.
35. That these outcomes can be affected in the first place by short-term factors such as civic education is no longer controversial, though the relative impact of short-term interventions versus long-term factors such as generational replacement or top-down actions from parties and political elites remains undetermined. See, e.g. Neundorf, "Democracy in Transition: A Micro Perspective on System Change in Post-socialist Societies."
36. Gine and Mansuri, "Together We Will: Experimental Evidence."
37. Moehler, *Distrusting Democrats*.
38. Finkel *et al.*, "Civic Education, Civil Society, and Political Mistrust."
39. Chong *et al.*, "Does Corruption Information Inspire?"
40. Sexton, "The Long Road to Accountable Democracy."
41. Reyntjens, "Briefing: Democratic Republic of Congo."
42. Crawford and Hartmann, *Decentralisation in Africa: A Pathway?*"; Dizolele, "The Mirage of Democracy in the DRC."
43. Englebert *et al.*, "Misguided and Misdiagnosed: The Failure of Decentralization Reforms in the DRC."
44. Ibid.
45. See Appendix (A1) for the exact encouragement script.
46. Random assignment to receive the encouragement was blocked at the village level.
47. Sovey and Green "Instrumental Variables Estimation in Political Science: A Readers' Guide."
48. Our dependent variable in all our models ($.\Delta DV_{v,i}.$) is the change in individuals' attitudes over the two waves ($.DV_{v,i,post} - \Delta DV_{v,i,pre}.$). This applies to the behavioral questions such as political discussion and non-institutional participation as well, so in those models the dependent variable represents the change in the individual's reported engagement in the various acts between the two waves of interviews.
49. Imai *et al.*, "Unpacking the Black Box of Causality"; Imai *et al.*, "Causal Mediation Analysis Using R."
50. The first-stage estimates in all of the IV models reported in this section produce F statistics ranging from 41 to 71, well above the generally accepted threshold of 10 for rejecting instruments as "weak".
51. Croke *et al.*,"Deliberate Disengagement: How Education Can Decrease Political Participation in Electoral Authoritarian Regimes"; also Chong *et al.*, Does Corruption Information Inspire?"
52. Gibson *et al.*, "Democratic Values and the Transformation of the Soviet Union," 332.
53. Moehler, *Distrusting Democrats*.
54. Blair, "Jump-Starting Democracy: Adult Civic"; Milner and Lewis. "It's What Happens on the Front Lines."
55. Gottlieb, "Why Might Information Exacerbate the Gender"; Johns and Sjoberg, "Partisan Responses to Democracy Promotion."

Acknowledgements

We thank Rakesh Sharma and Rola Abdul-Latif of IFES for overseeing the VOICE evaluation, Reynaldo Rojo-Mendoza for his earlier work on the project, and participants at the Ordinary Citizens in Autocracies conference at the University of Nottingham, June 2018, for comments, criticisms, and helpful suggestions.

Disclosure statement

No potential conflict of interest was reported by the author(s).

References

Azpuru, Dinorah, Steven E. Finkel, Aníbal Pérez-Liñán, and Mitchell A. Seligson. "Trends in Democracy Assistance: What Has the United States Been Doing?" *Journal of Democracy* 19, no. 2 (2008): 150–159.

Banerjee, Abhijit, Donald Green, Jennifer Green, and Rohini Pande. "Can Voters Be Primed to Choose Better Legislators? Experimental Evidence from Rural India." Paper presented at the political economics seminar, Stanford University, Palo Alto, CA. 2010. http://citeseerx.ist.psu.edu/viewdoc/download?doi=10.1.1.371.7626&rep=rep1&type=pdf

Blair, Harry. "Jump-Starting Democracy: Adult Civic Education and Democratic Participation in Three Countries." *Democratization* 10, no. 1 (2003): 53–76.

Bratton, Michael, Philip Alderfer, Georgia Bowser, and Joseph Temba. "The Effects of Civic Education on Political Culture: Evidence from Zambia." *World Development* 27, no. 5 (1999): 807–824.

Chong, Alberto, Ana L De La O, Dean Karlan, and Leonard Wantchekon. "Does Corruption Information Inspire the Right or Quash the Hope? A Field Experiment in Mexico on Voter Turnout, Choice, and Party Identification." *The Journal of Politics* 77, no. 1 (2015): 55–71.

Claassen, Christopher. "Does Public Support Help Democracy Survive?" *American Journal of Political Science* 64, no. 1 (2020): 118–134.

Collier, Paul, and Pedro C. Vicente. "Votes and Violence: Evidence from a Field Experiment in Nigeria." *The Economic Journal* 124, no. 574 (2014): 327–355.

Crawford, Gordon, and Christof Hartmann, eds. *Decentralisation in Africa: a Pathway out of Poverty and Conflict?* Amsterdam: Amsterdam University Press, 2008.

Croke, Kevin, Guy Grossman, Horacio A. Larreguy, and John Marshall. "Deliberate Disengagement: How Education Can Decrease Political Participation in Electoral Authoritarian Regimes." *American Political Science Review* 110, no. 3 (2016): 579–600.

Diamond, Larry. *Developing Democracy: Toward Consolidation*. Baltimore: JHU Press, 1999.

Dizolele, Mvemba Phezo. "The Mirage of Democracy in the DRC." *Journal of Democracy* 21, no. 3 (2010): 143–157.

Englebert, Pierre, and Emmanuel Kasongo Mungongo. "Misguided and Misdiagnosed: the Failure of Decentralization Reforms in the DR Congo." *African Studies Review* 59, no. 1 (2016): 5–32.

Finkel, Steve E., Christopher A. Sabatini, and Gwendolyn G. Bevis. "Civic Education, Civil Society, and Political Mistrust in a Developing Democracy: the Case of the Dominican Republic." *World Development* 28, no. 11 (2000): 1851–1874.

Finkel, Steven E. "Can Democracy Be Taught?" *Journal of Democracy* 14, no. 4 (2003): 137–151.

Finkel, Steven E., and Amy Erica Smith. "Civic Education, Political Discussion, and the Social Transmission of Democratic Knowledge and Values in a New Democracy: Kenya 2002." *American Journal of Political Science* 55, no. 2 (2011): 417–435.

Finkel, Steven E., Jeremy Horowitz, and Reynaldo T. Rojo-Mendoza. "Civic Education and Democratic Backsliding in the Wake of Kenya's Post-2007 Election Violence." *The Journal of Politics* 74, no. 1 (2012): 52–65.

Gibson, James L., Raymond M. Duch, and Kent L. Tedin. "Democratic Values and the Transformation of the Soviet Union." *The Journal of Politics* 54, no. 2 (1992): 329–371.

Giné, Xavier, and Ghazala Mansuri. "Together We Will: Experimental Evidence on Female Voting Behavior in Pakistan." *American Economic Journal: Applied Economics* 10, no. 1 (2018): 207–235.

Gottlieb, Jessica. "Greater Expectations: A Field Experiment to Improve Accountability in Mali." *American Journal of Political Science* 60, no. 1 (2016a): 143–157.

Gottlieb, Jessica. "Why Might Information Exacerbate the Gender Gap in Civic Participation? Evidence from Mali." *World Development* 86 (2016b): 95–110.

Imai, Kosuke, Luke Keele, Dustin Tingley, and Teppei Yamamoto. "Unpacking the Black Box of Causality: Learning About Causal Mechanisms from Experimental and Observational Studies." *American Political Science Review* 105, no. 4 (2011): 765–789.

Imai, Kosuke, Luke Keele, Dustin Tingley, and Teppei Yamamoto. "Causal Mediation Analysis Using R." In *Advances in Social Science Research Using R*, edited by H. Vinod, 129–154. New York, NY: Springer, 2010.

John, Peter, and Fredrik M. Sjoborg. "Partisan Responses to Democracy Promotion – Estimating the Causal Effect of a Civic Information Portal." *World Development* 130 (2020): 1–10.

Keefer, Philip, and Stuti Khemani. *Do Informed Citizens Receive More ... or Pay More? The Impact of Radio on the Government Distribution of Public Health Benefits.* Washington, DC: The World Bank, 2012.

Kuenzi, Michelle T. "Nonformal Education, Political Participation, and Democracy: Findings from Senegal." *Political Behavior* 28, no. 1 (2006): 1–31.

Lieberman, Evan S., Daniel N. Posner, and Lily L. Tsai. "Does Information Lead to More Active Citizenship? Evidence from an Education Intervention in Rural Kenya." *World Development* 60 (2014): 69–83.

Mattes, Robert, and Michael Bratton. "Learning About Democracy in Africa: Awareness, Performance, and Experience." *American Journal of Political Science* 51, no. 1 (2007): 192–217.

Milner, Henry. *Civic Literacy: How Informed Citizens Make Democracy Work.* Hanover, NH: University Press of New England, 2002.

Milner, Henry, and J. P. Lewis. "It's What Happens on the Front Lines of Civic Education Policy That Matters: Reflections on a Natural Experiment on Youth Turnout in Ontario." *Canadian Political Science Review* 5, no. 2 (2012): 136–146.

Moehler, Devra. *Distrusting Democrats: Outcomes of Participatory Constitution Making.* Ann Arbor, MI: University of Michigan Press, 2008.

Moehler, Devra C. "Democracy, Governance, and Randomized Development Assistance." *The ANNALS of the American Academy of Political and Social Science* 628, no. 1 (2010): 30–46.

Mvukiyehe, Eric, and Cyrus Samii. "Promoting Democracy in Fragile States: Field Experimental Evidence from Liberia." *World Development* 95 (2017): 254–267.

Neundorf, Anja. "Democracy in Transition: A Micro Perspective on System Change in Post-Socialist Societies." *The Journal of Politics* 72, no. 4 (2010): 1096–1108.

Norris, Pippa. *Democratic Deficit: Critical Citizens Revisited.* New York: Cambridge University Press, 2011.

Reyntjens, Filip. "Briefing: Democratic Republic of Congo: Political Transition and Beyond." *African Affairs* 106, no. 423 (2007): 307–317.

Sexton, Renard. "The Long Road to Accountable Democracy: Evidence from a Field Experiment in Peru." *Working Paper.*, 2018.

Sovey, Allison J., and Donald P. Green. "Instrumental Variables Estimation in Political Science: A Readers' Guide." *American Journal of Political Science* 55, no. 1 (2011): 188–200.

Verba, Sidney, and Gabriel Almond. *The Civic Culture: Political Attitudes and Democracy in Five Nations.* Princeton, NJ: Princeton University Press, 1963.

Vicente, Pedro C. "Is Vote Buying Effective? Evidence from a Field Experiment in West Africa." *The Economic Journal* 124, no. 574 (2014): 356–387.

Democratic Horizons: what value change reveals about the future of democracy

Christian Welzel

ABSTRACT
Recent accounts of democratic backsliding are negligent about the cultural foundations of autocracy-vs-democracy. To bring culture back in, I demonstrate that (1) the countries' membership in culture zones explains some 70% of the global variation in autocracy-vs-democracy and (2) that this culture-bound variation has remained astoundingly constant over time – in spite of all the trending patterns in the global distribution of regime types over the last 120 years. Furthermore, the explanatory power of culture zones over autocracy-vs-democracy roots in the cultures' differentiation on "authoritarian-vs-emancipative values." Against this backdrop, lasting regime turnovers happen as a corrective response to glacially accruing regime-culture misfits – driven by generational value shifts into a pre-dominantly emancipatory direction. Consequently, the backsliding of democracies into authoritarianism is limited to societies in which emancipative values remain under-developed. Contrary to the widely cited deconsolidation-thesis, the prevalent generational profile in people's moral orientations exhibits an almost ubiquitous ascension of emancipative values that will lend more, not less, legitimacy to democracy in the future.

"Pessimism is too often treated as an indication of superior intellect."

(inspired by John Kenneth Galbraight)

The new democratic gloom

In the face of surging populism seemingly everywhere in the world, media pundits and academics alike prophesize a groundbreaking erosion of democracy and its liberal principles.[1] The resilience and revival of autocratic rule among major powers, most notably China and Russia, as well as recently amassing evidence of a worldwide democratic recession[2], fuel a swelling pessimism about the future of democracy.[3] The new gloom magnifies older concerns about a creeping legitimacy crisis of democracy.

ⓑ Supplemental data for this article can be accessed https://doi.org/10.1080/13510347.2021.1883001.

These concerns are simmering since long throughout Western democracies[4], which all experienced the same worrisome trends. These include declining voter turnout, a weakening identification with mainstream political parties, shrinking membership of churches, trade unions and other voluntary associations, together with crumbling trust in key institutions, from the media to parliaments to government.[5]

The alleged erosion of trust in institutions raises the strongest concerns. Observers fear that fading public trust will cause social unrest and bring extremist parties to power, which then hollow out and eventually abandon democracy.[6] Raging dissatisfaction with democracy, evident in recent riots by the *gilets jaunes* in France, PEGIDA in Germany and the mob attack on Capitol Hill, further amplify these worries.

But a revisionist camp of scholars interprets the facts in a starkly contrasting manner.[7] Revisionists point out that the decline in public trust is by no means as uniform and sweeping as its advocates suggest.[8] Next, revisionists do not consider low levels of public trust as such a bad thing to begin with. On the contrary, they see low trust as a source of vitalizing impulses for democratic institutions. As the revisionists argue, a generational shift from authoritarian to emancipative values has elevated the normative standards under which people judge the performance of democratic institutions, turning undemanding subjects into "critical citizens."[9] Critical citizens feel more easily underwhelmed by the performance of their institutions, which is what low trust figures document. Criticalness motivates people to raise their voice in public. The resulting rise in civic protest heightens the pressure on elites to listen to people's demands. As a consequence, the institutions' responsiveness actually improves – not despite but because of low public trust and the related perpetuation of civic protest.

From the revisionists' point of view, dissatisfaction with the functioning of democracy in *practice* does not turn people away from democracy as a *norm*. Instead, revisionists cite evidence that support for democracy as the most desirable form of government persists since decades on an unchangingly high level in all Western countries.[10] More importantly, revisionists stress that the tectonic cultural shift from authoritarian to emancipative values has strengthened people's commitment to the most primordial principles of democracy, in particular freedom of choice and equality of opportunities – the two pivotal values of Enlightenment philosophy.[11]

Since a while, the debate is turning again in favor of the pessimists – and this time with a vengeance. Among the various streams in the gloomy turn, the recently advocated "deconsolidation-thesis" challenges the revisionists' optimistic interpretation of democratic legitimacy most profoundly. The deconsolidation-thesis posits that public support for democracy is crumbling all over the world, even among mature Western democracies. What seems to be particularly worrisome is that the postulated decline is most pronounced among the younger generations. The pessimists see the alleged erosion of democratic passion among Western youth as the primary source of the swelling popularity of illiberal populism.[12]

The counter-argument

Disputing the newly surging gloom, this article argues that the recent recession of democracy is an episode that reflects a temporary illiberal cycle in public mood.[13] Liberal-vs-illiberal swings in public mood have little transformative power because of their very cyclicality. The true transformative force resides in the cultural undercurrent on the surface of which liberal-vs-illiberal mood swings happen. This undercurrent brings a glacial and almost ubiquitous ascension of emancipative values over the generations. In the sections following this introduction, I present evidence supporting this proposition framed in a "cultural theory of autocracy-vs-democracy." The Online Appendix to this study (available at www.worldvaluessurvey.org) presents ample of supplementary evidence.

The cultural theory of autocracy-vs-democracy sees the driving psychological force of global regime evolution in the generational rise of emancipative values. These values idealize *universal* human freedoms and combine a *libertarian* emphasis on individual choice with an *egalitarian* emphasis on equality of opportunities.[14] Philosophically speaking, these are essentially the values that inspired the Enlightenment and the modern reinvention of democracy.[15]

Due to this cultural theory of regimes, the long-term dynamic propelling regime-culture coevolution follows a logic by which generational shifts in the populations' value orientations generate slowly but steadily increasing regime-culture tensions. At one point, these tensions grow so strong that they trigger a sudden and swift regime transition through which the tension resolves, thus reinstating a new regime-culture equilibrium. At the moment, many of the regime changes that scholars characterize as "backsliding" are cutting back liberal regime elements, most notably media freedom and judicial independence.[16] In many cases, including Hungary, Poland, Romania, Russia, and Turkey, this happens as a reaction to regime-culture misfits that emerged during the apex of the democratic euphoria after the collapse of Soviet communism. As a consequence, many regimes became overly liberal *relative* to their populations' values and are now experiencing a "regression to the mean" under the reign of illiberal populism. But considered through a wider temporal lens – namely, across the time horizon of a generation – the corrective function of regime turnovers has worked heavily in favor of democracy, and increasingly so over the past 115 years.[17]

Given that generational change points in most regions of the world from authoritarian to emancipative values, I hypothesize that the reproductive advantage of democracy over autocracy in global regime evolution is poised to recover from its current intercession and to bounce back mightily.

The point of departure of this model of regime-culture coevolution is the sweeping worldwide expansion of education and other cognition-, awareness- and intelligence-lifting consequences of modernization.[18] The essence of this pervasive process of "cognitive mobilization" is that it unlocks the most highly evolved human quality on a mass-scale: agency – our faculty to act with purpose and to think for ourselves. Where this happens, collective mentality patterns change profoundly. Most importantly, people do no longer want to be told what to believe and what to do. This psychological awakening is a force of nature that undermines the appeal of authoritarian rule and, instead, turns people towards emancipative values. It needs no civic education programme and no orchestrated political strategy to make this happen. As a consequence, the continuation of cognitively mobilizing dynamics feeds a cultural metamorphosis that places emancipative values on a glacially ascending trajectory in most places of the world, as we will see.

Since durability is the purpose of institutions, most political regimes do not change most of the time. Hence, cultural change is like an undercurrent that happens below the crusted surface of inert regime structures. Consequently, the generational ascension of emancipative values nurtures glacially accruing regime-culture misfits. In the long run, these misfits take shape in such fashion that they leave regimes too undemocratic, and increasingly so, given the emancipatory direction of their slow but steady cultural undercurrent. To be sure, there is no automatism of how these misfits translate into actual regime turnovers, which are in the end always the outcome of the purposeful acts of concrete actors. Nevertheless, accruing regime-culture misfits reshape the context of actor constellations. As they grow, regime-culture misfits open opportunity windows for regime-challenging counter-elites to rise, forge alliances and mobilize popular support – support in favor of turning regimes into the opposite direction of their misfit to the underlying culture. Within short-term illiberal swings in public mood, this logic might bring regime changes into an autocratic direction, as we see them more frequently during the recent democratic recession. But under the long-term ascension of emancipative values, regime turnovers into the democratic direction heavily outweigh those in the opposite direction in both number and scope, as we will also see.

Democracy's inspiration

The key inspiration of democracy[19] – the idea that people live in freedom and have an equal voice and vote in the public sphere – roots firmly in the Enlightenment view of human nature. According to this view, all humans are equipped with the faculty to think for themselves, make reasonable judgements, act with purpose and tame their self-interest in light of the common good. In cultures committed to build and train these human qualities, democracy is the natural order.[20]

To be understood and appreciated, democracy needs a citizenry among which the belief in these Enlightenment values[21] is solidly encultured. Where these values are under-developed, democracy might be sustained by exceptionally benevolent elites. But relying on benevolent elites is a naive bet on democracy. A merely elite-sustained democracy has no defense when autocratic temptations corrupt the elites' democratic commitment at one point. In fact, this is what the current resurgence of authoritarianism demonstrates in a number of backsliding democracies.

Since the Washington Consensus in the early 1980s, a steep increase in Western-funded democracy promotion, combined with the conditioning of international aid on electoral accountability, reshaped the incentive structure of the international system. Accordingly, rulers in many countries felt tempted to introduce electoral contestation and democratic constitutions.[22] The ensuing regional waves of democratization affected numerous countries in which large population segments lack an intrinsic appreciation of democracy's Enlightenment values. Seemingly widespread support for democracy all over the world is only hiding over the fact that the apparent avowal of the word "democracy" often lacks a firm foundation in values.[23] In countries where this lack of a profound value base is endemic, seeming support for democracy coexists – not surprisingly – with severe misunderstandings of what democracy actually means.[24] These are also the countries where democracy recedes under the surge of illiberal populism.

In the European Union, Romania, Hungary and Poland are cases in point. In fulfillment of the *Acquis Communautaire* during the accession to the EU, the governments of these countries institutionalized democracy in the early 1990s at a higher level than the values of their populations support.[25] Populist leaders intuitively recognize such regime-culture misfits, capitalize on them in their campaigns, win elections this way and eventually cut back on democracy's liberal qualities. Victor Orban's propagation of "illiberal democracy" is paradigmatic. One might actually conclude that the world has, in a sense, become "over-democratic" during the apex of the Third Wave and is now experiencing a "regression to the mean."[26]

Democracy's culture-bound ascension

Recurrent setbacks notwithstanding, the world as a whole has become gradually more democratic through two centennial trends: (1) a continuous rise of democratic standards among Western countries and (2) a sequence of regional waves of democratization into non-Western countries.[27] As of now, the world is still at a historic record level of democracy, although a mild recent backsliding to lower levels of democracy is apparent in most regions.[28] The key question is whether this recession will turn out to be a temporary intermission of the long-term trend or whether it will reverse the ascending democratic trajectory altogether.

I argue that greater awareness of democracy's cultural anchors helps us to answer this question with a greater sense of realism. These cultural anchors reveal themselves when we recognize the element of continuity that endures throughout all the democratic up- and downswings of recent decades. Mainstream scholarship is negligent about this element of continuity. It is, hence, overdue to pinpoint it.

Since the end of WWII, the global variation in autocracy-vs-democracy maps astoundingly tight on the countries' belongingness to Western and non-Western culture zones. In fact, the tightness of this cultural mapping is a temporal constant that accounts for a striking 70% of the global variation in autocracy-vs-democracy – in *any* given year from 1960 until today (Figure 1). This element of continuity indicates

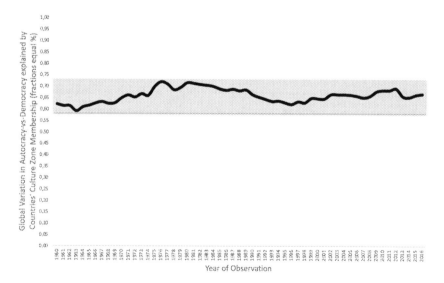

Figure 1. Temporal Constancy in the Global Variation in Autocracy-vs-Democracy due to the Countries' Culture Zone Membership.

Note: Data are from the Varieties of Democracy (V-Dem) project (www.v-dem.net) and cover 175 countries. See S. Lindberg, M. Coppedge and J. Gerring et al. (eds.). 2018. V-Dem Democracy Dataset (release version 2018). V-Dem Institute Gothenburg University, Sweden. Countries are attributed to culture zones due to Welzel's (2013) historically grounded culture zone scheme (see Figure 6 and https://www.cambridge.org/cl/files/8613/8054/8416/FreedomRising_OA.pdf). Introduced by Brunkert et al. (2018, cited in endnote 27), autocracy-vs-democracy is the product of V-Dem's electoral, participatory and liberal democracy component measures. To calculate culture zone averages in autocracy-vs-democracy, countries are weighted proportional to the size of their national population.

that, throughout all the various trending patterns, we always find countries from Western cultures at the forefront of democracy. In other words, the global average in democracy continued to rise constantly but the highest levels of democracy remain to be found in the West.

The fact that the global distribution of autocracy-vs-democracy maps in astounding constancy on the distinction between Western and non-Western cultures, and that this constancy persists in spite of the complex trending patterns in global regime dynamics, is to date largely unnoticed. This stunning observation calls for a theorizing of global regime dynamics in *cultural* terms, and quite profoundly so.

The cultural essence that underlies the Western/non-Western distinction is a dimension of moral values that I call *authoritarian*-vs-*emancipative* values.[29] Indeed, fully 56% of all the cultural differences between the Western and non-Western world[30] boil down to differences over authoritarian-vs-emancipative values (Figure 2). In light of this evidence, emphasis on emancipative values is the cultural signature of Western civilization.

Emancipative values combine a libertarian emphasis on freedom of choice with an egalitarian emphasis on equality of opportunities.[31] Emancipative values in this understanding reflect the origin of liberal democracy in Enlightenment thought. These values involve more than mere lip service to the catchword "democracy"; instead, emancipative values embody a principled commitment to the view of human nature from which democracy derives its original inspiration. That is the reason why the spread of emancipative values in a population has way more predictive power over the countries' actual level of democracy than is true for the percentage of people just saying to support democracy.[32]

To be sure, people who defy emancipative values are no less likely to express support for democracy than anyone else. But decoupled from emancipative values,

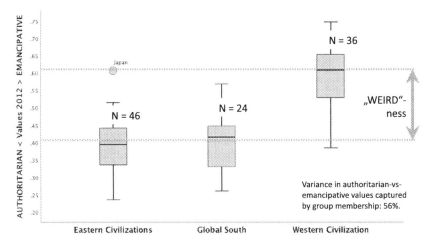

Figure 2. The Western/Non-Western Divide over Authoritarian-vs-Emancipative Values.

Note: Vertical axis displays Welzel's (2013) emancipative values index, with scores estimated for 2012 from current cohort differences, as explained in Section 2 of the Online Appendix. Estimations are based on data from the World Values Surveys (www.worldvaluessurvey.org) (Haerpfer, Inglehart, Moreno and Welzel et al., cited in endnote 8). "WEIRD"ness refers to Henrich's (2020) notion of "Western-Educated-Industrialized-Rich-Democratic" (in short: WEIRD) societies. See J. Henrich .2020. The WEIRDest People in the World. New York: Allen Lance. Due to Welzel's (2013) culture zone scheme, "Eastern Civilizations" include nations of the "Islamic East" (Middle East and Northern Africa), the "Orthodox East" (post-Soviet space), "Indic East" (South Asia) and "Sinic East" (East Asia). The "Global South" captures the nations of Latin America and Sub-Saharan Africa. "Western Civilization" covers the nations of the "Reformed West" (Protestant Europe), the "New West" (North America, Australia and New Zealand), the "Old West" (Catholic Mediterranean Europe) and the "Returned West" (ex-communist EU member states). See also Figure 6.

support for democracy often involves authoritarian misconceptions of what democracy truly means. Should these people take action in favor of what they believe democracy is, it is highly uncertain that such actions serve democracy in its real meaning. In stark contrast, support for democracy is genuine in conjunction with emancipative values because these values oppose any form of autocratic domination over people's beliefs and actions. Moreover, emancipation-minded people support democracy for the proper reasons because their values imply a deeply internalized appreciation of democracy's liberal-egalitarian inspiration. For this reason, emancipation-minded people resist authoritarian misinterpretations of democracy and support democracy for the freedoms by which it entitles the people.[33] Finally, emancipative values embody an expressive urge to voice shared concerns in public, which is why emancipation-minded people demonstrate in favor of democratic freedoms when these freedoms are denied or challenged, even in the face of autocratic repression.[34]

Obviously, whether a country attains or sustains democracy depends on the power balance between anti- and pro-democratic actors at the level of elites. But a key element in this elite-level power balance is how much public support the respective actors can muster in favor of their goals. This is exactly where the distribution of authoritarian-vs-emancipative values makes the critical mass-level factor: the more widespread emancipative values become, the more does mass support turn away from anti-democratic forces and lend itself towards pro-democratic forces. Therefore, the attainment, sustenance and deepening of democracy all become more likely as emancipative values gain momentum on a mass-scale.[35]

In support of this argument, the upper diagram of Figure 3 illustrates the astoundingly close correlation between authoritarian-vs-emancipative values and autocratic-vs-democratic regimes in 2002-2012, with values measured ten years *before* regimes.[36] Admittedly, in the absence of experimental control this evidence does not reveal the causal mechanism that accounts for its existence. But whatever that mechanism might be, the tightness of this relationship alone (with a 70% explained variance) provides a striking case for regime-culture congruence.

Moreover, a comparison with the lower scatterplot at least suggests a causal interpretation: in 1980, regimes also tended to be democratic in proportion to the extent to which the population endorsed emancipative values in 1970. But there was a group of "incongruent" societies – including, among others, Argentina, Chile, Uruguay, the Philippines, Hungary, Czechoslovakia, the GDR and South Africa – where the regimes have been way too autocratic relative to their populations' relatively advanced emancipative values. By no coincidence, a few years later all of these countries became prominent examples of transitions from autocracy to democracy.

The rise of emancipative values

Originally a domain of liberal philosophers, emancipative values began to spread into wider population segments when mass-scale economic progress profoundly improved the living conditions of ordinary people, giving them access to previously unknown goods, services and opportunities, plus the prospect of upward social mobility through educational merit. Taken together, these increasingly enabling living conditions enhance people's agency in taking their lives into their own hands, planning for themselves and making their own judgements. Once people have learnt to think for themselves, their need for doctrinal guidance in what to believe and to do fades;

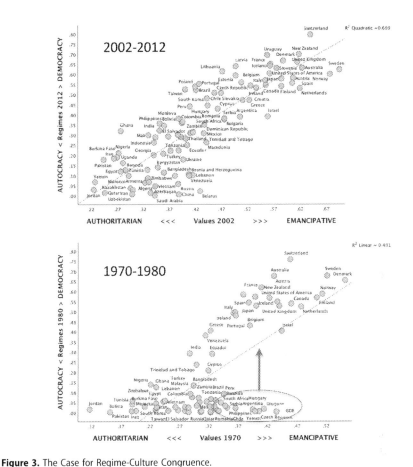

Figure 3. The Case for Regime-Culture Congruence.

Note: Horizontal axes display Welzel's (2013) emancipative values index, with scores estimated for 2002 and 1970 from current cohort differences, as explained in Section 2 of the Online Appendix. Estimations are based on data from the World Values Surveys (www.worldvaluessurvey.org) (Haerpfer, Inglehart, Moreno and Welzel et al., cited in endnote 8). The measure of the vertical axes is explained in the footer of Figure 1.

they no longer want to be told what decisions to make and what actions to take. In that moment, people find inherent appeal in emancipative values.[37]

In this Enlightenment moment, a drive towards liberation from domination of one's thoughts and actions awakes from dormancy. This awakening is a natural response of the human mind to increasingly enabling living conditions. For this reason, no ideological programme and no orchestrated strategy is needed to enculture emancipative values, once people experience enabling living conditions.[38] In other words, emancipative values are not the result of a top-down fabricated ideology; they evolve naturally bottom-up under expanding existential opportunities – no matter if those in power want this to happen or not. Supporting this enlightenment logic, Figure 4 documents that authoritarian-vs-emancipative values map tightly on how far a society's cognitive mobilization has advanced, that is, how pervasively education, information, communication, science and technology penetrate people's daily lives. Again, the relationship does not reveal which causal mechanism creates it. But by all means of plausibility, it is far more intuitive to assume that emancipative values rise in response to cognitive mobilization instead of the other way around.

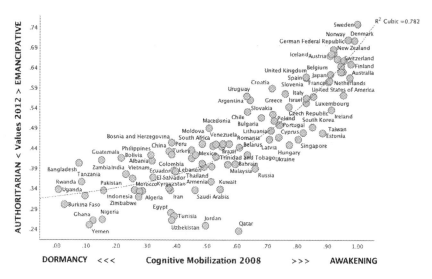

Figure 4. Emancipative Values as a Response to Cognitive Mobilization.

Note: Horizontal axis is the World Bank's knowledge index (divided by 100), which combines in a single index information on a population's average educational achievement, informational connectedness and per capita scientific output (e.g., patents per inhabitants). The vertical axis is Welzel's (2013) emancipative values index, with scores estimated for 2012 from current cohort differences, as explained in Section 3 of the Online Appendix. Estimations are based on data from the World Values Survey (www.worldvaluessurvey.org), (Haerpfer, Inglehart, Moreno and Welzel et al., cited in endnote 8).

Since several decades, rising living standards, falling mortalities, dropping fertilities as well as expanding education and other aspects of cognitive mobilization turn existential conditions more enabling in most parts of the world. Only a shrinking number of trouble spots remain excluded from this generally progressive trend.[39] Across the globe, existential opportunities, emancipative values and liberal democracy have been rising in baffling unison, promoting an encompassing trend towards human empowerment more broadly speaking (Figure 5). Consequently, emancipative values are spreading out beyond the borders of Western culture and are now ascending through generational replacement across all of the globe's culture zones (Figure 6). True, a firmly encultured emphasis on emancipative values still remains a Western singularity, yet the dynamic points to a ubiquitous rise of these values all around the world.

Cultural relativists would argue that there is no moral hierarchy in human values. Values just differ by culture and each culture is in an equally legitimate position to praise its own values.[40] Due to this view, authoritarian values are just as good or bad as emancipative values. This position might appear charming because of its seeming cultural neutrality. But the charm is deceptive because it denies an existing moral hierarchy that places emancipative values at an ethically more indiscriminate position than authoritarian values. This moral hierarchy relates to the fact that emancipative values unleash the brighter ethical qualities of human nature. Indeed, people who endorse emancipative values operate on a broader "mental bandwidth" in that their concerns go beyond the here and now and beyond the wellbeing of their close ingroup. In that sense, emancipative values embody a "transcendent mentality" that holds a more indiscriminately benevolent view of humans and the world – which means a higher ethical quality.[41]

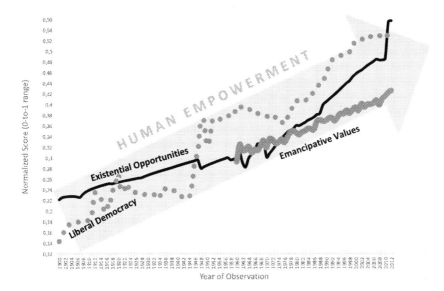

Figure 5. The Global Rise of the Three Ingredients of Human Empowerment.

Note: Existential opportunities combine per capita incomes, mean years of schooling, inverse fertility and inverse income inequality (GINI) into a single index, using a time-pooled cross-sectional factor analysis and standardizing the resulting country-by-year z-scores into a 0-to-1 scale. For times before the World Development Indicator Series starts (i.e., before 1960), the index shows predicetd scores using Vanhanen's index of power resources as the regressor. Emancipative values represent backward estimations of Welzel's (2013) index, as explained in Section 3 of the Online Appendix. Introduced by Brunkert et al. (citation in endnote 27), liberal democracy measures autocracy-vs-democracy by a multiplicative combination, of V-Dem's liberal, electoral and participatory democracy components. To calculate global averages for the three indices, national data are weighted in proportion to the respective country's population size. To adjust scores on liberal democracy such that its base level is comparable to the other two indices, the cubic root of the original scores is displayed.

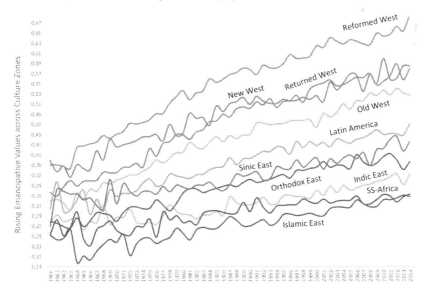

Figure 6. Trajectories and Cycles in the Global Rise of Emancipative Values by Culture Zones.

Notes: Emancipative values are backward estimations by transposing cohort differences in a recent survey into a time-series of annual observations, with trend and intercept adjustments, as explained in Section 3 of the Online Appendix. Trends displayed here are based on data from 79 nations, weighting national samples in proportion to the respective country's population size. Estimations are based on data are from the World Values Surveys (www.worldvaluessurvey.org) (Haerpfer, Inglehart, Moreno and Welzel et al., cited in endnote 8).

Illiberal scripts of modernity

Since Russia's anti-Western turn and China's global outreach, the power structure of the international system ceases to operate as uniformly in favor of democracy as it used to in the aftermath of the Cold War.[42] With Russia and China, two powers are gaining weight that propagate an explicitly illiberal script of modernity. This script is couched in a cultural narrative about non-Western geo-political identities that inspire illiberal missions of modernization, in open confrontation with the West's liberal model of modernity. Illiberal scripts of modernity had been influential in the past when major industrial powers, like Nazi Germany and fascist Japan in the 1930s and the Soviet Union during the 1950s, seemed to pursue with sweeping success a non-democratic course of modernization.

Already Barrington Moore[43] distinguished three paths into modernity and the democratic route was just one of them, next to fascism and communism. While fascism and communism have been trashed by history, we now see populist authoritarianism compete with liberal democracy for the better version of modernity. The mechanism is still the same though: rulers deny the values of the Enlightenment as a Western alienation of their own culture's values and try to pick from modernity those parts that make their nation more powerful, like technological progress, economic prosperity and military prowess, while avoiding modernity's disliked emancipatory consequences known from the West, most notably democracy.

Autocrats and populists deliberately compose narratives about national destinies and geo-political missions to breed a "culture of sanctity," in the hope that emancipative values remain dormant under the blanket of national allegiance and religious faith. To some extent, this strategy actually pays off, as we see from the upper diagram in Figure 7. As is obvious, the extent to which ruling elites succeed in feeding sanctity cults indeed diminishes the translation of cognitive mobilization into emancipative values, thus slowing down the liberating consequences of modernization. However, the more important information is entailed in the lower diagram of Figure 7. In comparison to Figure 4, we see here that the emancipatory effect of cognitive mobilization looks considerably weaker when we take into consideration the counter-acting role of sanctity cults. Nevertheless, the effect still shows up recognizably and turns out to be stronger than its counter-acting force (compare the explained variances: 52% in contrast to 31%). In a nutshell, authoritarian sanctity cults certainly slow down but do by no means entirely eradicate the emancipatory consequences of ongoing modernization.

Historically, fascist and communist versions of the illiberal script of modernity did not sustain. As concerns the contemporary versions of the illiberal script, the jury is still out. But the afore-shown evidence suggests that time is operating against the novel illiberal versions, too. Also, living conditions continue to become more enabling in most places of the world; and this enabling turn gives rise to emancipative values, irrespective of a culture's particular traditions. The evidence in Figure 6 above supports this conjecture using cohort-based projections of the emancipatory trajectory by culture zones.

The selective force in global regime evolution

Emancipative values are on a long-term rise and have evolved to ever new frontiers, with same-sex marriage and animal rights among the more recent extensions.

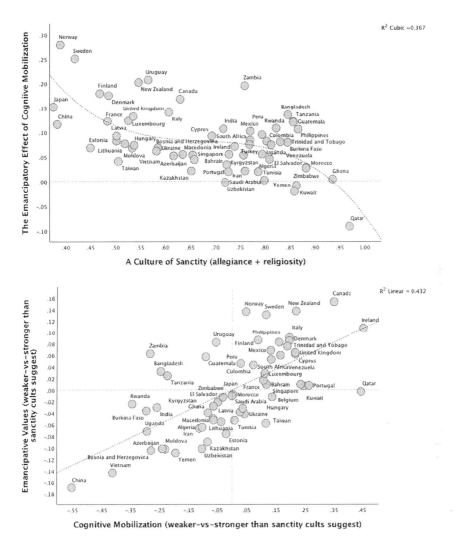

Figure 7. Sanctity Cults as a Decelerator of Modernity's Emancipatory Effect.

Note: Horizontal axis is the inverse of Welzel's (2013) secular values index (short version), thus measuring the combination of national pride, an urge to make one's parents proud, willingness to fight for one's country in the case of war, respect for authority and strength of religious belief as well as frequency of religious practice.
The vertical axis displays the residuals in emancipative values in 2012 unexplained by a country's advancement in cognitive mobilization (see Figure 4). Data are from the World Values Surveys (www.worldvaluessurvey.org) (Haerpfer, Inglehart, Moreno and Welzel et al., cited in endnote 8).
Note: Variables on the two axes are residuals of the same variables in Figure 4, obtained after controlling the effect of cognitive mobilization on emancipative values for sanctity in the diagram above.

Despite this ascending dynamic, the correlation between democracy and emancipative values is a temporal constant, exhibiting a persistently tight connection throughout the past decades (Figure 8). This evidence indicates that, despite democracy's recurrent up- and downswings, we always find those countries at the forefront of democracy whose populations have encultured emancipative values most firmly.

Global regime dynamics in autocracy-vs-democracy exhibit an intriguing simultaneity. On the one hand, democracy oscillates in recurrent cycles along an ascending

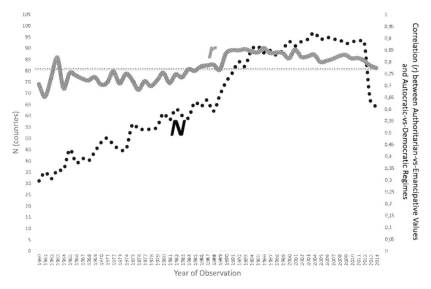

Figure 8. Temporal Constancy of Autocratic-vs-Democratic Regimes' Link to Authoritarian-vs-Emancipative Values.
Note: See footer of Figure 5 for data sources and measurement details.

trajectory. On the other hand, steadily rising emancipative values correlate with democracy at constant strength throughout all of democracy's cycles. This simultaneity can only exist because a two-fold regularity in global regime dynamics prevails: (1) during democratic upswings, countries with more widespread emancipative values are *more* likely to follow the trend and make shifts towards democracy; (2) during democratic downswings, countries with more widespread emancipative values are *less* likely to follow the trend and withstand shifts away from democracy. Should this be an accurate description, of which the available evidence suggests that it indeed is, then the dynamic of emancipative values is the decisive selective force in the global evolution of political regimes.

Challenging the deconsolidation-thesis

The evidence presented here casts doubts on the alarmist idea that democracy's cultural foundation is in a process of deconsolidation. The deconsolidation-thesis is most profoundly mistaken in its portrayal of inter-generational cultural change. Its advocates propagate that mass support for democracy is in decline all around the world, including most notably long-established democracies, and that it is the younger generations in particular who turn their back to democracy.

None of these claims is tenable, however. This is clear beyond reasonable doubt when looking at the World Values Surveys' complete country coverage and temporal scope, rather than cherry-picking particular countries and periods. In fact, mass support for democracy increased in more countries ($N = 26$) than it declined ($N = 14$) from the third round (1994-98) till the seventh round (2017-20) of polls. On average across the globe, mass support for democracy remained stable at 75% over this time span and age differences account for a minuscule 4% (*sic*) of the total individual-level variation in support for democracy.[44]

Much more importantly though, lip service to democracy as documented in surveys is an altogether inconclusive indicator of a culture's fitness for democracy. The reason is that overt support for democracy obscures deeply encultured differences in how people understand democracy. Some of these understandings are actually so strongly twisted into an authoritarian direction that the meaning of support for democracy reverts into its own negation – support for autocratic rule, that is. Where this is the case, people systematically mistake autocratic regime characteristics for democratic ones. Consequently, autocracy is likely to prevail or to revive in precisely these places.[45]

The propaganda of autocrats deliberately nourishes misperceptions of democracy as obedience to rulers. As a matter of fact, most autocracies portray themselves as democracies. China, for instance, depicts itself since recently as the world's "greatest democracy" and officials claim that cultural authenticity entitles each nation to develop its own version of democracy. The usual indoctrination denigrates Western democracies as overly liberal perversions of "true" democracy, which is then presented as a form of "guardianship" by which "wise" rulers govern in the best of people's interest. In return for such "enlightened" rulership, the people owe their leaders obedience.[46] Schools, the media and other institutions under government control all disseminate those guardianship tales, which vary from culture to culture in attire but not in content. Across the globe, the World Values Surveys exhibit an astoundingly large percentage of people (easily above 50%, to be precise) who indeed misunderstand democracy as "people obey their rulers" (Figure 9).

In the absence of emancipative values, people lack the moral stature to resist authoritarian propaganda. Therefore, autocrats have a vested interest in keeping

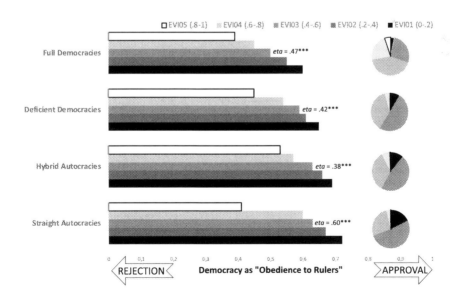

Figure 9. Misunderstandings of Democracy as "Obedience to Rulers" by Emancipative Values and Regime Type.
Note: Data are from the World Values Surveys (www.worldvaluessurvey.org), rounds 6 (2010-14) and 7 (2017-20). See Haerpfer, Inglehart, and Moreno et al. (citation in endnote 8). "Straight Autocracies": countries scoring 0-.25 on autocracy-vs-democracy. "Mixed Autocracies": countries scoring .25-.50 on autocracy-vs-democracy. "Deficient Democracies": countries scoring .50-.75 on autocracy-vs-democracy. "Full Democracies": countries scoring .75-1 on autocracy-vs-democracy. "Autocracy-vs-Democracy" uses Brunkert et al.'s (citation in endote 27) measure of "comprehensive democracy" based on V-Dem, as explained in the footer of Figure 1. For the countries covered in each regime category, see Section 4 in the Online Appendix.

emancipative values dormant.[47] To achieve this end, autocrats breed national sanctity cults that propagate a geo-political mission in explicit opposition to the West's emancipatory spirit. Cultural identity constructions are the most potent tool in this psychological game. Explicitly anti-Western constructions of cultural identity aim to rejuvenate modern forms of tribalism that de-individuate people to turn them into blind followers of their heroic rulers. In China, Russia, Turkey, Venezuela and other places where illiberal forces are in power, we witness these indoctrinations on a daily basis (Figure 10).

When emancipative values spread, misunderstandings of democracy as obedience to rulers recede. Strikingly, this effect is so sweeping that it unfolds regardless of the type of regime in place (Figure 9). Complementing this finding, we observe a current illiberal cycle in public mood throughout mature Western democracies. As a result, there is a noticeable rise in popular support for *"strong leaders who do not have to bother with parliaments and elections."* But this increase is largely limited to people with weak and mediocre emancipative values; it is not discernible among people with strong emancipative values. Consequently, authoritarian-vs-emancipative values differentiate Western publics more strongly than they did in the past over the approval-vs-rejection of strongmen rule (Figure 10). These observations reinforce the conclusion that strong emancipative values provide the mightiest antidote against authoritarian redefinitions of democracy.[48]

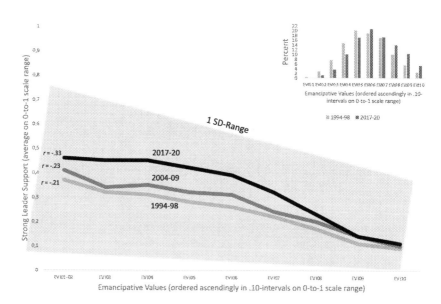

Figure 10. Strong Leader Support over Time and by Emancipative Values.

Note: Data are from the World Values Surveys (http://www.worldvaluessurvey.org/): Haerpfer, Inglehart and Moreno et al. (citation in endnote 8). Fractions are equivalent to percentages of national samples agreeing strongly or fairly with the statement that it is a good idea to have *"strong leaders who do not have to bother with parliaments and elections."* National samples are weighted in proportion to the respective country's population size and cover a constant set of mature Western democracies participating in rounds 3 (1994-98), 5 (2005-09) and 7 (2017-19) of the World Values Surveys, including: Australia, Finland, Germany, New Zealand, Norway, Spain, Sweden, Switzerland, the UK and the US.

A cultural theory of autocracy-vs-Democracy

What explains the tight link between emancipative values and liberal democracy and its constant strength over time?[49] In answering this question, I propose a cultural theory of autocracy-vs-democracy.[50] This theory conceptualizes the relationship between emancipative values and democratic institutions as a supply-demand link with respect to freedoms. In this relationship, democratic institutions constitute the elite-side supply of freedoms, while emancipative values constitute the mass-side demand for them. Now, while values change continuously but slowly through generational replacement, institutions change through rare but incisive ruptures, like revolutions, coup d'états, civil wars or foreign invasions. Hence, a co-evolutionary dynamic between these two differently paced processes can only follow a tectonic tension-release logic: incrementally changing demands for freedom build up an accruing tension with frozen supply levels, until this tension releases through a sudden regime turn that brings the supplies back into equilibrium with the demands. Accordingly, the direction and scope of regime change operates as a correction of the supply's once accrued misfit to the demand. This model implies three regularities:

(1) Where the supply of freedoms falls short of the demand, an occurring regime change shifts the supply *upward*. In this case, we observe democratization.
(2) Where the supply of freedoms exceeds the demand, an occurring regime change shifts the supply *downward*. In this scenario, we witness autocratization.
(3) Where the supply of freedoms roughly fits the demand, no regime change occurs and the supply stays where it was. This is the case of regime stability, which can be either democratic or autocratic stability.

The upper diagram in Figure 11 largely confirms these propositions. On the horizontal axis, one sees to what extent a country's supply of freedoms thirty years back in time underbid or overbid the population's demand back then. These regime-culture misfits explain what we see on the vertical axis: the direction and extent of subsequent regime changes over the following thirty years, that is, the timespan of a generation. The diagram exemplifies this logic by setting the timepoint t_{-30} at 1980 and the timepoint t_0 at 2010. Yet, the pattern is generalizable to any thirty-year interval between 1960–1995 and 1985–2015 (OA-Figures 6–8 in the Online Appendix).

Indeed, where regimes were too autocratic relative to the surrounding society's cultural values a generation ago, democratization happened at *some* point in the subsequent thirty-years period and did so in approximate proportion to the regime's initial misfit to its embedding culture. Vice versa, where regimes were too democratic relative to the surrounding society's cultural values, autocratization happened. And again, it did so in approximate proportion to the regime's once accrued misfit to its embedding culture. Likewise, neither democratization nor autocratization happened to a noteworthy extent where regimes roughly fit the culture of the society in which they are settled.

One qualification of this generalization is due, however. In the broad time perspective of a generation, democratic regime turnovers heavily outweigh autocratic turnovers in both number and scope, with Venezuela sticking out as the single most illustrative example for an enduring autocratic turnover. This observation highlights a striking asymmetry: when countries are too democratic relative to their populations' values, the resulting pressures to autocratize are apparently much weaker than are the

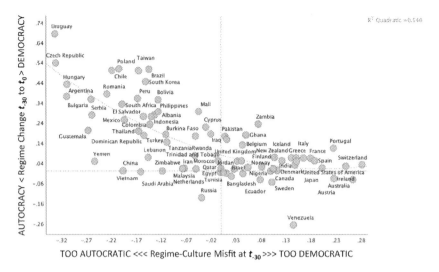

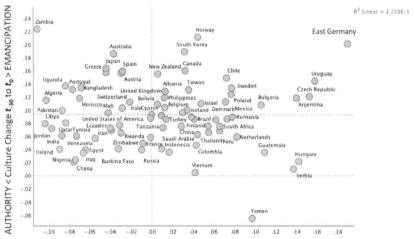

Figure 11. Regime-Culture Coevolution I: Misfits drive regime change but not culture change.

Notes: **Horizontal axis** measures the regime-culture misfit at time t_{-30} by regressing liberal demo-cracy at time t_{-30} on backward estimated emancipative values at time t_{-30} and plotting the residuals. Negative residuals suggest that the regime has been too autocratic relative to the population's emancipative values thirty years back in time. Positive residuals suggest that the regime has been too democratic relative to the population's emancipative values thirty years back in time.

Vertical axis measures change in liberal democracy from time t_{-30} till time t_0. In this diagram, t_{-30} is 1980 and time t_0 is 2010. Yet, the pattern exemplified here is generalizable to other thirty-year intervals: Regimes change as a function of their once accrued misfit to the surrounding culture. The backward Estimation of emancipative values is explained in the Online Appendix.

Notes: **Horizontal axis** measures the culture-regime misfit at time t_{-30} by regressing backward estimated emancipative values at time t_{-30} on liberal democracy at time t_{-30} and plotting the residuals. Negative residuals suggest that culture has been too author-itarian relative to the regime's democraticness (or lack thereof) thirty years back in time. Positive residuals suggest that the culture has been too emancipatory relative to the regime's democraticness (or lack thereof) thirty years back in time.

Vertical axis measures change in estimated emancipative values from time t_{-30} till time t_0. In this diagram, t_{-30} is 1980 and time t_0 is 2010. Yet, the pattern exemplified here is generalizable to other thirty-year intervals: Values do NOT change as a function of their once accrued misfit to regime institutions.

pressures to democratize when countries are too autocratic relative to their populations' values. Accordingly, authoritarian cultures seem to be more tolerant of democratic institutions than emancipatory cultures are of autocratic institutions. A reason for this pattern could be that authoritarian cultures prevail under less enabling living conditions, in which case most people lack the means, skills and maybe even urge to enforce an opposing regime preference.

Rethinking regime-culture coevolution

Once more, over the thirty-year timespan of a generation, democratization heavily outweighs autocratization in both the number of regime changes and their scope. This holds true throughout *every* thirty-year period between 1900 and 2015 – a barely noticed piece of evidence (OA-Figure 7 in the Online Appendix). In its face, we have to conclude that there is a truly massive democratic advantage in regime dynamics. It just needs a wider time window to see it. The main reason for this long-term democratic advantage in regime dynamics, I suppose, is that cultural values around the world have been predominantly shifting from an idolization of authoritarianism towards an emphasis on emancipation. This prevalent direction in cultural evolution has made unchanging regimes too undemocratic relative to their cultural undercurrent, and increasingly so. Consequently, the misfit-correcting function of regime change operates mostly to the favor of democracy – and increasingly as time passes by.

Due to this evidence, the undercurrent cultural change drives global regime dynamics in such fashion that generationally transforming values build up regime-culture misfits that get at some later point in time resolved through a sudden rupture that turns a regime into the opposite direction of its misfit to the undercurrent culture. Consequently, regime-culture coevolution advances as the interplay between cultural change as the misfit-*creating* force and regime change as the misfit-*resolving* force, as illustrated in Figure 12.

As far as the evidence suggests, the causal direction in regime-culture coevolution is such that cultural dynamics drive regime dynamics, much more so than the other way around. This becomes glaringly obvious when comparing the upper diagram in Figure 11 with the lower diagram. Indeed, the lower diagram reverses the causal direction, yet without uncovering any significant effect. In fact, while the upper diagram shows that regime changes happen in response to previously accrued regime-culture misfits, the lower diagram illustrates that the reverse does not hold true at all: cultural change does not proceed in response to previously accrued culture-regime misfits. The main reason, I suppose, why the causal direction in regime-culture coevolution is so one-sided in the long run is two-fold: (1) living conditions have turned more enabling since the Industrial Revolution in most places of the world; (2) autocracy slows down but certainly does not stop emancipative values from rising where this enabling turn happens.

The Temporality of democracy's reproductive advantage

Because cultural change proceeds steadily but slowly, we must widen the temporal horizon to make considerable changes in cultural values visible. And since generational replacement determines the rhythm of cultural change, thirty-year time intervals seem to provide the most appropriate temporal lens. Now, if regime dynamics respond indeed to cultural change, it follows suit that with regime dynamics, too, a thirty-year perspective reveals clearer patterns than shorter perspectives.

Figure 13 confirms this proposition in stunning clarity. Only a tiny 1.1% of all 15,282 regime observations between 1900 and 2015 are regime changes from one

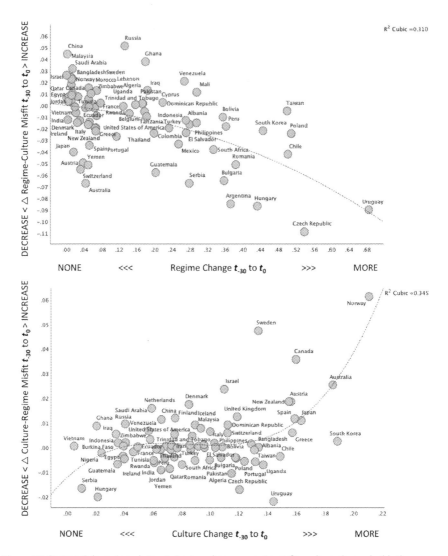

Figure 12. Regime-Culture Coevolution II: Regime change corrects misfits, culture change builds them.

Notes: **Horizontal axis** measures change in autocracy-vs-democracy from t_{-30} till t_0 (i.e., the pure amount of change disconsidering its direction). **Vertical axis** measures change in absolute regime-culture misfit scores (square-root of squared residuals) from t_{-30} till t_0. In this diagram, t_{-30} is 1980 and t_0 is 2010. Yet, the pattern exemplified with this temporal choice is generalizable to other 30-year intervals since 1970: regime change functions to **diminish** regime-culture misfits.

Notes: **Horizontal axis** measures change in estimated authoritarian-vs-emancipative values from t_{-30} till t_0 (i.e., the pure amount of change disconsidering its direction).
Vertical axis measures change in absolute culture-regime misfit scores (square-root of squared residuals) from t_{-30} till t_0. In this diagram, t_{-30} is 1980 and t_0 is 2010. Yet, the pattern exemplified with this temporal choice is generalizable to other 30-year intervals since 1970: cultural change funcitons to **magnify** culture-regime misfits.

year to the next. By implication, 98.9% of all regime observations are instances of regime stability from one year to the next. Such a powerful indication of stability should strike us as natural because political orders are made to last. Accordingly, the evolutionary advantage of democracy is hardly visible in a one-year perspective: of the 1.1% regime changes in any one-year timespan between 1900 and 2015, 0.8%

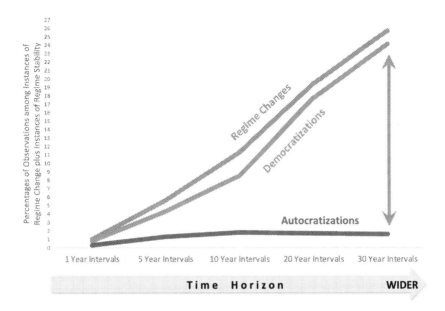

Figure 13. The Evolutionary Advantage of Democracy over Autocracy in Temporal Perspective..

Notes: Source is the V-Dem dataset (Lindberg et al. 2018), release version 2018. I measure regime change by subtracting a country's score on the Comprehensive Democracy Index (CDI) at an earlier time from that at a later time, using varying temporal spans. I count as autocratization any temporal change on the CDI surpassing -.10 into the negative and as democratization any temporal change on the CDI surpassing +.10 into the positive. All temporal changes on the CDI below these thresholds are counted as instances of regime stability. Observations are country-years. N varies from 15,282 for all 1-year changes between 1900 and 2015 and 10,848 for all 30-year changes between 1930 and 2015.

are democratizations and 0.3% are autocratizations – which does not come over as a towering advantage in favor of democracy.

By contrast, when we widen the temporal lens to cover thirty years, 25.7% of all 10,848 regime observations between 1900–1930 and 1985–2015 represent regime changes over a thirty-year timespan. Now, the evolutionary advantage of democracy surfaces potently: of these 25.7% regime changes over a generational timespan, 24.1% are democratizations and only 1.6% (!) are autocratizations. Accordingly, democratizations outnumber autocratizations only by a factor of 2.7 in a one-year serial perspective but by a factor of 15.1 in a thirty-year serial perspective. In other words, democratization follows a temporally *cumulative* dynamic, while autocratization follows a temporally *episodic* dynamic. These observations suggest that the recent democratic recession is a cyclical episode. Within shorter time-windows, regime dynamics from 1900 till 2015 have shown many democratic recessions – yet never in the long run. The question, of course, is if we have good reasons to rely on the endurance of democracy's long-term advantage. The generational profile of emancipative values suggests that we do.

OA-Figure 7 shows that the long-term reproductive supremacy of democracy over autocracy is not only huge but has been continuously increasing over the twentieth century. Even under recognition of the more recent reduction of the democratic advantage, this advantage remains monumental, with democratizations outnumbering autocratizations by a factor of 38 over the period 1985-2015.

Conclusion

In its essence, democracy is about freedoms – freedoms that entitle people to self-determine their private lives and to have a voice and vote in the public sphere of which they are part. In that very sense, democracy operates on our species' most highly evolved natural quality: human agency, that is. On a mass scale, democracy in this understanding existed nowhere, until the Industrial Revolution brought enabling living conditions to ordinary people. The reason for democracy's tie to mass-level enabling living conditions is simple: democracy is a demanding system that requires encultured qualities from the people among which it is practiced. Most notably, people need to endorse the values that make them appreciative of practicing the freedoms to which democracy entitles them. In short, these are emancipative values.

The long-term democratic trend over the past 120 years reflects the fact that globally progressing modernization plays more action resources into the hands of ordinary people and that this empowering turn in living conditions is giving rise to emancipative values. In perspective, these trends make modern mass publics more capable and eager to defend and demand freedoms. Since these groundbreaking empowering trends are spreading and accelerating, the long-term odds are tilted heavily in favor of democracy and against autocracy – in spite of the momentary democratic downcycle. The prevalent generational profile in emancipative values reinforces this conclusion. By the same token, the countries' vulnerability to the democratic downcycle varies with the differential prevalence of emancipative values in their populations.

This conclusion does not deny that even mature democracies are currently going through troubled waters, which involves grown class polarization over authoritarian-vs-emancipative values and greater readiness among those at the authoritarian end of this polarity to resort to violent political action. Still, if the pro-democratic forces manage to mobilize their support base and to elevate voter turnout, illiberal populism faces electoral defeat, as the recent European Parliament and US Presidential elections have just shown. In light of the ascendant generational profile of emancipative values, the momentary challenges to democracy are unlikely to completely revert democracy's long-term rise. For genuine democrats, this is not a reason for complacency but – on the contrary – a reason to struggle harder for their cause, precisely because it is far from being hopeless.

Summing up, a proper understanding of democracy's cultural anchors informs a two-fold, albeit succinct, conclusion. Negatively expressed, the prospects of democracy are bleak where emancipative values remain weak. Positively turned, wherever emancipative values come to light, democracy is about to shine bright.

Notes

1. Y. Mounk, *The People vs. Democracy*. Levitsky and Ziblatt, *How Democracies Die*.
2. Luehrmann et al. ("How Much Democratic Backsliding," "A Third Wave of Autocratization is There") attest a new wave of autocratization since the 2010s. By contrast, Lauth, Schlenkrich and Lemm, "Democracy Matrix," dispute a global democratic recession and diagnose instead a growing hybridization among both democracies and autocracies.
3. Foa and Mounk, "The Dangers of Deconsolidation," "The Signs of Deconsolidation."
4. Crozier, Huntington and Watanuki, *The Crisis of Democracy*.
5. Putnam and Pharr. *Disaffected Democracies*.
6. Bellah et al., *Habits of the Heart*.

RESILIENCE OF DEMOCRACY 145

7. Dalton, *Democratic Challenges – Democratic Choices*. Dalton, *Political Realignment*. Inglehart, *Modernization and Postmodernization*. Inglehart and Welzel, *Modernization, Cultural Change and Democracy*. Norris, *Democratic Phoenix*. Norris, *Democratic Deficit*.
8. Against alarmist voices, the largest collection of public opinion data around the globe, the World Values Surveys (www.worldvaluessurvey.org), shows no overall breakdown of public trust (Haerpfer et al., *World Values Surveys*
9. Norris, *Democratic Deficit*.
10. Again, and once more against alarmist voices, the data cited in endnote 8 exhibit neither a uniform nor an overall worldwide breakdown in public support for democracy. For proof, see Section 3.2 in the Online Appendix.
11. Alexander and Welzel, "The Myth of Deconsolidation." Voeten, "Are People Really Turning away from Democracy?." See also the public opinion trends documented in Section 3 of the Online Appendix.
12. Foa and Mounk, op. cit.
13. The concept of "public mood" describes regular cyclical fluctuations in illiberal-vs-liberal preferences in public opinion among the citizenries of mature democracies (Stimson, *Ideology in America*).
14. The concept of "emancipative values" describes an internalized appreciation of universal human freedoms (Welzel, *Freedom Rising*).
15. Pinker, *Enlightenment Now*.
16. Luehrmann et al., op. cit.; Lauth, Schlenkrich and Lemm, op.cit.
17. Evidence in support of these points follows further below and in Section 4 of the Online Appendix.
18. "Intelligence-lifting" is to be understood literally and refers to the famous "Flynn effect," which denotes the generational rise of average IQ-scores among the populations of postindustrial knowledge economies (Flynn, *Are We Getting Smarter?*).
19. From a human empowerment perspective, which is at the heart of most of democratic theory, I consider democracy first and foremost as a system of entitlements provided, protected and enforced by the state—entitlements in the form of civil rights that allow people self-determination in personal affairs, that give them an equal voice and vote in public affairs and that protect them from oppression and discrimination (Kymlicka, *Multicultural Citizenship*; Brettschneider, *Democratic Rights*).
20. Dahl, *Polyarchy*; Held, *Models of Democracy*.
21. As Enlightenment values I define the view of human nature due to which our humanity resides in our faculty to think for ourselves and that this faculty entitles us to be trained in this faculty and then to utilize it for personal self-determination and political participation (Grayling, *Toward the Light of Liberty*).
22. Yilmaz, "The International Context."
23. Kirsch and Welzel, "Democracy Misunderstood." Kruse, Ravlik and Welzel, "Democracy Confused."
24. Ibid.
25. Inglehart and Welzel, op. cit.
26. Welzel and Inglehart, "Political Culture, Mass Beliefs and Value Change."
27. Brunkert, Kruse and Welzel, "A Tale of Culture-Bound Regime Evolution."
28. Luehrmann et al., op. cit. But see Lauth, Schlenkrich and Lemm, op.cit., who dispute an autocratization trend and diagnose, instead, a "hybridization" of both democracies and autocracies.
29. Welzel, op. cit.
30. Underlying the statistics is the historically grounded scheme of global cultural zones by Brunkert et al., op. cit.
31. Using data from the World Values Surveys for about a hundred countries, emancipative values measure support for universal freedoms by combining responses to four themes, each of which comprises three questions, including (1) gender equality (support for women's equal access to education, jobs and politics), (2) child autonomy (independence, imagination and non-obedience as desired child qualities), (3) public voice (support for freedom of speech and public participation in local, job and national affairs) and (4) reproductive freedoms (tolerance of homosexuality, abortion and divorce). Index scores vary between 0 at the authoritarian end and 1.0 at the emancipatory end, with multiple decimal fractions for intermediate positions.

146 RESILIENCE OF DEMOCRACY

Section 1 of the Online Appendix documents the index construction. Besides, there is a dispute about the measurement equivalence of emancipative values. Alemán and Woods ("Value Orientations from the World Values Surveys") and Sokolov ("The Index of Emancipative Values") claim that emancipative values do not measure the same concept across countries because the constituent items show different factor loadings in different countries. Brunkert, Inglehart and Kruse et al. ("Non-Invariance?"), by contrast, demonstrate that "compositional substitutability" allows different items to substitute each other's function in different countries, for which reason non-invariance in factor loadings is no measurement problem.

32. Welzel and Inglehart (op. cit.) find that the predictive power of support for democracy over the countries' actual levels of democracy is entirely conditional: only that part of support for democracy which is tied to emancipative values predicts subsequent levels of democracy, whereas the part of support for democracy which is decoupled from emancipative values shows no posterior regime effect at all. Claassen, by contrast, finds that mass support for democracy underlies cyclical fluctuations (rather than showing a glacial decline as postulated by Foa and Mounk, op. cit.) and that these cycles drive corresponding cycles in regime dynamics towards more and less democracy, in line with Soroka and Wlezien's (*Degrees of Democracy*) thermostatic model of public opinion-policy interactions. Claassen's ("Does Public Support Help Democracy to Survuve?") evidence does not contradict Welzel and Inlgehart's findings because he does not divide support for democracy into its emancipatory and non-emancipatory partition. In light of the findings of Ruck et al. ("The Cultural Foundations of Modern Democracies") who show that the generational rise of emancipative values drove the global trend towards democracy over recent decades, it can be assumed that Claassen's findings would come out even stronger, had he measured support for democracy on the condition that this support is coupled with emancipative values.

33. Kirsch and Welzel, op. cit. Kruse, Ravlik and Welzel, op. cit.

34. Deutsch and Welzel, "Emancipative Values and Nonviolent Protest." For further proof, see Section 3.3 of the Online Appendix.

35. While the close relationship between emancipative values and levels of democracy is undisputed, its causal nature is a matter of debate, reflecting a division over whether the causal arrow in regime-culture coevolution runs from regimes to culture or the other way around. Against the proposition that rising emancipative values drive the ascension of democracy, Spaiser et al. ("The Dynamics of Democracy, Development and Cultural Values") as well as Dahlum and Knutsen ("Democracy by Demand?") claim that emancipative values mature under the imprint of democracy. The recent analyses by Brunkert et al. and Ruck et al. (op. cit.) and in this article resolve this dispute in favor of the claim that culture drives regimes more than the other way around.

36. It is an established insight that people reach a stable setpoint in their value orientations once their formative socialization is completed. Therefore, value change advances through generational replacement, which also means that current cohort differences in value orientations show the footprints of value change in the past. This allows one to transpose cohort differences in emancipative values from a recent national survey into a time series of annual measures by projecting the average emancipative values of people from the same birth year into the year in which these people were of a certain age. Section 2 of the Online Appendix documents these backward projections. For a similar procedure, see Ruck et al., op. cit.

37. Welzel and Inglehart, op. cit.

38. Ibid.

39. Rosling, Rosling and Rosling Roennlund, *Factfulness*. Goldstone and Diamond, "Demography and the Future of Democracy." Pinker, op. cit.

40. This position has been propagated by the defenders of authoritarian rule in the Asian values debate, while avoiding the term "authoritarian" values and calling them "collectivist" values instead (Yew, "Culture Is Destiny").

41. Emancipative values bring to dominance humans' better ethical qualities because these values embody a more indiscriminately benevolent view of people and the world. This is visible in the fact that emancipative values associate with higher out-group trust, stronger respect for human rights and a more universal sense of altruism. Ample evidence for this claim is presented in Welzel, op. cit. (ch. 6).

42. van den Bosch, "Introducing Regime Cluster Theory."

43. Moore, *The Social Origins of Democracy and Dictatorship*.
44. See the evidence in Section 3.2 of the Online Appendix.
45. Kirsch and Welzel; Kruse, Ravlik and Welzel, 2018 (op.cit).
46. One of the World Values Survey items actually phrases the meaning of democracy as "people obey their rulers" and this notion of democracy finds high levels of support in non-Western cultures.
47. Brown, "From Democratization to 'Guided' Democracy."
48. For a more detailed picture of the modest global increase in public support for strongmen rule, see Section 3.4 of the Online Appendix.
49. Brunkert et al.; Ruck et al. (op. cit.).
50. Welzel, Inglehart and Kruse, op. cit.

Disclosure statement

No potential conflict of interest was reported by the author(s).

Funding

This work was supported by Russian Science Foundation [Grant Number Russian Academic Excellence Project's 5-100's].

Bibliography

Alemán, J., and D. Woods. "Value Orientations from the World Values Survey." *Comparative Political Studies* 49 (2016): 1039–1067.

Alexander, A. C., and C. Welzel. "The Myth of Deconsolidation." *Journal of Democracy* 28 (2017. online debate forum.

Bellah, R. N., R. Madson, W. M. Sullivan, A. Swidler, and S. M. Tipton. *Habits of the Heart*. Berkeley: University of California Press, 1996.

Brown, A. "From Democratization to 'Guided' Democracy." *Journal of Democracy* 12 (2001): 35–41.

Brettschneider, C. *Democratic Rights*. Princeton: Princeton University Press, 2007.

Brunkert, L., S. Kruse, and C. Welzel. "A Tale of Culture-Bound Regime Evolution: the Centennial Democratic Trend and its Recent Reversal." *Democratization* 26 (2019): 422–443.

Brunkert, L., R. Inglehart, and S. Kruse. "Non-Invariance? On Overstated Problem with Misconceived Causes." *Sociological Methods and Research* 50 (2021. forthcoming.

Claassen, C. "Does Public Support Help Democracy to Survive?" *American Journal of Political Science* 64 (2020): 118–134.

Crozier, M. J., S. P. Huntington, and J. Watanuki. *The Crisis of Democracy*. New York: New York University Press, 1975.

Dahl, R. A. *Polyarchy*. New Haven: Yale University Press, 1973.

Held, D. *Models of Democracy*. Stanford: Stanford University Press, 1997.

Dahlum, S., and C. H. Knutsen. "Democracy by Demand?" *British Journal of Political Science* 45 (2015): 43–58.

Dalton, R. J. *Democratic Challenges – Democratic Choices*. Oxford: Oxford University Press, 2004.

Dalton, R. J. *Political Realignment*. Oxford: Oxford University Press, 2019.

Deutsch, F., and C. Welzel. "Emancipative Values and Non-Violent Protest: The Importance of 'Ecological' Effects." *British Journal of Political Science* 42 (2012): 465–479.

Foa, R. S., and Y. Mounk. "The Dangers of Deconsolidation." *Journal of Democracy* 27 (2016): 5–17.

Foa, R. S., and Y. Mounk. "The Signs of Deconsolidation." *Journal of Democracy* 28 (2017): 5–15.

Goldstone, J. A., and L. Diamond. "Demography and the Future of Democracy." *Perspectives on Politics* 17 (2020): 1–14.

Haerpfer, C., R. Inglehart and A. Moreno et al. (eds.). *World Values Surveys: Time Series 1981-2020* (release version 11/2020). Madrid: JD Systems Archive. 2020.

Inglehart, R. *Modernization and Postmodernization*. Princeton: Princeton University Press, 1997.

Inglehart, R., and C. Welzel. *Modernization, Cultural Change and Democracy*. New York: Cambridge University Press, 2005.

Flynn, J. R. *Are We Getting Smarter? Rising IQ in the 21st Century*. New York: Cambridge University Press, 2012.

Grayling, A. C. *Toward the Light of Liberty*. New York: Walker, 2007.

Kirsch, H., and C. Welzel. "Democracy Misunderstood." *Social Forces* 91 (2018): 1–33. S.

Kruse, S., M. Ravlik, and C. Welzel. "Democracy Confused." *Journal of Cross-Cultural Psychology* 49 (2018): 1–21.

Kymlicka, W. *Multicultural Citizenship*. Oxford: Oxford University Press, 1995.

Lauth, H.-J., O. Schlenkrich, and L. Lemm. "Democracy Matrix (DeMaX) Version 3 goes online." (www.democracymatrix.com). 2020.

Levitsky, S., and D. Ziblatt. *How Democracies Die*. New York: Crown Publishing Group, 2018.

Luehrmann, A., V. Mechnikova, and S. Lindberg. "How Much Democratic Backsliding?" *Journal of Democracy* 28 (2018): 162–169.

Luehrmann, A., and S. Lindberg. "A Third Wave of Autocratization is Here: What is new About it?" *Democratization* 26 (2019): 1095–1113.

Marquez, G. *Non-Democratic Politics*. London: Palgrave, 2016.

Moore, B. *The Social Origins of Democracy and Dictatorship*. Boston: Beacon Press, 1966.

Mounk, Y. *The People vs. Democracy*. New York: Cambridge University Press, 2018.

Norris, P. *Democratic Phoenix*. New York: Cambridge University Press, 2002.

Norris, P. *Democratic Deficit*. New York: Cambridge University Press, 2011.

Pinker, S. *Enlightenment Now*. New York: Penguin Books, 2018.

Putnam, R. D., and S. Pharr, eds. *Disaffected Democracies*. New Jersey: Princeton University Press. 2000.

Rosling, H., O. Rosling, and A. Rosling Roennlund. *Factfulness*. New York: Flatiron Books, 2018.

Ruck, D. J., L. J. Matthews, T. Kyritsis, et al. "The Cultural Foundations of Modern Democracies." *Nature - Human Behavior* 4 (2019): 264–269.

Sokolov, B. "The Index of Emancipative Values." *American Political Science Review* 113 (2018): 1–14.

Soroka, A., and C. Wlezien. *Degrees of Democracy*. New York: Cambridge University Press, 2014.

Spaiser, V., S. Ranganathan, R. P. Mann, and D. J. D. Sumpter. "The Dynamics of Democracy, Development and Cultural Values." *PLoS One* 9 (2014): 1–11.

Stimson, J. A. *Ideology in America*. New York: Cambridge University Press, 2012.

van den Bosch, J. J. J. "Introducing Regime Cluster Theory: Framing Regional Diffusion Dynamics of Democracy and Autocracy Promotion." *International Journal of Political Theory* 4 (2020): 71–102.

Voeten, E. "Are People Really Turning Away from Democracy?" *Journal of Democracy* 28 (2017. online debate forum.

Welzel, C. *Freedom Rising*. New York: Cambridge University Press, 2013.

Welzel, C., and R. F. Inglehart. "Political Culture, Mass Beliefs and Value Change." In C. Haerpfer, P. Bernhagen, and R. F. Inglehart, et al. (eds.), op.cit., 134–157, 2019.

Yew, L. K. "Culture Is Destiny." *Foreign Affairs* 73 (1994): 109–126.

Yilmaz, H. "The International Context." In *Democratization* (2nd fully revised edition), edited by C. Haerpfer, P. Bernhagen and R. F. Inglehart et al., 103–118. Oxford: Oxford University Press, 2019.

ð OPEN ACCESS

Disrupting the autocratization sequence: towards democratic resilience

Anna Lührmann **ⓘ**

ABSTRACT
Contemporary autocratization is typically the result of a long sequence of events and gradual processes. How can democratic actors disrupt such autocratization sequences in order to enhance democratic resilience? To address this question, this conclusion presents an ideal-typical autocratization sequence and entry points for democratic resilience. It builds on the findings of this special issue, extant research and a novel descriptive analysis of V-Party data. In the first autocratization stage, citizens' discontent with democratic institutions and parties mounts. Remedies lie in the areas of a better supply of democratic parties and processes as well as in civic education. During the second stage, anti-pluralists – actors lacking commitment to democratic norms – exploit and fuel such discontent to rise to power. In order to avoid the pitfalls of common response strategies, this article suggests "critical engagement", which balances targeted sanctions against radicals with attempts to persuade moderate followers; and has the aim of decreasing the salience of anti-pluralists' narratives by means of democratic (voter) mobilization. Thirdly, once autocratization begins, weak accountability mechanisms and opposition actors enable democratic breakdown. Thus, resilient institutions and a united and creative opposition are the last line of democratic defense.

The articles in this Special Issue demonstrate that processes of autocratization are multi-faceted and multi-causal. Because diverse factors may contribute to democratic failure,[1] strategies for democratic resilience are heterogenous. Nevertheless, many contemporary processes of autocratization share one commonality: democracy rarely dies overnight. Rather, "incumbents who accessed power in democratic elections gradually but substantially undermine democratic institutions".[2] Such processes of democratic erosion often span many years. In each step along that path, anti-pluralists – actors lacking "commitment to key democratic processes, institutions, and norms"[3] – challenge the resilience of democracies.

Building on such insights, I propose to schematize the process of autocratization and its drivers into three ideal-typical stages: first, citizens' discontent with democratic

---

This is an Open Access article distributed under the terms of the Creative Commons Attribution-NonCommercial-NoDerivatives License (http://creativecommons.org/licenses/by-nc-nd/4.0/), which permits non-commercial re-use, distribution, and reproduction in any medium, provided the original work is properly cited, and is not altered, transformed, or built upon in any way.

parties and democracy mounts (Stage 1), which enables adept anti-pluralists to rise to power in elections (Stage 2) and then to erode democracy to the extent that is possible given existing constraints (in Stage 3) (see Figure 1).

The articles in this special issue explore individual parts of this autocratization sequence. Welzel focuses on the role of democratic norms and values for autocratization and democratic resilience.[4] Finkel and Lim present evidence on how civic education may foster such traits.[5] Meléndez and Rovira Kaltwasser shed light on the voter potential of the most prevalent type of anti-pluralist party in Western Europe: the Populist Radical Right.[6] Somer, McCoy and Luke demonstrate that pernicious polarization, which many such actors actively promote through wilful political action, enables them to foster an autocratization agenda.[7] Laebens and Lührmann show how accountability mechanisms may halt autocratization even after it has begun.[8] Boese et al. distinguish between factors contributing to the onset of autocratization and those fostering the subsequent breakdown of democracy.[9]

The contributions show that autocratization is not inevitable. Many democratic regimes are able to "*prevent or react to challenges without losing its democratic character*".[10] What entry points do democratic actors – citizens, politicians, civil society groups, civil servants – have in this autocratization sequence where they can enhance such democratic resilience?

This article addresses this question as follows. Firstly, I develop the idea of an autocratization sequence and demonstrate the central role of anti-pluralist parties in this sequence using data from V-Dem and the V-Party project.[11] In the subsequent three sections, I elaborate on each of the three stages of autocratization in detail, and outline sources of democratic resilience. I conclude with a summary of the main resilience strategies and recommendations for future research.

The autocratization sequence: three stages to democratic breakdown

Structural and contextual challenges heighten the risk of autocratization. These include an economic or financial crisis, inequality, migration, the salience of polarizing cleavages, the rise of new communications technologies and cultural transformation.[12] Such challenges are one of several drivers and mediating factors that determine the

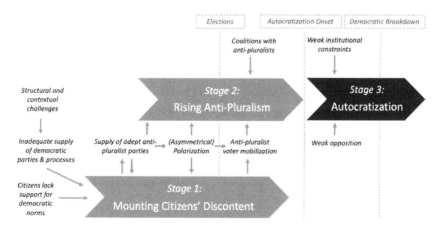

Figure 1. The autocratization sequence.

"success" of the autocratization sequence. Addressing them in a timely and effective manner shapes democratic resilience. Figure 1 includes some relevant challenges in italics. The list is not exhaustive.

Building on the contributions to this special issue, I argue that the rise of anti-pluralists to power becomes more likely if the following three factors are contributing to citizens' discontent with democratic parties and institutions: Firstly, an *inadequate supply of democratic parties and processes;* secondly, *lacking support for democratic norms,* which may be fuelled by *(asymmetrical) polarization;* and thirdly, *appealing anti-pluralist leaders and parties* that skilfully fuel and then exploit such discontent. In order to achieve power, they need to win elections or be invited to join a *coalition government.* Anti-pluralist mobilization and a lack of mobilization for democratic alternatives contribute to such electoral success.

Even if anti-pluralists are in power, they do not have free reign to erode democracy. Therefore, Boese et al. distinguish between onset and breakdown resilience.[13] In particular, constraints on the power of the executive may halt autocratization once it has started. *Institutions* (legislature, judiciary, public administration) as well as *opposition* actors (political parties, civil society groups, citizens) create such accountability mechanisms.[14] These are critical for limiting the damage to democratic institutions, halting autocratization, and paving the way for democratic recovery.

However, once anti-pluralists are in power, autocratization becomes more likely, as Figure 2 illustrates. V-Party measures the degree of anti-pluralism in political parties as the extent to which they lack *"commitment to (i) the democratic process; (ii) the legitimacy of political opponents; (iii) peaceful resolution of disagreements and rejection of political violence; and (iv) unequivocal support for civil*

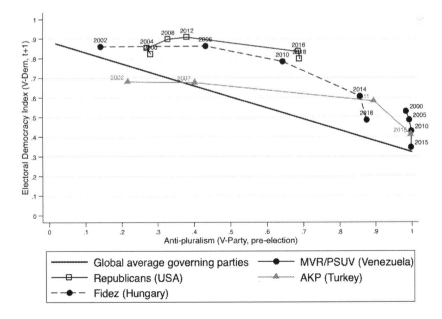

Figure 2. Anti-pluralist party traits and electoral democracy (2000–2019).

Note: The Electoral Democracy Index ranges from 0 (not democratic) to 1 (fully democratic). The Anti-Pluralism Index ranges from 0 (pluralist) to 1 (anti-pluralist). $N = 682$.

liberties of minorities.[15] The thick black line on Figure 2 shows that the relationship between the pre-electoral anti-pluralist traits of all (future) governing parties (2000–2019) (x-axis) and V-Dem's Electoral Democracy Index the year after the election is negative.[16] Thus, the more anti-pluralist parties appear before an election, the lower the level of democracy when they take or regain power. Lührmann, Medzihorsky and Lindberg demonstrate that this relationship in democracies holds in further statistical tests.[17]

Some parties have demonstrated unequivocally anti-pluralist positions from early on, such as the Fifth Republic Movement (MVR), which brought Chavez to power in Venezuela in 1998 and later evolved into the United Socialist Party of Venezuela (PSUV) (black circles on the right). The story is different for the Fidesz Party in Hungary (dashed line) and the AKP in Turkey (grey line with triangle markers), which only gradually became more anti-pluralist and subsequently eroded democratic institutions step-by-step. In other cases, new party leaders or leading candidates have shifted their party into an anti-pluralist direction, such as Donald Trump in the United States in 2016 (line with squares).

Such anti-pluralists often use populist rhetoric to claim that they – and only they – are the legitimate representatives of "the people" and that "the elites" are not to be trusted.[18] While a certain degree of skepticism of elites may be healthy for a democracy, anti-pluralists use anti-elitism to undermine democratic political competition. They challenge the pluralist foundation of democracy, which embraces "that societies are composed of several social groups with different ideas and interests".[19] Such actors may gain votes, but should not gain democratic legitimacy in a normative sense, because their actions prevent citizens from exercising their democratic rights in the future.[20]

Stage 1: mounting citizens' discontent with democratic parties and institutions

Democracies are consolidated if democracy is the "only game in town".[21] Thus, support for democracy among elites and citizens is conducive to democratic resilience. Elites tend to support democratic norms if they trust political opponents to play by the rules as well.[22] Such mutual trust is limited in countries with weak democratic institutions and a history of autocratization. This might explain why autocratization is more likely in such countries, as Boese et al. demonstrate in this issue.[23]

Contemporary autocratizers typically come to power through popular vote and not military coups, which gives citizens an important role in autocratization processes. Citizens turn away from democratic parties and candidates for two reasons: firstly, out of discontent with the way democratic governments and parties perform (a lack of specific support); secondly, because they are explicitly discontented with basic democratic norms and procedures (a lack of diffuse support).[24] These sources of discontent can be interrelated and reenforce each other. For instance, declining specific support may activate already existing diffuse non-support.

Rising discontent with democratic options increases the demand for alternatives, but by far not all discontented citizens vote for anti-pluralist parties and candidates. Therefore, it is also important to understand the supply side and how anti-pluralist parties mobilize voters, which will be the focus of the next section (Stage 2).

Declining specific support: insufficient supply of effective democratic responses to structural and contextual challenges

Dissatisfaction with the performance of democratic governments and parties is a major source of discontent with democracy.[25] Petrarca et al. have demonstrated a clear empirical link between declining trust in government institutions and a decline in vote share for established parties, which "opens a window of opportunity for challenging outsider parties"[26] such as the Populist Radical Right. Low and declining public trust in institutions increases the probability of regime change from democracy to autocracy as well as the other way around.[27]

Such dissatisfaction and lack of trust can be due to the actual failure of governments to respond to new structural or contextual challenges or due to the mere perception that they have failed to do so. As Meléndez and Rovira Kaltwasser summarize the state of the research in this issue, many contemporary supporters of anti-pluralist parties "are not predominantly 'economic losers' in an objective sense, but individuals who at the *subjective* level feel left behind because of ongoing cultural and economic transformations that negatively affect their social status".[28] Historical comparative studies show that economic recession,[29] weak economic development,[30] corruption,[31] and inequality[32] predict democratic discontent and – further down the line – autocratization. Thus, policies which effectively address such grievances can be seen as fostering democratic resilience.

At the same time, we are witnessing tectonic shifts in the social fabric of our societies.[33] The labour market has become more flexible and the economy globalized. Ways of life are more individualized and less pre-determined. Two-dimensional party systems are a consequence of these developments: economic status matters less in how people vote while the salience of cultural issues has increased.[34] The Internet has revolutionized the way we communicate and form political opinions and has opened the door for disinformation. At the same time, traditional "gatekeepers" of the political system – newspapers and established political parties – have lost much of their power.[35]

Thus, many analysts view the rise of anti-pluralist parties as a symptom of the failure of established democratic parties "to adapt to [this] new social reality".[36] After they have de-aligned with established parties, some voters realign with new parties.[37] This creates a window of opportunity for anti-pluralist mobilization. Historically, similar processes have occurred. For instance, Cornell, Møller and Skaaning attribute democratic resilience in Denmark and United Kingdom during the interwar years to "the ability of conventional parties to channel the frustrations resulting from the repeated interwar crisis episodes".[38]

A lack of diffuse support for democratic norms: a driver for autocratization?

We have strong evidence that citizens with weak commitment to democratic norms – those who show a lack of support for democracy,[39] and exhibit authoritarian values[40] and populist attitudes – are more likely to vote for anti-pluralists.[41] In Germany for instance, 75% of the voters for the anti-pluralist party AfD approve of law-and-order authoritarianism, racism and evince distrust in democracy.[42] However, such attitudes have not increased in the German population since 2014 – unlike the AfD's share of the vote.[43]

Globally, there is mixed evidence on the development of democratic values. Christian Welzel shows in this issue that mass support for democracy has increased in many more countries (26) than it declined in (14) from the third round (1994–98) of the World Value Survey (WVS) to the seventh round (2017–20).[44] Figure 3 shows that the share of citizens supporting a democratic system has remained at the consistently high level of around 90% in democracies since the 1990s (small-dashed line).[45] Other surveys paint a similar picture. For instance, it remains "absolutely" important for 52% of EU citizens to live in a democracy and not important for only 3.5%.[46]

However, at the same time, some of these respondents might be "democrats in name only".[47] For instance, support for "strong leaders who do not have to bother with parliaments and elections" has increased by 14% – from 38% in the 2005–2009 wave to 51% in 2017–2020 (dashed/dot line Figure 3).[48] Nevertheless, 90% of WVS respondents continue to value free elections as an important part of democracy (black line). They even support a key principle of liberal democracy: that the protection of civil rights is "essential" (dashed line).[49] Complementing this evidence, Christian Welzel points out in this issue that "emancipative values" – gender equality, child autonomy, public voice and reproductive freedoms – have been globally on the rise.[50]

Strengthening citizens' support for democracy to enhance democratic resilience

While we do not have clear evidence for a drastic decline in global commitment to democratic norms, citizens with a weak commitment to democratic norms are more likely to vote for anti-pluralists. The average vote share for anti-pluralist parties in

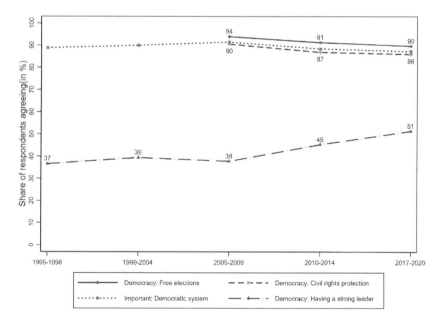

Figure 3. The attitude of citizens living in a democracy towards democracy since the mid-1990s (WVS). Source: Inglehart et al., "World Values Survey". Includes only citizens in countries classified as democracies at the beginning of the WVS wave by the Regimes of the World measure. Coppedge et al. "V-Dem dataset V10."

the world's democracies has increased from 17.8% in the period 1994–98 to 22.7% in 2016–19.[51] What explains this? In the literature, we find four hypotheses: rollback due to *over-liberalization*; *activation* of authoritarianism; rising *protest vote*; and *ignorance* of democratic threats. How can such insights help to strengthen democratic resilience?

In this issue, Christian Welzel argues that some of the recent processes of autocratization such as in Poland and Hungary, are the result of an *over-liberalization* of the regimes. He argues that prior to autocratization, these regimes had liberalized more than the advancement of emancipative values in their respective electorates would naturally support.[52] Skilful demagogues may intuitively capture and capitalize on such misalignments between values and the regime and use such window of opportunity for autocratization.[53] Emancipative values are fostered by modernization – "rising living standards, falling mortality rates, dropping fertility rates as well as expanding education".[54] Such existential conditions are improving across the world – a further increase in emancipative values is likely to follow the same pattern, which might be conducive to re-democratization.[55]

The *activation hypothesis* claims that the rise of anti-pluralist parties is (partially) due to their mobilization of previously unaligned voters.[56] These could be voters who lack a commitment to democratic norms. For example, as Meléndez and Rovira Kaltwasser summarize in this special issue, the Populist Radical Right (PRR) combines populism and anti-pluralism/authoritarianism with nativism – the longing for a homogenous nation state.[57] Malka et al. show that cultural conservativism and authoritarian attitudes are closely related.[58] Thus, the cultural conservative agenda of anti-pluralists such as Victor Orbán might have activated such voters. Furthermore, anti-immigration policies and euro-skepticism matter a lot to the voters for these parties.[59]

In response to such challengers, pro-democratic actors have to avoid merely enhancing the salience of those issues that many voters attribute anti-pluralist parties as having the main competence in – such as immigration.[60] Attempts of centre parties to adopt a tough stance on immigration typically do not result in electoral success.[61] On the contrary, such parroting maneuvers might actually undermine the credibility of centre parties while at the same time risk strengthening the anti-immigration agendas of anti-pluralist parties.[62]

At the same time, some citizens turn away from democratic parties in *protest* against the way democratic parties and governments perform and not because of a lack of support for democratic norms.[63] Those who think that politicians do not represent their views are more likely to be dissatisfied with democracy. A meta-study of 3,500 country surveys reported that, globally, the proportion of citizens dissatisfied with the performance of democracy rose by 10% between 1995 and 2019, from 48% to 58%.[64]

Thus, it is paramount that democratic parties get better at responding to legitimate grievances and societal changes. To revitalize democratic parties, Bertoa and Rama propose a potpourri of remedies: building new and strong party organizations which capitalize on new technologies; leadership by example and without corruption; and embracing the democratic imperative of consensus.[65] Others suggest that democratic parties should appeal more to the emotions and show empathy towards those people who feel that globalization and cultural modernization has devalued their experience and accomplishments.[66]

Nevertheless, the question remains: Why would citizens who support democratic norms in principle jeopardize them by voting for anti-pluralist parties? Here the literature holds several answers, which can be summarized as *ignorance* out of a lack of awareness, knowledge or alternative priorities. Citizens might prioritize other issues such as anti-abortion, their economic situation, and anti-immigration policies. They might not be aware that a party or politician has anti-pluralist tendencies or they might not recognize anti-pluralism as a threat to democracy. Many citizens hold a majoritarian view of democracy, thinking that democracy simply means the majority should get what they want (and they also often falsely assume that the majority wants the same as them).[67] For example, 41% of US citizens support the notion that the US President should act without bothering with institutional procedure if "a large majority of the American people believe the president should act".[68] Furthermore, anti-pluralist actors turn the political contest into an "us-versus-them" game where their ideological wins are perceived as more important than democratic norms.[69] Such pernicious polarization increases apathy in relation to authoritarian and illiberal behaviour.[70] For instance, in several survey experiments, voters were shown to prioritize their ideological preferences over democratic norms in polarized societies.[71]

In order to foster democratic awareness, knowledge and commitment among ordinary citizens, civic education is an important tool.[72] Civic education and engagement is a key pillar of external democracy promotion activities. Given the contemporary challenges, even established democracies could learn from these well-established methodologies.[73] Therefore, this special issue features a study by Finkel and Lim demonstrating how a civic education programme in the Democratic Republic of Congo (DRC) enhanced political participation in non-electoral activities, as well as knowledge and the feeling of efficacy and tolerance.[74] They attribute the success to the programme's "active and participatory approach".[75] However, the programme also decreased support for democracy in the DRC and satisfaction with an ongoing decentralization programme. Such mixed effects are not uncommon.[76] Finkel and Lim point out that in the studied case, civic education had fostered an understanding of what democracy and decentralization *should* look like – a normative ideal that did not match the dire realities of the DRC.[77] Thus, they concluded that future programmes should better account for the "discrepancy between democracy in theory and in practice".[78]

Stage 2: anti-pluralists rising to power

Discontent with democracy as such does not bring down democracies. *Anti-pluralist political leaders or parties* do. These actors skilfully claim to address democratic discontent while fuelling it, and mask their anti-democratic aspirations with populist rhetoric. They also fuel and benefit from *polarization*.

In democracies, most autocratizers come to power through free and fair elections.[79] Thus, understanding how the *electoral arena* enables or constrains them is critical for blocking their access to power. The key variables here are the mobilization of voters – for the anti-pluralist challenger as well as for democratic parties and the institutions and coalitions which translate votes into power.

Adept anti-pluralist parties: populist narratives for claiming legitimacy[80]

Populist rhetoric helps anti-pluralists to conceal how dangerous their ideas are for democracy. As discussed earlier, they claim to stand for "true democracy" while their actions are likely to undermine it. To a limited extent, the totalitarian movements of the last century shared such populist traits and appealed to legal justifications.[81] As Hannah Arendt noted, both fascists and communists "use[d] and abuse[d] democratic freedoms in order to abolish them".[82]

Many anti-pluralist parties attract voters beyond a radical base by avoiding explicit autocratic statements. Consequently, their parties suffer from internal tensions between such *reformers* aiming at broad coalitions and *radicals* prioritizing protest.[83] Grahn, Lührmann and Gastaldi show that the demise of European far right parties has occurred mainly due to internal factors such as "internal splits, changes in leadership and corruption scandals".[84] The authors recommend that democratic actors should amplify such scandals and internal conflicts and "develop creative strategies" seeking to deepen divisions within anti-pluralist parties.[85] This includes parliamentary initiatives that force MPs of anti-pluralist parties to show their true colours, e.g. their views on the Nazi regime. Others suggest the toolkit of a "militant democracy": "pre-emptive, prima facie illiberal measures to prevent those aiming at subverting democracy with democratic means from destroying the democratic regime".[86] Such reasoning builds on Karl Popper's "paradox of tolerance": If a tolerant society tolerates the intolerant, the latter will eventually undermine the foundations of tolerance.[87] In effect, the constitutions of many democracies – most conspicuously Germany – include measures allowing constitutional courts to subdue actors and behaviour that would undermine the liberal order; for instance banning extremist parties. Repressive strategies include "hard" responses such as party/organization bans, prosecution and surveillance, but also "softer" strategies such as state officials excluding anti-pluralistic organizations and teachers.[88]

Such measures are often not effective in containing contemporary challengers of democracy, who conceal an anti-democratic agenda behind a populist façade and thus do not meet the legal criteria for the application of such measures. Furthermore, critiques of militant democracy fear that governments will use such measures not to defend democracy, but to subvert it.[89] Juan Linz rightly worries that indiscriminate, exclusionary measures might push supporters of anti-pluralist actors more into their arms.[90] Thus, they may foster polarization.

The accelerator: pernicious polarization

Anti-pluralists – in particular populist ones – often use a stark rhetoric separating a society into the "people" (us), and its enemies (them). Ultimately, as Somer, McCoy and Luke point out in this special issue, "society is split into mutually distrustful us vs. them camps in which political identity becomes a social identity".[91] Such pernicious or "toxic polarization" goes beyond healthy, controversial debates about policy preferences and impedes trustful interactions between citizens with different points of views.

As Somer, McCoy and Luke emphasize, polarization is the result of a deliberate strategic choice of political actors to exploit and exaggerate pre-existing cleavages for their own political ends rather than an automatic consequence of such structural preconditions.[92] Two or more sides may intentionally foster polarization. It may also occur "asymmetrically," that is, be pushed from only one side as in recent years in the US, where Republicans increasingly placed their own political ends over democratic norms.[93] However, democratic actors may also foster a vicious circle of polarization by mounting vigorous counterattacks.[94]

158 RESILIENCE OF DEMOCRACY

In this issue, Somer, McCoy and Luke show, using a cross-national data set (1900–2019), that countries that are more polarized are more likely to autocratize.[95] Thus, polarization seems to be a key accelerating factor in the autocratization sequence. It helps anti-pluralists to fuel discontent with democratic parties, and muster support.

Furthermore, supporters of polarizing political leaders tend not to trust information from a non-partisan or opposing source, and they communicate less with people with opposing views.[96] Arendt observed similar processes when studying the supporters of totalitarian movements.[97] The social media algorithms aggravate this problem.

Democratic actors have to be aware of such toxic dynamics of pernicious polarization and address them thoughtfully in order to disrupt the autocratization sequence.[98] This does not imply that both sides are the culprits for democratic malaise. Furthermore, addressing polarization does not imply avoiding polarizing policy debates at all costs. On the contrary, *"transformative repolarization"* may be successful if it "seeks to change the axis of polarization away from the Manichean line emphasized by the polarizing incumbent and toward one that is more flexible and programmatic, such as those based on democratic or social justice principles".[99] For example, the successful protest movement in South Korea in 2016–17 moved the cleavage from "conservative vs. liberal" to "executive accountability vs. corruption/authoritarianism" with the help of innovative methods.[100]

In other cases, *"active depolarization"* has been successful: social and political action which places new issues on the political agenda and forges new alliances, cutting across the polarizing cleavage.[101] Similarly, Norris and Inglehart stress that "[polarization] calls above all for leaders who can help to bridge divisions – and not exacerbate them".[102] Such strategies have contributed to the 2019 opposition victories in local elections in Turkey and Hungary.[103] Conversely, reactive strategies such as "reciprocal polarization" along the same cleavage entail the risk of backfiring as in Turkey in 2007 and 2008, and in Venezuela in recent years.[104]

Thus, the key to hindering pernicious polarization is increasing unity and common ground through the invention of "communication tools, campaign strategies and alliances with social movements and civic organization, recruitment methods, use of emotion and symbols, and narratives".[105]

The electoral arena: voter mobilization and coalition building

Anti-pluralist parties polarize, which limits their potential to mobilize voters. Meléndez and Rovira Kaltwasser analyse such "electoral ceilings" for the case of the Populist Radical Right in Western Europe in this special issue.[106] They conclude that in 2019 about 50% of the electorate clearly opposed such parties – in Meléndez and Rovira Kaltwasser's words thy had a "negative identity" towards them – while only about 10% identify positively with the parties of that family.[107] At the same time, citizens who support such parties are somewhat more likely to actually vote than those with a negative identity (83% versus 76%).[108] Thus, while the potential for electoral success for the Populist Radical Right in Western Europe is limited, specific electoral outcomes depend on who mobilizes their support base better: democratic parties or anti-pluralists.

The rejection of anti-pluralists can be important in mobilizing the democratically-minded voters.[109] Strategies of passive depolarization run the risk of demobilizing them.[110] The 2020 US election has demonstrated once more how critical electoral mobilization is. While Donald Trump mobilized more voters than in 2016 (from 63 million to 74 million); Joe Biden won because the Democratic vote increased even more (from 66 million in 2016 to 81 million in 2020).[111] For many Biden voters, preventing four more years of Donald Trump was an important argument.[112] Thus, *counter-mobilization* may give democratic parties an electoral advantage.[113] However, it also runs the risk of increasing the salience of anti-pluralist agendas, which can be avoided by appealing to a broad base and cutting through polarizing cleavages.

To what extent votes translate into political power depends on the electoral system. While several studies have pointed to presidential systems being more prone to autocratization,[114] the effects of specific electoral rules have not been systematically tested. The exception is perhaps the introduction of a minimal threshold for achieving parliamentary representation, which is said to preserve the parliamentary capacity to act by avoiding fractionalization.[115]

Issues of institutional design are relevant to consider for long-term reform processes. In the short-term, after elections in systems with proportional representation, parties between the centre and the extremes ("border parties") can become "kingmakers" as they choose between a coalition of democratic parties or one with anti-pluralists. If their main strategic goal is vote maximization, they are likely to "follow their voters" and move towards the extremes.[116]

Some scholars argue in favor of *accommodating* anti-pluralist parties in coalitions. Such parties might perform badly in government with mundane issues (such as "fixing potholes"[117]), distracting them from their radical policies. This might disappoint their support base and eventually present the anti-pluralist party with the choice of leaving government or losing electoral support.[118] Other scholars suggest that inclusion in government forces such parties to deradicalize.[119] However, in several cases such deradicalization has not materialized.[120] Even parties that became slightly less radical while in office re-radicalized as soon as they joined the opposition again.[121]

In Europe in the 1920s to 1930s, the accommodation of anti-pluralists – intended to keep them under control – enabled them to dominate government.[122] Similarly, in already autocratic settings, the cooptation of democratic parties has cemented dictatorships multiple times, e.g. in Kenya and Zimbabwe.[123] Some pact transitions (e.g. in Chile after 1989) and the broad-based coalition in post-revolutionary Tunisia were perhaps more positive for democratization.[124]

Critical engagement: addressing polarization and the legitimacy claims of anti-pluralists

Anti-pluralists claim to be democratically legitimate, while at the same time fuelling pernicious polarization. This creates a strategic dilemma for democratic actors (see Figure 4). Democratic responses may have contrary effects on the legitimacy of anti-pluralists (y-axis) and on pernicious polarization (x-axis).

On the one hand, democratic actors aim to signal clearly that anti-pluralists are not legitimate actors in a democratic sense, because while they may gain some electoral support, they are not playing by democratic rules. To achieve such an aim, a strategy of *exclusion* seems promising – placing anti-pluralists in a "cordon sanitaire" to limit their agenda-setting power[125] and using the tools of militant democracy discussed above such as party bans (low-right quadrant). On the other hand, such measures

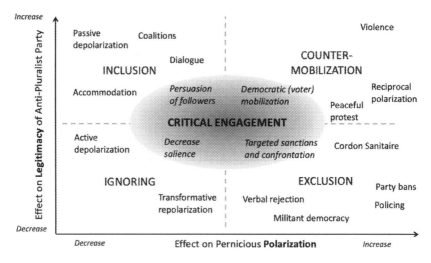

Figure 4. Effects of democratic actors' strategies towards anti-pluralist parties. Source: Author.

may fuel the vicious circle of pernicious polarization. Actors aiming to prevent this from happening often call for a more *inclusionary* approach of accommodation, which could help to depolarize societies (top-left quadrant).[126] However, by tolerating them or even forming a coalition with anti-pluralists, democrats give such actors a veneer of democratic legitimacy – a gift, which they can scarcely take back.[127]

The aim of depolarization could also be fostered by a strategy of *ignoring* anti-pluralist provocations (low-left quadrant). This avoids anti-pluralists framing themselves as "victims" of the establishment.[128] Similarly, Somer, McCoy and Luke discuss in this issue various strategies for reducing the salience of the polarizing divide with "active depolarization" and "transformative repolarization" (see above).[129] The downside of such activities is that they might not actively challenge the legitimacy of anti-pluralists at least in the short term. In the long run, they might decrease anti-pluralist legitimacy by reducing the salience of the issues that render them legitimate in the eyes of their supporters in the first place. Conversely, extreme *counter-mobilization* strategies (top-right quadrant), such as "fighting fire with fire"[130] with violent counter-attacks, intend to delegitimize anti-pluralists but might actually enhance their legitimacy by creating plausible victim narratives. They also risk fuelling polarization. Other types of counter-mobilization seem more suitable such as civic engagement and peaceful protest even though they may also fuel polarization.

An effective strategy of democratic resilience could use "critical engagement" as a leitmotif combining the advantages of all four response strategies while avoiding their pitfalls. *Targeted sanctions and confrontation* use the exclusionary tool kit of militant democracy, including policing, party-bans, and verbal delegitimization, but focus interventions on the most radical anti-pluralists and in particular their leaders.

Thus, pro-democratic actors should only engage in measures that suppress anti-pluralist actors if there is clear evidence that they threaten the democratic order and that such tools are proportionate and effective. Trusted arbiters such as courts can help to differentiate between what is legitimate opposition within a democratic system and what is undemocratic and thus illegitimate.[131] In particular, it is important to differentiate between the threat posed by groups and individuals.[132] Arguably, the threat level posed by an organized group is higher than the danger posed by individual citizens. Thus, while some anti-pluralist groups and group activities could be the subject of militant measures, societies should avoid actions that "vilify supporters" of anti-pluralists.[133]

Persuasion aims at convincing moderately illiberal citizens that democratic values and institutions work for them; and at unifying people around what they have in common. Linz suggests that such "semi-loyal" actors should be integrated as much as possible.[134] On their own, authoritarian radicals are rarely able to take and sustain power in a democracy. They need the support or at least toleration of more moderately-oriented reformers within their party or other parties or groups in society.[135] A source of democratic resilience is thus to drive a wedge between those groups. Such a strategy needs to make it more attractive for reform-oriented followers of anti-pluralist groups to turn towards democratic alternatives than to stay with the anti-pluralists. This includes engaging in dialogue, a more attractive supply of democratic candidates, and fostering civic education, and, for potential defectors from authoritarian governments, guarantees for future participation.

However, many polarizing actors use deliberate lies, disinformation and hatred to advance their agendas. Merely talking risks legitimizing and amplifying such narratives. In public debates, red lines need to be drawn to protect minorities and separate facts from lies. At the same time, democratic actors should not mirror unfair and aggressive tactics.[136] Rather, as Michele Obama put it in 2016 "when they go low, we go high" should be the leitmotif. For instance, in Slovakia, Caputova won the 2019 presidential elections against a severely polarizing incumbent while not engaging in demonization and disinformation due to support from civil society and his focus on anti-corruption.[137]

Such *democratic mobilization* demonstrates the strength of the democratic side of the political spectrum and creates the momentum for democratic candidates to win elections. Democratic mass protests and civic engagement can also help to educate citizens about democratic values and processes while creating spaces for democrats to collaborate.[138] At the same time, democratic mobilization should avoid merely reacting to anti-pluralists' provocations along the polarizing cleavage in order to *decrease the salience* of the issue "owned" by anti-pluralists (e.g. immigration).

Stage 3: autocratizers dismantle democratic institutions

Boese et al. show that resilience to democratic breakdown, or *breakdown resilience* – limiting the extent to which autocratization damages democratic institutions – is contingent on several factors.[139] Strong institutions of accountability and democratic experience ("democratic stock") make such breakdown less likely.[140] This applies in particular for judicial constraints, but not for the role of the legislature – at least not on average.[141]

In individual cases, the parliament has been relevant for breakdown resilience for instance when the South Korean legislature impeached then-president Park Geun-heye in 2017.[142] However, the legislature responded mainly because other accountability actors – civil society and the media – mounted pressure and public opinion turned against Park Geun-heye after a major corruption scandal came to light.[143]

Therefore, Laebens and Lührmann argue that accountability mechanisms – constraints on the power of the executive – are key for breakdown resilience.[144] This includes: parliamentary and judicial oversight and an independent administration (horizontal accountability), pressure from civil society and the media (diagonal accountability), and electoral competition between parties and within parties (vertical accountability).[145] Such mechanisms may halt autocratization if multiple accountability actors work together and contextual factors shift the "balance of power between the incumbent and accountability actors".[146]

Such contextual factors include corruption scandals, economic downturns and approaching term of office limits, but only if the opposition or intra-party elites exploit them for mobilization against the incumbent. Thus, "creative" opposition strategies are critical, particularly during advanced stages of autocratization, where formal accountability institutions may not be independent, but still be perceived as legitimate.[147] As Boese et al. demonstrate, democracies are more likely to break down the longer the autocratization process lasts.[148] Therefore, a quick response is of the essence.

Conclusions

Democracies typically do not die overnight. Contemporary autocratization is typically the result of a long sequence of events and processes – ranging from mounting discontent with democratic institutions and parties, to anti-pluralists rising to power, to the failure of accountability constraints. The articles assembled in this special issue shed light on specific stages in this autocratization sequence.

The good news is that each step along this sequence is also an entry point for enhancing democratic resilience. While no "silver bullet" exists, democratic actors – citizens, politicians, civil servants – have many options to choose from.[149] As Boese et al. show in this issue, only one in five democracies survive autocratization once it has started.[150] Thus, the most important avenue for democratic resilience is preventing it from starting.

For such *onset resilience*, firstly, democratic actors need to avoid discontent with democratic institutions and parties. Here, the most important parameter seems to be an attractive supply of democratic parties and politicians that address structural and contextual challenges as well as organize inclusive and participatory political processes. The latter gives citizens a sense of political efficacy, which enhances support for democratic norms. If the gap between democratic ideals and reality is wide, the effects of civic education on support for democracy are limited.[151] Thus, an inclusive, participatory, and effective political process also enhances the effectiveness of civic education, which in general should be expanded in order to foster support for democratic norms.

Secondly, as democratic actors try to block anti-pluralists' access to power, they face several dilemmas: Should they choose exclusionary approaches and risk fuelling pernicious polarization; or inclusionary approaches, which might give anti-pluralists a veneer of undeserved legitimacy? Should they ignore anti-pluralist provocations or rather counter-mobilize? Based on the articles assembled in this special issue and other research, I suggest balancing the advantages and pitfalls of conventional approaches with a strategy of *critical engagement*. Borrowing from exclusionary strategies, targeted sanctions and confrontation could limit the reach of the most radical anti-pluralist actors, groups and causes. At the same time, the inclusionary idea that more moderate followers could be persuaded to follow democratic causes might have some merits, while coalitions with anti-pluralists appear too risky. Finally, it seems important to decrease the salience of anti-pluralist issues and campaigns while at the same time mobilizing democratic citizens for elections, peaceful protest and civic engagement. Here, it is important to build shared values, visions and priorities, which cut through polarizing cleavages.

Once an anti-pluralist has come to power, institutional constraints and skilful opposition strategies may limit the extent of autocratization. To build such *breakdown resilience*[152] it seems advisable to enhance the independence and strength of judicial oversight, of public administration, the media and civil society.

Future research needs to empirically test the notions presented here more extensively, in particular regarding the effects of democratic strategies vis-à-vis anti-pluralists. Multiple bottlenecks and circles of reverse causality make such endeavors challenging, but data availability has improved in recent years, – for instance with the V-Dem and V-Party datasets.[153] The list of factors contributing to the autocratization sequence addressed in this special issue is explicitly not exhaustive. For instance, we have not addressed how the rise of social media relates to processes of autocratization and how online debates could become more civil and fact-based. Future studies should shed light on this important topic. The same applies to international factors. To foster democratic resilience, "democracy protection"[154] needs to happen across borders.

Notes

1. For excellent reviews see: Waldner and Lust, "Unwelcome Change", Hyde, "Democracy's Backsliding."
2. Laebens and Lührmann, "What Halts Democratic Erosion?," 2.
3. Lührmann, Medzihorsky and Lindberg, "Walking the Talk," 9. Anti-pluralism is a contested notion that not both editors of this issue agree to.
4. Welzel, "Democratic Horizons."
5. Finkel and Lim, "The Supply and Demand Model."
6. Meléndez and Rovira Kaltwasser, "Negative Partisanship."
7. Somer, McCoy and Luke, "Pernicious Polarization."
8. Laebens and Lührmann, "What Halts Democratic Erosion?."
9. Boese et al., "How Democracies Prevail."
10. Merkel and Lührmann, "Introduction."
11. Coppedge et al., "V-Dem." Lührmann et al. "V-Party."
12. See next section, contributions to this issue and Waldner and Lust, "Unwelcome Change."
13. Boese et al., "How Democracies Prevail."
14. Laebens and Lührmann, "What Halts Democratic Erosion?."
15. Lührmann, Medzihorsky and Lindberg, "Walking the Talk."
16. The Pearson's correlation of −0.83 is statistically significant. On the Electoral Democracy Index see Coppedge et al., "V-Dem Dataset v10." Ruling parties are identified in the V-Party data set by the variable v2pagovsup. Lührmann et al., "V–Party Dataset." Both datasets rely on expert coding, which is aggregated by a custom-built measurement model to enhance comparability across countries and time. Pemstein et al., "V-Dem Measurement Model."
17. Lührmann, Medzihorsky and Lindberg, "Walking the Talk," 9.
18. Populism as such is a contested concept. For more detail, see Melendez and Rovira Kaltwasser's article in this special issue.
19. Mudde and Rovira Kaltwasser, "Exclusionary vs. inclusionary populism", 152.
20. For a similar argument, see Karl Popper's work on the paradox of freedom (1945/2003, 130).

164 RESILIENCE OF DEMOCRACY

21. Linz and Stepan, *Problems of Democratic Transition and Consolidation*.
22. Przeworski, *Sustainable Democracy*, 11; Dahl, *Polyarchy*, 40.
23. Boese et al., "How Democracies Prevail," 19.
24. On the difference between specific and diffuse support, see Easton, "A Re-assessment."
25. On the link between perceived government performance and democratic discontent, see Dahlberg, Linde, and Holmberg, "Democratic Discontent."
26. Petrarca, Giebler, and Weßels. "Support for Insider Parties," 1.
27. Ruck, Matthews and Kyritsis, "Cultural Foundations."
28. Meléndez and Rovira Kaltwasser, "Negative Partisanship," 11, emphasis mine. On status anxiety, see also Gidron and Hall, "The Politics of Social Status."
29. Bernhard, Nordstrom, and Reenock, "Economic Performance."
30. Svolik, "Authoritarian Reversals"; Przeworski et al., *Democracy and Development*.
31. Dahlberg, Linde, and Holmberg, "Democratic Discontent."
32. Leininger, Lührmann, and Sigman, "The Relevance of Social Policies"; Haggard and Kaufman, *Dictators and Democrats*.
33. See e.g. Norris and Inglehart, *Cultural Backlash*.
34. Mair, *Ruling the Void*.
35. Levitsky and Ziblatt, *How Democracies Die*, 55–6.
36. Casal Bertoa and Rama, "The Antiestablishment Challenge," 40. See also: De Vries and Hobolt, *Political Entrepreneurs*.
37. Mair, *Ruling the Void*; Hooghe and Marks, "Cleavage Theory Meets Europe's Crises."
38. Cornell, Møller and Skaaning, *Democratic Stability*, 12.
39. Todd, "Authoritarian Attitudes."
40. Norris and Inglehart, *Cultural Backlash*, 279; MacWilliams, "Trump Is an Authoritarian." https://www.politico.com/news/magazine/2020/09/23/trump-america-authoritarianism-420681
41. Van Hauwaert and van Kessel, "Beyond Protest and Discontent."
42. Zick, Küpper, and Berghan, "Verlorene Mitte."
43. Ibid.
44. Welzel, "Democratic Horizons", 13. See also Wuttke et al., "Grown Tired of Democracy?."
45. Respondents viewing democracy as a "fairly" or "very" good way of "governing this country" (Inglehart et al., "World Values Survey").
46. Schmitt et al., "European Parliament Election."
47. Wuttke et al., "Grown Tired of Democracy?."
48. Respondents viewing a "strong leader" as a "fairly" or "very" good way of "governing this country" (Inglehart et al., "World Values Survey"). See also Wuttke et al., "Grown Tired of Democracy?."
49. Respondents selecting 5 or higher on a 0–10 scale.
50. Ibid., 6; Alexander and Welzel, "The Myth of Deconsolidation."
51. This includes all parties scoring higher than 75% of the parties in democracies in this millennium on the V-Party Anti-Pluralism Index (0.4395). Lührmann et al. "V–Party Dataset."
52. Welzel, "Democratic Horizons," 6.
53. Ibid., 8.
54. Ibid., 9.
55. Ibid., 16–19.
56. Pardos-Prado, Lancee and Sagarzazu, "Immigration and Electoral Change."
57. Meléndez and Rovira Kaltwasser, "Negative Partisanship," 3.
58. Malka et al., "Open to Authoritarian Governance."
59. Meléndez and Rovira Kaltwasser, "Negative Partisanship", 13. Hainmueller and Hopkins, "Public Attitudes Toward Immigration."
60. On issue ownership, see Pardos-Prado, Lancee, and Sagarzazu, "Immigration and Electoral Change."
61. Abou-Chadi and Wagner, "The Electoral Appeal"; Spoon and Klüver, "Responding to Far Right"; Hutter and Kriesi, "Politicising Immigration."
62. Akkerman and Rooduijn, "Pariahs or Partners?"; Heinze, "Strategies of Mainstream Parties."
63. Dahlberg, Linde, and Holmberg, "Democratic Discontent," 24f.
64. Foa et al., "The Global Satisfaction with Democracy Report."

65. Casal Bertoa and Rama, "The Antiestablishment Challenge," 47f.
66. Urbanska and Guimond, "Swaying to the Extreme." Wigura and Kuisz, The Guardian, 11 Dec 2020, https://www.theguardian.com/commentisfree/2019/dec/11/populist-politicians-power-emotion-loss-change.
67. In a survey experiment, Grossman et al. show that citizens often do not object to undemocratic actions by elected leaders. Grossmann et al., *The Majoritarian Threat*.
68. Drutman, "Democracy Maybe," 5.
69. Somer, McCoy and Luke, "Pernicious Polarization."
70. See for example McCoy and Somer, "Toward a Theory of Pernicious Polarization."
71. Svolik, "When Polarization Trumps"; Graham and Svolik, "Democracy in America?."
72. Finkel and Lim, "The Supply and Demand Model."
73. Thomas Carothers has made a similar call, see *Foreign Policy*, January 27, 2016; https://foreignpolicy.com/2016/01/27/look-homeward-democracy-promoter/
74. Finkel and Lim, "The Supply and Demand Model."
75. Ibid., 18.
76. Ibid., 2.
77. Ibid., 18.
78. Ibid., 18.
79. Medzihorsky, Lührmann, and Lindberg, "Autocratization by Elections."
80. For similar arguments see Lührmann et al., *Resource Guide*.
81. Linz, *The Breakdown of Democratic Regimes*; Cavazza, "War der Faschismus populistisch?."
82. Arendt, *The Origins of Totalitarianism*, 312.
83. See, for example, Schroeder and Weßels, *Smarte Spalter*.
84. Grahn, Lührmann and Gastaldi, "Resources for Democratic Politicians," 53.
85. Ibid., 53. Downs recommends a similar approach, see Downs, "How Effective Is the Cordon Sanitaire?," 49.
86. Müller, "Militant Democracy," 1253.
87. Popper, *Open Society*, 293.
88. Müller, "Protecting Popular Self-government."
89. For a detailed discussion of this controversy, see Müller, "Militant Democracy."
90. Linz, *The Breakdown of Democratic Regimes.*
91. Somer, McCoy and Luke, "Pernicious Polarization," 1.
92. Somer, McCoy and Luke, "Pernicious Polarization," 6.
93. Levitsky and Ziblatt, *How Democracies Die.*
94. Somer, McCoy and Luke, "Pernicious Polarization," 6.
95. Somer, McCoy and Luke, "Pernicious Polarization," 8.
96. Somer, McCoy and Luke, "Pernicious Polarization," 12.
97. Members of a totalitarian movement are "well-protected against the reality of the non-totalitarian world" (Arendt, *The Origins of Totalitarianism*, 367).
98. Somer, McCoy and Luke, "Pernicious Polarization," 28.
99. Somer, McCoy and Luke, "Pernicious Polarization," 19.
100. Somer, McCoy and Luke, "Pernicious Polarization," 21. See also Laebens and Lührmann, "What Halts Democratic Erosion?"
101. Somer, McCoy and Luke, "Pernicious Polarization," 19.
102. Norris and Inglehart, *Cultural Backlash*, 265.
103. Somer, McCoy and Luke, "Pernicious Polarization," 22, 26.
104. Ibid., 14–15; Cleary and Öztürk, "When Does Backsliding Lead to Breakdown?"; On Venezuela see also: Rovira Kaltwasser, "Populism," 502.
105. Somer, McCoy and Luke, "Pernicious Polarization," 19–20.
106. Meléndez and Rovira Kaltwasser, "Negative Partisanship."
107. Ibid., 14.
108. Ibid., 13.
109. Ibid., 14.
110. Somer, McCoy and Luke, "Pernicious Polarization," 18.
111. *CNN*, 2016; https://edition.cnn.com/election/2020/results/president; https://edition.cnn.com/election/2016/results

112. *Forbes*, August 13, 2020; https://www.forbes.com/sites/jackbrewster/2020/08/13/poll-56-of-biden-voters-say-theyre-voting-for-him-because-hes-not-trump/?sh=2ba442266132
113. See Grahn, Lührmann, Gastaldi, "Resources for Democratic Politicians"; Müller, *What Is Populism?*, 84.
114. Linz, *The Perils of Presidentialism*; Stepan and Skach, "Constitutional Frameworks"; *Washington Post*, February 4, 2021; Carey, "Did Trump Prove."
115. Carey and Hix, "The Electoral Sweet Spot."
116. Capoccia, *Defending Democracy*, 17 (based on Sartori).
117. Berman, "Taming Extremist Parties."
118. Heinisch, "Success in Opposition."
119. Ibid., Berman, "Taming Extremist Parties."
120. Akkerman and Rooduijn, "Pariahs or Partners?"; Akkerman, "Conclusions," 279.
121. Akkerman, "Conclusions," 276.
122. Somer, McCoy and Luke, "Pernicious Polarization," 16. Casal Bertoa and Rama, "The Antiestablishment Challenge," 40; Grahn, Lührmann, Gastaldi, "Resources for Democratic Politicians."
123. Somer, McCoy and Luke, "Pernicious Polarization," 16.
124. Somer, McCoy and Luke, "Pernicious Polarization," 16–17.
125. Norris, *Radical Right*; van Spanje, "Contagious Parties," 485; Minkenberg, "The Radical Right."
126. Heinze, "Strategies of Mainstream Parties"; Downs, "Pariahs in their Midst"; Grahn, Lührmann, Gastaldi, "Resources for Democratic Politicians."
127. Heinze, "Strategies of Mainstream Parties."
128. However, anti-pluralists may use such narratives even if they are in government – think about Donald Trump.
129. Somer, McCoy and Luke, "Pernicious Polarization," 12–15.
130. See Rovira Kaltwasser, "Populism," 489–503.
131. Linz, *The Breakdown of Democratic Regimes.*
132. See also Müller, "Protecting Popular Self-government"; Popper, *Open Society*, 293; Lührmann et al., *Resource Guide*, 19.
133. Somer, McCoy and Luke, "Pernicious Polarization," 14.
134. Linz, *The Breakdown of Democratic Regimes*, 34.
135. See for example Bermeo, *Ordinary People in Extraordinary Times*; Ziblatt, *Conservative Parties.*
136. Somer, McCoy and Luke, "Pernicious Polarization," 14.
137. Somer, McCoy and Luke, "Pernicious Polarization," 14.
138. Norris and Inglehart, *Cultural Backlash*; Bermeo, "Reflections."
139. Boese et al., "How Democracies Prevail."
140. Boese et al., "How Democracies Prevail," 19.
141. Ibid.;. Staton, Reenock and Holsinger, *Can Courts be Bulwarks of Democracy?*
142. Laebens and Lührmann, "What Halts Democratic Erosion?"
143. Ibid., 11–12.
144. Laebens and Lührmann, "What Halts Democratic Erosion?"
145. On the concept of accountability see Lührmann, Marquardt and Mechkova, "Constraining Governments."
146. Laebens and Lührmann, "What Halts Democratic Erosion?," 15.
147. Somer, McCoy and Luke, "Pernicious Polarization," 14, 15.
148. Boese et al., "How Democracies Prevail."
149. For an overview of options see Lührmann et al., *Resource Guide.*
150. Boese et al., "How Democracies Prevail," 1.
151. Finkel and Lim, "Supply and Demand Model."
152. Boese et al., "How Democracies Prevail."
153. Coppedge et al., "V-Dem Dataset v10"; Lührmann et al., "Varieties of Party Identity and Organization (V–Party) Dataset."
154. https://www.die-gdi.de/en/the-current-column/article/time-is-ripe-for-a-global-democracy-summit/

Acknowledgements

I would like to thank the authors of this issue as well as Paulina Fröhlich, Christal Morehouse, Bernhard Wessels, Daniel Ziblatt, participants at the Berlin Democracy Conference (11/2019), V-Dem research seminar (2/2021) and Cornell University's Peace and Conflict Studies Institute's reading group (2/2021) for helpful comments on earlier versions of this article and inspiring discussions. I highly appreciate the skilful research assistance of Lisa Gastaldi, Sandra Grahn, Dominik Hirndorf, Palina Kolvani, Martin Lundstedt, and Shreeya Pillai.

Disclosure statement

No potential conflict of interest was reported by the author(s).

Funding

The Berlin Democracy Conference has been funded by the Open Society Initiative for Europe (OSIFE, Grant OR2018-45627). My work on the special issue has been supported by the Swedish Research Council, Grant 2018-01614.

ORCID

Anna Lührmann http://orcid.org/0000-0003-4258-1088

Bibliography

Abou-Chadi, Tarik, and Michael Wagner. "The Electoral Appeal of Party Strategies in Post-Industrial Societies: When Can the Mainstream Left Succeed?" *The Journal of Politics* 81, no. 4 (2019): 1405–1419.

Akkerman, Tjitske. "Conclusions." In *Radical Right-Wing Populist Parties in Western Europe*, edited by Tjitske Akkerman, Sarah L. De Lange, and Matthijs Rooduijn, 268–282. Oxon: Routledge, 2016.

Akkerman, Tjitske, and Matthijs Rooduijn. "Pariahs or Partners? Inclusion and Exclusion of Radical Right Parties and the Effects on Their Policy Positions." *Political Studies* 63, no. 5 (2015): 1140–1157. doi:10.1111/1467-9248.12146.

Alexander, Amy C., and Christian Welzel. "The Myth of Deconsolidation: Rising Liberalism and the Populist Reaction". *Journal of Democracy*: online debate forum (2017). https://www. journalofdemocracy.org/online-exchange-democratic-deconsolidation/.

Arendt, Hannah. *The Origins of Totalitarianism.* New York: Harcourt, Brace and Company, 1951.

Berman, Sheri. "Taming Extremist Parties: Lessons from Europe." *Journal of Democracy* 19, no. 1 (2008): 5–18. doi:10.1353/jod.2008.0002.

Bermeo, Nancy. *Ordinary People in Extraordinary Times: The Citizenry and the Breakdown of Democracy.* Princeton, NJ: Princeton University Press, 2003.

Bermeo, Nancy. "Reflections: Can American Democracy Still Be Saved?" *The ANNALS of the American Academy of Political and Social Science* 681, no. 1 (2019): 228–233. doi:10.1177/0002716218818083.

Bernhard, Michael, Timothy Nordstrom, and Christopher Reenock. "Economic Performance, Institutional Intermediation, and Democratic Survival." *The Journal of Politics* 63, no. 3 (2001): 775–803. http://www.jstor.org/stable/2691713.

Boese, Vanessa A., Amanda B. Edgell, Sebastian Hellmeier, Seraphine F. Maerz, and Staffan I. Lindberg. "How Democracies Prevail: Democratic Resilience as a Two-Stage Process." *Democratization* 5 (2021): 1–23.

Capoccia, G. *Defending Democracy: Reactions to Extremism in Interwar Europe*. Baltimore: Johns Hopkins University Press, 2005. doi:10.1353/book.3332.

Carey, John. "Did Trump Prove that Governments with Presidents Just Don't Work?" *Washington Post* (4 Feb 2021), https://www.washingtonpost.com/outlook/did-trump-prove-that-govern ments-with-presidents-just-dont-work/2021/02/04/9e9c69f2-5f3f-11eb-9430-e7c77b5b0297_story. html?fbclid=IwAR0sKpgvNSrxTKNozrljDuvRDhN6TmUZ3FuGo8LJck3wrEUK19Xps5ASXXM.

Carey, John M, and Simon Hix. "The Electoral Sweet Spot: Low-Magnitude Proportional Electoral Systems." *American Journal of Political Science* 55, no. 2 (2011): 383–397. doi:10.1111/j.1540-5907.2010.00495.x.

Casal Bértoa, Fernando, and José Rama. "The Antiestablishment Challenge." *Journal of Democracy* 32, no. 1 (2021): 37–51. doi:10.1353/jod.2021.0014.

Cavazza, Stefano. "War der Faschismus populistisch? Überlegungen zur Rolle des Populismus in der faschistischen Diktatur in Italien (1922–1943)." *Totalitarismus und Demokratie* 9, no. 2 (2012): 235–256.

Cleary, Matthew R., and Aykut Öztürk. "When Does Backsliding Lead to Breakdown? Uncertainty and Opposition Strategies in Democracies at Risk." *Perspectives on Politics* (2020): 1–17. doi:10.1017/S1537592720003667.

Coppedge, Michael, John Gerring, Carl Henrik Knutsen, Staffan I. Lindberg, Jan Teorell, David Altman, Michael Bernhard, et al. "V-Dem Dataset v10." *Varieties of Democracy (V-Dem) Institute* (2020). doi:10.23696/vdemds20, 2020.

Cornell, A., J. Møller, and S. Skaaning. *Democratic Stability in an Age of Crisis: Reassessing the Interwar Period*. Oxford: Oxford University Press, 2020.

Dahl, Robert A. *Polyarchy: Participation and Opposition*. New Haven, CT: Yale University Press, 1971.

Dahlberg, Stefan, Jonas Linde, and Sören Holmberg. "Democratic Discontent in Old and New Democracies: Assessing the Importance of Democratic Input and Governmental Output." *Political Studies* 63 (2015): 18–37. doi:10.1111/1467-9248.12170.

De Vries, Catherine E., and Sara B. Hobolt. *Political Entrepreneurs: The Rise of Challenger Parties in Europe*. Princeton, NJ: Princeton University Press, 2020.

Donovan, Todd. "Authoritarian Attitudes and Support for Radical Right Populists." *Journal of Elections, Public Opinion and Parties* 29, no. 4 (2019): 448–464. doi:10.1080/17457289.2019.1666270.

Downs, William M. "How Effective Is the Cordon Sanitaire? Lessons from Efforts to Contain the Far Right in Belgium, France, Denmark and Norway." *Journal für Konflikt- und Gewaltforschung* 4, no. 1 (2002): 32–51.

Downs, William M. "Pariahs in Their Midst: Belgian and Norwegian Parties React to Extremist Threats." *West European Politics* 24, no. 3 (2001): 23–42. doi:10.1080/01402380108425451.

Drutman, Lee, Joe Goldman, and Larry Diamond. "Democracy Maybe. Attitudes on Authoritarianism in America." Democracy Fund (June 2020). https://www.voterstudygroup.org/publication/democracy-maybe.

Easton, David. "A Re-assessment of the Concept of Political Support." *British Journal of Political Science* 5, no. 4 (1975): 435–457. doi:10.1017/S0007123400008309.

Finkel, Steven E., and Junghyun Lim. "The Supply and Demand Model of Civic Education: Evidence from a Field Experiment in the Democratic Republic of Congo." *Democratization* (2020): 1–22.

Foa, Roberto Stefan, Andrew Klassen, Micheal Slade, Alex Rand, and Rosie Collins. "The Global Satisfaction with Democracy Report 2020." Cambridge: Centre for the Future of Democracy, 2020.

Gidron, Noam, and Peter A. Hall. "The Politics of Social Status: Economic and Cultural Roots of the Populist Right." *British Journal of Sociology* 68, no. S1 (2017): S57–S84. doi:10.1111/1468-4446.12319.

Graham, Matthew H., and Milan W. Svolik. "Democracy in America? Partisanship, Polarization, and the Robustness of Support for Democracy in the United States." *American Political Science Review* 114, no. 2 (2020): 392–409. doi:10.1017/S0003055420000052.

Grahn, Sandra, Anna Lührmann, and Lisa Gastaldi. "Resources for Democratic Politicians and Political Parties." In *Defending Democracy against Illiberal Challengers: A Resource Guide*, edited by Anna Lührmann, Lisa Gastaldi, Dominik Hirndorf, and Staffan I. Lindberg, 45–53. Gothenburg: Varieties of Democracy Institute/University of Gothenburg, 2020.

Grossman, Guy, Dorothy Kronick, Matthew Levendusky, and Marc Meredith. "The Majoritarian Threat to Liberal Democracy." *Journal of Experimental Political Science* (2021): 1–10.

Haggard, Stephan, and Robert R. Kaufman. *Dictators and Democrats: Masses, Elites, and Regime Change*. Princeton: Princeton University Press, 2016.

Hainmueller, Jens, and Daniel J. Hopkins. "Public Attitudes Toward Immigration." *Annual Review of Political Science* 17, no. 1 (2014): 225–249. doi:10.1146/annurev-polisci-102512-194818.

Heinisch, Reinhard. "Success in Opposition-Failure in Government: Explaining the Performance of Right-Wing Populist Parties in Public Office." *West European Politics* 26, no. 3 (2003): 91–130. doi:10.1080/01402380312331280608.

Heinze, Anna-Sophie. "Strategies of Mainstream Parties Towards Their Right-Wing Populist Challengers: Denmark, Norway, Sweden and Finland in Comparison." *West European Politics* 41, no. 2 (2018): 287–309. doi:10.1080/01402382.2017.1389440.

Hyde, Susan D. "Democracy's Backsliding in the International Environment." *Science* 369, no. 6508 (2020): 1192–1196. doi:10.1126/science.abb2434.

Inglehart, Ronald, Christian Haerpfer, Alejandro Moreno, Christian Welzel, Kseniya Kizilova, Jaime Diez-Medrano, Lagos Marta, et al., eds. "World Values Survey: All Rounds – Country-Pooled Datafile." ([dataset]; accessed March 3, 2021). http://www.worldvaluessurvey.org/WVSDocumentationWVL.jsp, 2020.

Laebens, Melisa, and Anna Lührmann. "What Halts Democratic Erosion? The Changing Role of Accountability." *Democratization* 5 (2021): 1–21.

Leininger, Julia, Anna Lührmann, and Rachel Sigman. "The Relevance of Social Policies for Democracy." Discussion Papers 7/2019, *German Development Institute (DIE)* (2019).

Levitsky, Steven, and Daniel Ziblatt. *How Democracies Die*. New York: Broadway Books, 2018.

Linz, Juan. *The Breakdown of Democratic Regimes: Crisis, Breakdown & Reequilibration*. Baltimore: Johns Hopkins University Press, 1978.

Linz, Juan. "The Perils of Presidentialism." *Journal of Democracy* 1, no. 1 (1990): 51–69. muse.jhu.edu/article/225694.

Linz, Juan, and Alfred Stepan. *Problems of Democratic Transition and Consolidation: Southern Europe, South America, and Post-Communist Europe*. Baltimore, MD: Johns Hopkins University Press, 1996.

Lührmann, Anna, Nils Düpont, Masaaki Higashijima, Yaman Berker Kavasoglu, Kyle L. Marquardt, Michael Bernhard, Holger Döring, et al. "Varieties of Party Identity and Organization (V–Party) Dataset V1." Varieties of Democracy (V-Dem) Project, https://www.v-dem.net/en/data/data/v-party-dataset/?edit_off=true, 2020.

Lührmann, Anna, Lisa Gastaldi, Dominik Hirndorf, and Staffan I. Lindberg, eds. *Defending Democracy against Illiberal Challengers: A Resource Guide*. Gothenburg: Varieties of Democracy Institute/University of Gothenburg, 2020.

Lührmann, Anna, and Staffan I Lindberg. "A Third Wave of Autocratization Is Here: What Is New about It?" *Democratization* 26, no. 7 (2019): 1095–1113. doi:10.1080/13510347.2019.1582029.

Lührmann, Anna, Kyle L Marquardt, and Valeriya Mechkova. "Constraining Governments: New Indices of Vertical, Horizontal, and Diagonal Accountability." *American Political Science Review* 114, no. 3 (2020): 811–820. doi:10.1017/S0003055420000222.

Lührmann, Anna, Juraj Medzihorsky, and Staffan I. Lindberg. "Walking the Talk: How to Identify Anti-Pluralist Parties." *V-Dem Working Paper* (2021).

Mair, Peter. *Ruling the Void: The Hollowing-Out of Western Democracy*. London: Verso, 2013.

Malka, Ariel, Yphtach Lelkes, Bert N. Bakker, and Eliyahu Spivack. "Who Is Open to Authoritarian Governance within Western Democracies?" *Perspectives on Politics*, First View (2020): 1–20. doi:10.1017/S1537592720002091

McCoy, Jennifer, and Murat Somer. "Toward a Theory of Pernicious Polarization and How It Harms Democracies: Comparative Evidence and Possible Remedies." *The Annals of the American Academy of Political and Social Science* 681, no. 1 (2019): 234–271. doi:10.1177%2F0002716218818782.

170 RESILIENCE OF DEMOCRACY

Medzihorsky, Juraj, Anna Lührmann, and Staffan Lindberg. "Autocratization by Elections: Arena or Trigger of Democratic Decline?" Paper presented at the Annual Meeting of the American Political Science Association (APSA) (2019).

Meléndez, Carlos, and Cristóbal Rovira Kaltwasser. "Negative Partisanship Towards the Populist Radical Right and Democratic Resilience in Western Europe." *Democratization* 5 (2021): 1–21.

Minkenberg, Michael. "The Radical Right in Public Office: Agenda-Setting and Policy Effects." *West European Politics* 24, no. 4 (2001): 1–21. doi:10.1080/01402380108425462.

Mudde, Cas, and Cristóbal Rovira Kaltwasser. "Exclusionary vs. Inclusionary Populism: Comparing Contemporary Europe and Latin America." *Government and Opposition* 48, no. 2 (2013): 147–174. doi:10.1017/gov.2012.11.

Müller, Jan-Werner. "Militant Democracy." In *The Oxford Handbook of Comparative Constitutional Law*, edited by Michel Rosenfeld, and András Sajó. Oxford University Press, 2012. doi:10.1093/oxfordhb/9780199578610.013.0062.

Müller, Jan-Werner. "Protecting Popular Self-Government from the People? New Normative Perspectives on Militant Democracy." *Annual Review of Political Science* 19 (2016): 249–265. doi:10.1146/annurev-polisci-043014-124054.

Müller, Jan-Werner. *What Is Populism?* Philadelphia: University of Pennsylvania Press, 2017.

Norris, Pippa. *Radical Right: Voters and Parties in the Electoral Market*. Cambridge: Cambridge University Press, 2005.

Norris, Pippa, and Ronald Inglehart. *Cultural Backlash: Trump, Brexit, and Authoritarian Populism*. Cambridge: Cambridge University Press, 2019. doi:10.1017/9781108595841.

Pardos-Prado, Sergi, Bram Lancee, and Iñaki Sagarzazu. "Immigration and Electoral Change in Mainstream Political Space." *Political Behavior* 36, no. 4 (2014): 847–875. doi:10.1007/s11109-013-9248-y.

Pemstein, Daniel, Kyle L. Marquardt, Eitan Tzelgov, Yi-ting Wang, Juraj Medzihorsky, Joshua Krusell, Farhad Miri, and Johannes von Römer. "The V-Dem Measurement Model: Latent Variable Analysis for Cross-National and Cross-Temporal Expert-Coded Data". *V-Dem Working Paper* 21. 5th edition. (2020). doi:10.2139/ssrn.2704787.

Petrarca, Constanza Sanhueza, Heiko Giebler, and Bernhard Weßels. "Support for Insider Parties: The Role of Political Trust in a Longitudinal-Comparative Perspective." *Party Politics* (2020). doi:10.1177/1354068820976920.

Popper, Karl. *Open Society and Its Enemies*. London: Routledge, 1945/2003.

Przeworski, Adam. *Sustainable Democracy*. Cambridge: Cambridge University Press, 1995.

Przeworski, Adam, Michael E. Alvarez, Jose Antonio Cheibub, and Fernando Limongi. *Democracy and Development: Political Institutions and Material Well-being in the World, 1950–1990*. Cambridge: Cambridge University Press, 2000.

Rovira Kaltwasser, Cristóbal. "Populism and the Question of How to Respond to it." In *The Oxford Handbook of Populism*, edited by Cristóbal Rovira Kaltwasser, Paul Taggart, Paulina Ochoa Espejo, and Pierre Ostiguy. Oxford: Oxford University Press, 2017. doi:10.1093/oxfordhb/9780198803560.013.21.

Ruck, Damian J, Luke J Matthews, Thanos Kyritsis, Quentin D Atkinson, and R. Alexander Bentley. "The Cultural Foundations of Modern Democracies." *Nature Human Behaviour* 4, no. 3 (2020): 265–269. doi:10.1038/s41562-019-0769-1.

Schmitt, Hermann, Sara B. Hobolt, Wouter Van der Brug, and Sebastian Adrian Popa. "European Parliament Election Study 2019, Voter Study". GESIS Data Archive, Cologne. (2020). https://doi.org/10.4232/1.13473.

Schroeder, Wolfgang, and Bernhard Weßels. *Smarte Spalter*. Bonn: Dietz Verlag J.H.W. Nachf, 2019.

Somer, Murat, Jennifer McCoy, and Russell Evan Luke, IV. "Pernicious Polarization, Autocratization and Opposition Strategies." *Democratization* 5 (2021): 1–20.

Spoon, Jae-Jae, and Heike Klüver. "Responding to Far Right Challengers: Does Accommodation Pay Off?" *Journal of European Public Policy* 27, no. 2 (2020): 273–291. doi:10.1080/13501763.2019.1701530.

Staton, Jeffrey, Christopher Reenock, and Jordan Holsinger. Can Courts be Bulwarks of Democracy? *Judges and the Politics of Prudence*. Cambridge: Cambridge University Press, forthcoming.

Stepan, Alfred, and Cindy Skach. "Constitutional Frameworks and Democratic Consolidation: Parliamentarianism versus Presidentialism." *World Politics* 46, no. 1 (1993): 1–22. doi:10.2307/2950664.

RESILIENCE OF DEMOCRACY

Svolik, Milan. "Authoritarian Reversals and Democratic Consolidation." *American Political Science Review* 102, no. 2 (2008): 153–168. doi:10.1017/S0003055408080143.

Svolik, Milan W. "When Polarization Trumps Civic Virtue: Partisan Conflict and the Subversion of Democracy by Incumbents." *Quarterly Journal of Political Science* 15, no. 1 (2020): 3–31.

Urbanska, Karolin, and Serge Guimond. "Swaying to the Extreme: Group Relative Deprivation Predicts Voting for an Extreme Right Party in the French Presidential Election." *International Review of Social Psychology* 31 (2018): 1–12. doi:10.5334/irsp.201.

Van Hauwaert, Steven M., and Stijn Van Kessel. "Beyond Protest and Discontent: A Cross-National Analysis of the Effect of Populist Attitudes and Issue Positions on Populist Party Support." *European Journal of Political Research* 57, no. 1 (2018): 68–92. doi:10.1111/1475-6765.12216.

van Spanje, Joost. "Contagious Parties: Anti-immigration Parties and their Impact on other Parties' Immigration Stances in Contemporary Western Europe." In *The Populist Radical Right: A Reader*, edited by Cas Mudde, 474–492. Oxon: Routledge, 2017.

Waldner, David, and Ellen Lust. "Unwelcome Change: Coming to Terms with Democratic Backsliding." *Annual Review of Political Science* 21 (2018): 93–113. doi:10.1146/annurev-polisci-050517-114628.

Welzel, Christian. "Democratic Horizons: What Value Change Reveals about the Future of Democracy." *Democratization* (2021): 1–25.

Wuttke, Alexander, Konstantin Gavras, and Harald Schoen. "Have Europeans Grown Tired of Democracy? New Evidence from Eighteen Consolidated Democracies, 1981–2018." *British Journal of Political Science* (2020): 1–13. doi:10.1017/S0007123420000149.

Ziblatt, Daniel. *Conservative Parties and the Birth of Democracy*. Cambridge: Cambridge University Press, 2017. doi:10.1017/9781139030335.

Zick, Andreas, Beate Küpper, and Wilhelm Berghan. "Verlorene Mitte – Feindselige Zustände. Rechtsextreme Einstellungen in Deutschland 2018/19." *Friedrich-Ebert-Stiftung*. Bonn: Dietz, 2019.

Index

Note: Page numbers in **bold** refer to tables and those in *italics* refer to figures.

accelerator 157–8
accountability: actors 45;
 de facto constraints 44;
 defined 40–1; diagonal 44–5; executive
 and *46*; horizontal 44; incumbents 45; "low
 quality" democracies 45–6; miscalculation
 scenario 46; power balance mechanism 46;
 research design and case selection 46–7;
 societal constraints 44; vertical 41, 44
activation hypothesis 155
active depolarization 9, 71–5
anti-abortion 156
anti-and pro-democratic actors 130
anti-immigration policies 156
anti-incumbent electoral coalitions 67
anti-pluralist mobilization 151, 153
Asia and the Pacific (AP) 23
authoritarian 1–2
authoritarianism 1, 83
authoritarian-*vs.*-emancipative values 129, *136*
autocratic regression 2
autocratization 153–4; democratic
 performers 3; description 2; episodes in
 democracies *24*, *25*; scholars 3; sequence
 149, *150*; third wave of 3, 17
autocratizers 161–2
average causal mediation effect (ACME)
 113, 116
average direct effect (ADE) 113

backsliding 126
Benin (2007–2012): accountability,
 activation of 49; accountability actors 48–9;
 executive 48
Bertelsmann Foundation 82
Boese, Vanessa A. 8
Boîtes à Images community workshop 108–
 11, *110*

breakdown resilience 5, 8, 18, 19, *19*, 22, **24**
Burnell, Peter 3

Calvert, Peter 3
christian democratic and conservative
 parties 86
citizens, profile of: analysis and interpretation
 89–93, **90**; measurement and method 88–9;
 positive vis-à-vis negative partisanship
 93–4, *94*
Civic Competence variables 106
civic education (CE): corruption 107;
 electoral autocracies 105; mediated
 through democratic demand
 (efficacy) **118**; mediated through
 (perceived) democratic supply **117**; positive
 democratic outcomes 104; post-Cold
 War period 103; supportive democratic
 values 104; treatment 108–9
closed autocracies 64
cognitive mobilization 126, *132*
Complier Average Causal Effect
 (CACE) 112
consolidated democracies *19*, 19–20
constitutional checks and balances 6
contemporary autocratizers 152
Cornell, Agnes 3
Costa Pinto, António 3
counter-argument 125–7
counter-polarization strategies **67**
Countries' Culture Zone Membership *128*
coups and regime transitions *20*, 20–1
critical engagement 159–61
criticalness 125
cultural identity constructions 138
cultural relativists 132
cultural theory of autocracy-vs-democracy
 126, 139–41

INDEX

culture-bound ascension 128–30
culture zones 11, *133*

Decelerator of Modernity's Emancipatory
Effect *135*
Decentralization in the Democratic Republic
of the Congo 109
deconsolidation-thesis 125, 136–8
democracy-in-crisis-literature 11
democratic breakdown: anti-pluralists 156–61;
autocratizers 161–2; democratic parties and
institutions 152–6; national elections 104;
structural and contextual challenges 150–1
democratic civic education *106*
democratic decline concept **42**
democratic erosion process 3, 41–2,
41–3, **47**, **52**
democratic institutions 2
democratic orientations 10
democratic regression 2
Democratic Republic of Congo (DRC) 103,
106, 156
democratic resilience: autocratization
(*see* autocratization); citizens' attitudes
and behaviours 4; citizens, political
community of 5; contributions 8–11;
defined 2, 3, 19; descriptive analysis 18;
erosion of 6–8; executive aggrandizement 5;
focused theory frames 4; four-level
approach 5; functionalist perspective 4;
liberal 2; polarization 5; political parties 4;
political regimes 4; structural-functionalist
concept 6
diagonal accountability 44–5
distrustful democrats 107

Eastern Europe and Central Asia (EECA) 23
economic factors 26
Ecuador (2008–2010) 49–50
electoral ceiling 85
electoral/defective democracies 3
electoral democracy 20, 20–1, *151*
Electoral Democracy Index 48
elevated polarization **66**
emancipative values 11, 129–33, *138*
enlightenment values 127–8
Entites TerritorialeDecentralise (ETD) 108
Episodes of Regime Transformation (ERT) 18,
21, 27, 47
equal political rights 6
estimation strategy 112–13
European Parliament 85
executive aggrandizement 42
executive constraints 25–6
expressive partisanship 84

feeling-thermometer/sympathies
approach 85
Fifth Republic Movement (MVR) 152
Finkel, Steven 10
focused theory frames 4–6
freezing hypothesis 83

global regime evolution 134–6
green parties 86
group-identity approach 85

heightened polarization **66**
high-quality democracy 41
horizontal accountability 44

"incongruent" societies 130
independent media 8
individual liberty 6
instrumental partisanship 84
Intent to Treat (ITT) 112
International Foundation for Electoral
Systems (IFES) 108

Kaltwasser, Cristóbal Rovira 9–10, 153
knowledgeable sceptics 86

liberal parties 86
Lim, Junghyun 10
Limongi, Fernando 26
Lipset's theory 26
low-quality democracy 41
Luke, Russell 9

Maddison project 28
majoritarian *vs.* consociational institutions 43
Maletz, Donald J. 4
McCoy, Jennifer 9
Meléndez, Carlos 9–10, 153
mental bandwidth 132
Middle East and North Africa (MENA) 23
miscalculation scenario 46
Mishler, William 86
modernity, illiberal scripts 134
Moehler's characterization of participation 107
Møller, Jørgen 3
monitory civil society 8

National Civic Education Programme
(NCEP) 104
national parliament 85
native group ("the nation") 83
nativism 83
negative partisanship 10, 87
neighbourhood effects 26–7
nonnatives ("alien") 83

"Obedience to Rulers" *137*
O'Donnell, Guillermo 44
onset resilience 5, 8, 18, 19, *19*, 22, **22**, **29**

pandemic backsliding 7
parliamentary *vs.* presidential forms of
government 43
party family 83
passive depolarization 69–70
perils of presidentialism 27
pernicious polarization: autocrats 62;
citizens and political actors 62; democratic
oppositions 66–7; and democratic
quality 63–6; exogenous factors 62;
mechanisms 63; polarization strategies
67, 67–8; political entrepreneurs 63; process
and condition 62
persuasion 161
Pinochet-era market approach 70
political polarization, Liberal Democracy
(1900–2019) **65**
political tolerance 104
popular sovereignty 6
populism 9–10, 83
populist-authoritarian 72
populist leaders 127
populist narratives 156–7
populist radical right (PRR) parties 10, 81, 82,
84, 86, 153
positive partisanship 10, 87
power balance mechanism 46
predicted probabilities, onset and breakdown
resilience *30*
previous democratic experience 27
proactive counter-polarization strategies 71
Przeworski, Adam 2, 26

raging dissatisfaction 125
ratchet effect 7–8
reciprocal counter-polarization strategy:
passive depolarization 69–70; reciprocal
polarization 68–9
Regime-Culture Coevolution I *141*
Regime-Culture Coevolution II *142*
Regime-Culture Congruence *131*
Regimes of the World classification 22
Regimes of the World typology 64
regional parliament 85
regional trends, onset resilience *23*
reputational shield 84

revisionists 125
"The Role of the Citizen" 109
Rose, Richard 86

Schmitt, Carl 9
"semi-loyal" actors 2
severe polarization **66**
Skaaning, Svend-Erik 3
social democratic parties 86
social tolerance 104
Somer, Murat 9
South Korea (2008–2016) 50–1
strategic manipulation of elections 42
sub-Saharan Africa (SSA) 23
"supply and demand" model 103–7
Support for Democratic Values 106
supportive democratic orientations 102
survey instrument and field
work **111**, 111–12

Teixeira, Conceição Pequito 3
Teo, Victor 3
Tocqueville, Alexis de 4
transcendent mentality 132
transformative repolarization strategy
9, 71, 72
two-stage concept 8

United Socialist Party of Venezuela
(PSUV) 152

Varieties of Democracy project 41, 63
V-Dem data set 6
V-Dem electoral democracy index (EDI) 18,
21, 27–8, 47
vertical accountability 41, 44
voter mobilization and coalition
building 158–9
Voter Opinion and Involvement through Civic
Education (VOICE) programme 103; civic
competence **114**; perceived democratic
supply **113**; political participation **116**;
values and norms **114**, **115**; *see also* civic
education (CE)

Welzel, Christian 11, 155
Western Europe 83, **84**
western/non-western divide over
authoritarian-vs-emancipative values *129*
World Value Survey (WVS) 137, 154, *154*

Printed in the United States
by Baker & Taylor Publisher Services